HADLEY

blue water sailing
manual

blue water sailing
manual

Barry Pickthall

CONTRIBUTING EDITORS:
Sir Chay Blyth CBE, BEM
Andrew Roberts
Dr. Campbell Mackenzie R.D.
Mike Golding
David Houghton
Pete Goss OBE
Hood Sails
Brookes and Gatehouse

International Marine / McGraw-Hill
Camden, Maine • New York • Chicago • San Francisco •
Lisbon • London • Madrid • Mexico City • Milan • New
Delhi • San Juan • Seoul • Singapore • Sydney • Toronto

The **McGraw·Hill** Companies

1 2 3 4 5 6 7 8 9 IMP IMP 9 8 7 6

Published by International Marine/McGraw-Hill
PO Box 220
Camden, Maine 04843
www.internationalmarine.com

First published in 1985 under the title *Blue Water Racing*
Second edition published 2006

ISBN–10: 0-07-148768-9
ISBN–13: 978-0-07-148768-9

A CIP catalogue record for this book is available from the
Library of Congress.

This book is produced using paper that is made from
wood grown in managed, sustainable forests. It is
natural, renewable and recyclable. The logging and
manufacturing processes conform to the environmental
regulations of the country of origin.

Designed by Ed White, PPL
Typeset in Utopia Roman 9.5pt
Printed and bound in in Singapore by Star Standard

contents

introduction

Blue Water Racing, the original edition of this book published in 1985, distilled the immense experience amassed from two winning Whitbread Round the World races over an 8-year period by Dutch skipper Cornelis van Rietschoten and his *Flyer* crews.

At the time, we questioned whether an owner/skipper would ever again win two successive campaigns, and two decades on, Van Rietschoten's record remains true. But in the interim, **Sir Chay Blyth** has become very much the Pied Piper within the offshore world of yachting, leading a succession of amateur sailors around the world in four Global Challenge races, and encouraging others like Mike Golding, Sam Brewster and Dee Caffari to take on the challenge alone. Together, these adventurous challenges amount to 50 circumnavigations, with other Global Challenge races scheduled for the future. These add up to an enormous amount of experience, and it is with considerable gratitude to Sir Chay and **Andrew Roberts**, who was the Challenge Business Project Director responsible for overseeing the design and maintenance of the fleet of Challenge yachts for 16 years, that they were prepared to contribute so much towards this second edition.

Our prime objective has been to provide a well researched manual for all those aspiring to compete or cruise across oceans. I am also indebted to **Dr Campbell Mackenzie RD* FRCP(Edin)** who marked his retirement from the Royal Navy by joining the *Rhone Poulenc* crew in the first British Steel Challenge race. He followed much of the medical advice given in the first edition by the two *Flyer* doctors, Bert Diskema and Julian Fuller, then built on his own experience to advise successive Global Challenge crews to become one of the most authoritive yachting medics in the world.

Another authoritive voice is **Mike Golding** who has become one of Britain's most successful blue water sailors. The former fireman cut his teeth leading *Group 4 Securitas* in two Global Challenge races, finishing 2nd in the first event in 1992/3 before winning the second by a wide margin in 1996/7. He has since sailed around the world a further three times, and became the first British yachtsman to win the IMOCA world championship. A consummate sailor in both crewed and single-handed races, he has dominated the Open 60 class with thirteen podium positions between 1999 and 2006.

David Houghton was the Senior Weather Forecaster at Britain's National Meteorological Centre before his retirement. A life-long sailor, he has been the weather advisor for Britain's Olympic sailing team since the early 1980s and provided weather routing and training for Conny Van Rietschoten's winning Whitbread round the world race crew on *Flyer.* His original contribution to the first edition remains as a weather bible for all who venture offshore.

Pete Goss OBE has completed more than 250,000 sea miles, many of them as the training skipper for the first Global Challenge races. His job was to whittle the applicants down from several thousand to final 120, then train them in the necessary skills to withstand the rigours of the Southern Ocean. Rising at dawn and working with the volunteers until late at night, Pete got the crews fit and focused on working together in teams so that they understood every aspect of sailing and their role on board. It was Pete's ability to motivate and instill enthusiasm in the crews, coupled with his unwavering attention to detail in the planning, preparation and safety, that played a major part in the overall success of the first Challenge races. His rescue of French yachtsman Raphael Dinelli from his stricken vessel deep in the Southern Ocean during the Vendee Globe solo non-stop round the world race, won him worldwide acclaim and the Legion d'Honneur. His own competitiveness was also underlined when he had to operate on himself to repair ruptured muscles around his left elbow. Even with these setbacks he became the fastest British Vendee skipper to sail around the world single-handed with a time of 126 days and 21 hours.

Hood Sails were key to the success of Conny van Rietschoten's two *Flyer* campaigns, and Ted Hood, Chris Bouzaid and Geoff Prior contributed greatly to the first edition of this book.

Hood is also the sole supplier of sails to the Challenge yachts, and we are thankful to **Tim Woodhouse,** the Managing Director, for his tireless help in working with us to update the rig and sail chapters.

Another key supplier to both *Flyer* campaigns and the Challenge yachts is **Brookes & Gatehouse,** and we are indebted to both the company and their race specialist, **Nat Ives**, who has updated the original detailed chapter on tactronics to include instruction on how to interpret and interpolate all the information that now floods in to the modern navigation station.

Our thanks also go to the Hydrographer of the Navy for allowing us to quote from the British Admiralty *Ocean Passages for the World*, Stan Darling, one of Australia's most successful navigators for his observations on whales, Dr Don Proudford from the Royal Australian Air Force Special Reserve for his advice on survival, and last but by no means least, to the editorial team at *Yachting World* magazine who have worked with Andrew Roberts to research so many of the lessons learned from following the Challenge yachts around the world.

Barry Pickthall

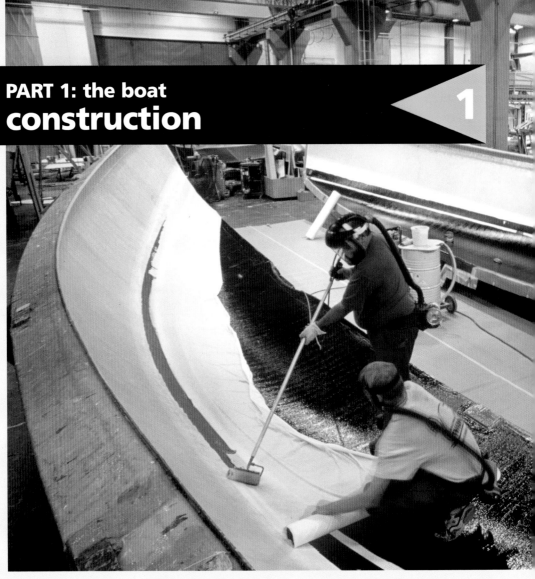

The layup for a modern composite yacht like this Nautor Swan is a complex matrix of Kevlar, carbon and glassfibre designed to maximise strength and minimise weight.

The need to minimise weight in a boat and centre it as low as possible, has long been realised by designers, builders and sailors. The Tudor warship _Mary Rose_, which capsized and sank with all hands in the Solent back in 1545, and later the _Wasa_, which rolled over and sank at her launching in Stockholm harbour in 1628, are monuments to faulty design.

The problems for these ships stemmed from a failure on the part of their architects to realise the harm a battalion of fully armoured men might have, not an enemy, but on their own calculations!

There have been other expensive mistakes made by over designing too.

Independence, the 140ft (42.67m) America's Cup defender, launched in 1901, was built of bronze and alloy with an internal space frame of braces, struts and rods – all tensioned with turnbuckles. Not only did the yacht suffer excessive electrolysis, but the internal structure was continually breaking as the crew worked feverishly at the pumps in a vain attempt to keep pace with the 4,000 gallons of water that the twisting hull took in each hour. *Independence* retained the Cup, but having done so, was then quietly scrapped. Three months after her launch, she cost her owner more than £5 million at today's values.

Despite the wealth of experience gathered during the intervening years, the same mistakes occasionally reappear when designers fail to heed those expensive lessons from the past in their search for possible break throughs in design. *Drum*, the 76ft (23.16m) maxi built for pop star Simon Le Bon, lost her keel and capsized during the 1995 Fastnet Race when the lead-filled alloy fabrication, made to save the cost of machine-casting the keel, suffered weld failure around the top plate. Her crew worked around the clock for six weeks to get the yacht shipshape once more to enter the Whitbread Round the World Race, but the Kevlar/carbon hull then suffered catastrophic delamination problems during a storm off South Africa, which effectively put her out of contention.

Phillips Innovation was another supposedly hi-tech craft built for Pete Goss

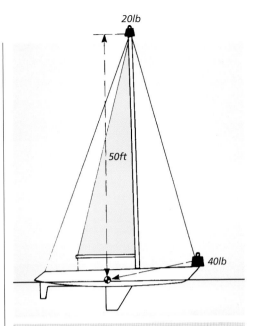

Excess weight in the ends causes speed-destroying pitching. Designers try to concentrate weight in the centre of the boat.
Pitching moment = lbxft².
A mast weighing 20lb (9.07kg) heavier at head, 50ft (15.24m) away from centre of pitching, contributes (20x50ft²) 50,000ft²/lb.
40lb (18.14kg) extra weight at the bow, contributes (40 x 20²) 16,000ft²/lb.
200lb (90.72kg) crewman at bow contributes 80,000ft²/lb.

to shatter the non-stop round the world record in 2000. The tandem-masted catamaran had the dimensions of a tennis court but was as brittle as a brandy snap.

An example of a high-strength composite layup utilising a lightweight Kevlar honeycomb sandwiched between carbon laminates.

One bow section snapped off during her maiden voyage and the £2 million carbon catamaran broke up completely on her second outing.

In yacht construction, there is a finite balance between strength and weight. Any decisions on choice and weight of materials have to be balanced against their strength. Disregard one for the other and the boat will not be competitive or ride well through the waves: it will either have the handling characteristics of a brick, or break up under the opposing forces exerted on it by rig and keel. Quality of construction is equally important, for while one material or building system may appear superior to another, a well built yacht engineered in almost any material, will perform better than one that is badly built from superior materials.

Whatever the material, the underlying requirement is to minimise weight at the ends and to centre heavy items as close to the keel as possible. This applies to cruising designs as much as to racing yachts because any extraneous weight will have a noticeable effect on motion through waves.

There is nothing more nauseating than a yacht that hobby-horses or yaws badly. That is why an increasing number of production and semi-custom yachts are constructed using stronger, lighter and invariably more expensive materials such as carbon, Kevlar and Alustar aluminium to add strength and reduce overall weight. The same applies to rigs and fittings, with items like carbon spars and titanium fittings no longer the exclusive reserve of stripped-out racing yachts. If weight saved at the extremities can be converted into ballast, then the boat's motion and ability to carry sail longer will be all the better for it. This is why production builders like Nautor Swan now mould their decks in carbon.

After the Frers-designed maxi *Flyer* had won line and handicap honours in the 1981 Whitbread Round the World Race, she was returned to her builder, The Royal Huisman Shipyard, for conversion into a cruiser for owner, Cornelis van Rietschoten, to sail leisurely around the world once more and take in the America's Cup in Fremantle. The changes, which included fitting out the interior and replacing the rig with one that had roller furling headsails and main, was a great success, but the addition of a washing machine in the forepeak with its 70lb (31.75kg) of stabilising concrete over the drum, had a noticeable effect on the yacht's handling.

The same applies to rigs. A carbon mast may cost seven times more than its alloy counterpart, but it offers a 20% weight saving. 20lb (9.07kg) saved at the head of a 50ft (15.24m) mast for instance, equates to a 50,000ft^2/lb saving as far as pitching moment!

The requirements of a construction material in terms of density and specific strength, change with the size of the yacht. While heavier materials like aluminium or steel can be weight-effective in maxi-sized yachts and above, the rig loading and panel stiffness requirements become more acute as size is reduced. With smaller boats, up to 30ft (9m) in length, a laminated wood epoxy provides the most cost effective strength/weight ratio, though an all-carbon hull offers a better ratio if cost is not an issue.

The greatest advantage fibre reinforced plastic (FRP) construction has is that the materials can be tailored accurately to the mechanical properties required in local areas within the hull. The high modulus of carbon can be used to stiffen key load areas around the mast, keel and rudder, while Kevlar's exceptional strength and impact resistance (which is why it is used in bullet-proof clothing and armour plating) can be utilised to lessen panel weight. Glassfibre also has special properties where compressive strength is required, especially S or R-glass and special hybrid weaves, which have been formulated to provide higher strength factors than regular E-glass.

There are two schools of thought as far as laminates are concerned. The first is to produce a rigid monocoque moulding with lightweight end-grain balsa or a polyurethane foam core separating the inner and outer skins. The second is to support the single skin with a hollow FRP framework of integral stringers and frames, which is bonded to the hull while it is still in the mould as Nautor is now doing with its latest models. This internal space-frame can also act as a conduit for wiring, and second as fresh air ducting for the heads to carry smells to watertight dorades at the stern. Builders will argue that as far as panel stiffness is concerned, there is no substitute for thickness, but with the increasing use and understanding of finite element software programmes, coupled with greater precision over resin/cloth ratios and lay-up techniques, the single skin and frame method can produce a lighter, more cost effective and stronger product as far as overall deflection is concerned.

One major advance is in pre-preg moulding techniques where the layers of cloth are supplied ready wetted with resin and the entire hull is laid up under a vacuum pressure of around 10lb/sq in (0.7kg/sq cm) and cured in an oven to produce an accurate 60/40 fibre/resin ratio.

Conventional aluminium and steel construction has advantages for bigger yachts, chiefly because these metals are immensely strong and easy to survey, repair or modify. If performance is a prime requisite, then aluminium (particularly Alustar alloy, which is 20% stronger and offers a 12% weight saving over conventional marina alloy) can provide a viable alternative to FRP for boats above 60ft in length. Steel provides a cheaper, stronger but heavier solution, but is an ideal material for vessels like the one-design Global Challenge yachts which only race against each other and require great reserves of strength to sail against the prevailing winds and currents in the Southern Ocean. The problem with using sheet metals for constructing boats below 60ft is that the plate thickness required to give adequate panel stiffness, represents a massive overkill as far as strength is concerned and will have a detrimental effect on motion and performance.

Global Challenge yacht construction details

The initial idea for the 67ft (20.42m) David Thomas/Thanos Condylis designed Challenge fleet was to build the yachts in laminated wood/epoxy – until British Steel stepped in to sponsor the first race in 1992. Steel has remained the construction method ever since, and the second generation fleet of Rob Humphrey designed 72 footers (21.95m) which, between them, have now undergone 50 circumnavigations and well over 3 million nautical miles across the most inhospitable waters in the world. The lessons learned from racing hard in such testing conditions have raised questions about the fundamental design and suitability of much of the equipment and materials that ordinary sailors take for granted, and have led to some major reappraisals.

'When a design or manufacturing problem occurs on one yacht, the marine industry has a habit of burying the evidence. When the same fault occurs across an identical fleet of yachts within the glare of international press coverage, then the problems get investigated and solutions are found,' says Andrew Roberts, who was Project Director of the Challenge Business for 16 years. He speaks from considerable experience. When the rigging bottle screws began to snap on one yacht after another during the second leg of the first British Steel Challenge in 1992, and ironically led to the dismasting of the main sponsor's own yacht *British Steel 2*, the analysis showed up not only significant differences in their engineering, but wide variances in the metallurgy of the forged steel. Andrew Roberts further explained, 'There is nothing special about a bottle screw. They have been used on yachts and more significantly on aircraft where tolerance levels are so much tighter, ever since the first days of flight. Yet our investigations showed up some manufacturers were not providing anything like the levels of quality control required for such heavily loaded fittings.'

In the second race four years later, a pressed stainless steel 'strip' toggle that linked the spreader end fabrication and the D3 shroud led to *Concert* being dismasted in almost the same position as *British Steel 2* had been four years earlier – a design issue that

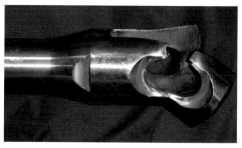

Tested to destruction. Following the bottle screw failures experienced during the first Global Challenge Race, Andrew Roberts commissioned a series of destructive tests which showed up wide variations in their metallurgy.

Roberts believes also caused the bottle screw failures four years before. With 20 yachts in their fleet and 200 lives to consider during any one race, not to mention the expense of flying new spars and heavy rigging half way around the world, the Challenge Business chose to manufacture their own terminal connections in conjunction with design engineer Roger Scammell, rather than rely on standard products. The company did exactly the same in other areas such as the spars and sheet

Construction of one of the 72ft (21.85m) Global Challenge yacht. The steel framing and outer plating was laser cut and supplied in flat-pack form so that these one-design yachts could be constructed to close tolerances anywhere in the world.

Never underestimate the power of the sea. Save the Children *caught on camera moments before dropping like a stone into the trough of a wave.*

tracks, to the extent of buying their own mast manufacturer, Atlantic Spars at Dartmouth, England, to ensure uniform quality. The first improvement was a headsail sheet track. 'Many companies produce a low profile extrusion or expect the tracks to be recessed into the deck, but we didn't need either,' Roberts explains, adding: 'In fact, we need these tracks to double as a foothold for crew as they make their way along the leeward deck, just like a toe rail set further inboard. We also produce our own low-profile cars which, last much longer and are quieter.' The 'clatter-factor' is an important consideration when the off-watch is asleep below deck, and at £400 a-piece from a proprietary supplier, there were big savings to be made when producing 90 of them .

The design specification of the 67ft (20.42m) Challenge yacht, and to a large extent, its 72ft (21.95m) successor, was drawn up around the primary winch. 'It's completely backwards from the way in which most yachts are designed, but at the time of the first yachts, the Lewmar 66 primary winches were priced at £1800 each. The next size up added a further £1000 to the cost. Multiply that by two for each of the ten yachts and your budgets run riot,' Roberts recalled.

Sir Chay Blyth, who conceived the idea for the Global Challenge races, worked with Roberts to calculate the maximum sail area that the Lewmar 66 could handle, and from that, they determined the design's optimum length and displacement. Another important consideration was the need for a moderately stiff hull; one that would be as easy on the crew as it would be on the gear and equipment. 'We wanted a yacht that could continue to sail to windward at 5-7 knots in 60-70 knot winds, yet have the handling and straight line sailing characteristics to look after itself if needs be,' Roberts added. By the time they approached designer David Thomas, the two had worked up a very exact brief. All that changed was the overall length, which jumped from 65ft (19.81m) to 67ft (20.42m) to provide the necessary accommodation for 11 fee-paying crew.

The specification for this first design exceeded the construction rules laid down by Lloyds and Veritas, the two premier structural classification organisations. Yet the yachts still suffered problems, which showed up weaknesses in these rules as much as to highlight the extreme pounding these yachts (and their crews) had to withstand when bashing their way the 'wrong way' around the world. All the yachts suffered cracked ring frames; one experienced a cracked skeg, and almost all finished up with their bows taking up the concaved panel shape of an upturned bonnet on a Citroen 2CV car.

The design of the latest 72ft (21.95m) yachts takes account of the lessons learned

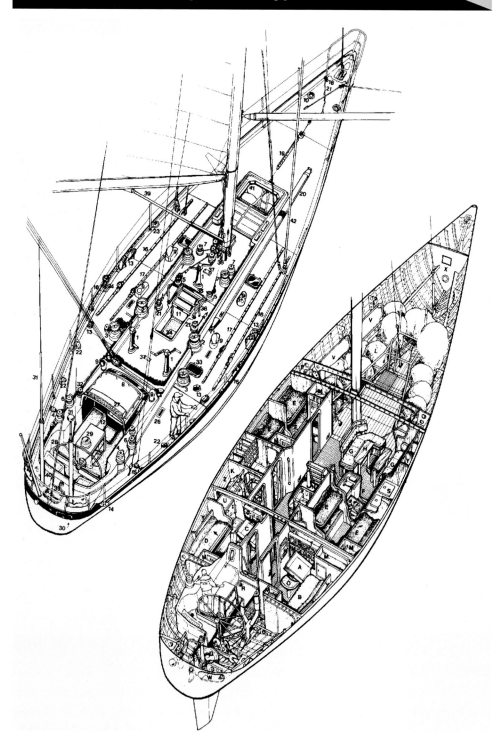

Deck Layout

1. Pedestal grinders
2. Primary winches
3. Spinnaker winches
4. Self-tailing winches for runners
5. Self-tailing winches for reefing lines
6. Self-tailing mainsheet winches
7. Self-tailing halyard winches
8. Doghouse
9. Air vents
10. Deck Lights
11. Companionway down to main saloon
12. Aft companionway leading to skipper and navigator cabins
13. Footblocks
14. Swivel sheet blocks
15. Runner blocks
16. Headsail sheet tracks
17. Inner sheet tracks
18. Recessed forestay attachment
19. Inner forestay track
20. Spinnaker pole
21. Spinnaker pole downhaul
22/4. Eye bolts to attach snatch blocks for barberhaulers
25. Liferaft
26. Prism deck light
27. Computerised sailing instrumentation
28. Backstay
29. Main compass
30. Dan-buoy stowage
31. Radio and sat/nav antenna
32. Mainsheet traveller winches
33. Cabin ventilation hatches
34. Central cockpit with access hatch to gas bottle stowage
35. Collapsible canvas dodger
36. Protective hand hold
37. Runners
38. Mast turning-blocks
39. Hydraulic boom-vang
40. Hydraulics backstay adjuster
41. Foredeck hatch with access to sail locker
42. Cap shroud

Interior Layout

A. Tiltable chart table
B. Navigator's berth
C. Tiltable table in radio cabin
D. Skipper's berth
E. Crew berths
F. Galley
G. Dinette seating
H. Dinette table
I. Heads
J. Stowage for crew's toiletry
K. Heated drying locker
L. Sail stowage
M. Crew lockers
N. Engine compartment
O. Navigator's seat
P. Shroud chain plates
Q. Steering quadrant
R. Cockpit drains
S. Freezer
T. Sailing instrumentation
U. SSB radio
V. Pipe cots
W. Stowage for Dan-buoy
X. Forward bulkhead
Y. Stowage areas
Z. Inner lining to reduce condensation

in building, racing and maintaining the sixteen 67ft (20.42m) yachts in Global races. Speed of construction and ease of survey were major considerations, as well as improving downwind speed without detracting from their upwind performance.

Like the 67ft (20.42m) model, the 72ft (21.95m) Challenge yachts are monocoque in construction; with the 4mm (0.157in) steel sheeting that makes up the hull, welded to a framework of stringers, set over an external jig fastened to the yard floor. Starting amidships, the 3ft (0.91m) wide plating, which is bent over the frame by hand rather than preformed, is welded in place vertically on both sides in sequence. This means that as the plating moves out to the ends, any distortion will be the same on both sides. In practice, the technique produces a fair and stable shape and requires little more than 330lb (150kg) of epoxy filler to fair up the lines – a small amount for yachts of this size.

To overcome the problems of 'dishing' in the bow sections, caused by the hammering these yachts receive in the Southern Ocean, two extra frames were added to the 67ft (20.42m) design to reduce panel size, and the plating on the existing fleet was bent back into shape with hydraulic rams, which, in the case of mild steel, actually improves the metallurgy rather than weakens it.

The 72ft (21.95m) Challenge yacht was designed by Rob Humphreys to be assembled from a flat-pack of steel plates cut with laser precision so that they could be built anywhere in the world, yet remain true to their strict one-design ethos. 'With the 67 footers (20.42m), it was just not economic to cut lightening holes in the frames, but with the laser cutting technology employed in producing the 72ft kits, the plates could be tailored exactly to their design specification. This made a considerable contribution to weight saving

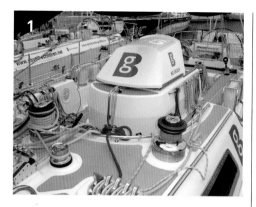

Deck detail on the 72ft (21.95m) Challenge yachts.
1. Safe central crew pit surrounding the main companionway. Crew face forward when winding winches so that they can see the waves coming.
2. Protective canvas 'catch-fencing' to protect crew from being washed into the wheel.
3. Liferaft stowage in the stern with dan-buoys ready to be launched from their stowage within the cockpit coamings.
4. Halyards and control lines lead back either side of mast to central crew pit.

measures, and also simplified production,' comments Roberts.

While the hulls are under construction in one part of the yard, their decks, cockpit, coamings and coachroof are fabricated in another from 316 grade stainless steel to minimize rusting and thus maintenance. The two are then welded together in a process that takes around 18 weeks from jig to finished hull. Three levels of quality checks are then made on the welds: visual by the welder, followed by a magnetic particle inspection which shows up any surface defects, The final tick follows a random X-ray test by specialist surveyors to check against internal voids.

A 1.5in (40mm) thick coating of epoxy foam is then sprayed on to the interior surfaces above the waterline in order to reduce condensation, provide a high level of thermal and sound insulation, and also prevent corrosion.

The greatest concern with mild steel is its susceptibility to rusting, but judging by the gleaming condition of the Challenge fleet when the yachts have returned from successive circumnavigations, this is another area where the Challenge Business has improved the process. International Paints, which, along with its parent company Courtaulds, sponsored yachts in two successive Global Challenge races, supply the painting system exclusively. The hulls are initially shot blasted to remove all rust, and from then on the treatment is similar to finishing any alloy or composite hull. After moving the hull into an atmospherically controlled bay to maintain a curing temperature of 30°C it is first sprayed with three coats of epoxy across the topsides and four below the waterline. Then comes the laborious job of filling and fairing before the hull is pressure-washed and two coats of polyurethane undercoat are applied. After a final rubdown, two coats of high gloss polyurethane/acrylic top coat are sprayed, and once cured, the graphics are then applied.

The greatest advantage steel and aluminium construction have over composite technology is the ease with which the hulls can be updated – or repaired. After *Pride of Teesside* suffered a cracked skeg during the 1992 British Steel Challenge, all ten yachts within this 67ft (20.42m) class had their foils cut off and a modified design welded back in their place.

During the third running of the race in 2000/01 *Quadstone* tee-boned into *Save The Children* during a frenetic start to the fourth leg from Wellington, New Zealand across the Tasman Sea to Sydney. The damage sustained by these two 42 ton, 72ft (21.95m) yachts as they powered into each other at 9 knots was considerable and had this happened to composite yachts, at least one would have been ruled out by the amount of repair work required.

The force of impact was such that *Save the Children* skipper Nick Fenton was thrown over the wheel and smashed his face against the deck, breaking his nose and cheekbone. The damage to his yacht was even worse, with more than 6ft (2m) of the hull having to be cut away, the framework reconstructed, deck gear reinstalled and wiring replaced.

Remarkably, the work to *Save the Children* was completed within 18 days, just in time to re-join the fleet, albeit starting from Hobart, on leg five across the Southern Ocean to Cape Town where *Quadstone* finished 3rd and *Save the Children,* which suffered only superficial damage to her bows, finished 5th!

The many lessons learned from these Challenge yachts, both in construction and equipment, are now filtering through to cruising yachts, for the good of the whole sailing community.

sails and their setting

2

Developments in sailcloth technology, particularly since the introduction of Mylar, carbon and Kevlar, have moved at a fast pace, but even before polyester was a twinkle in the research chemist's eye back in the 1940s, the search for exotic materials to overcome the high stretch characteristics of common cottons was no less intense.

In the early 1900s, the term 'exotic' referred to a rare cotton grown in Florida which was available only to those with large wallets and who were invariably involved in the America's Cup. The 'Auld Mug' events have long been the principle test bed for rig and sail developments. In 1937 for instance, the American defender *Ranger* carried a lightweight silk genoa that had to be lowered hurriedly at the first sign of rain for fear that water would destroy its shape!

The first radical development in sailcloth stemmed from the Second World War with the invention of polyester by the British company ICI. Continuous filaments of polyester formed from long chain polymers were twisted together to produce a high tenacity yarn that was far superior both in strength and durability to the best cottons of the day. In 1953, Dupont began to manufacture the yarn under licence in America, using the trade name Dacron. Essentially, these two products are the same, despite the separate research and development programmes conducted by the two chemical giants ever since. Another 30 years passed before any further radical improvements were made in material technology. First came the introduction of the aramid fibre Kevlar, a yellow coloured yarn developed by Dupont, initially as a core bracing for radial tyres, which has ten times the tensile strength of polyester. This was followed by the introduction of polyester film – Mylar and Melinex are its common trade names – which, when applied to a weave, can increase the strength and stability of the cloth threefold, as well as provide protection against ultraviolet light – something to which aramid based yarns are particularly susceptible to.

Spectra, another high-strength fibre, which has 4.5 times the stretch resistance of Kevlar for its weight and is impervious to flex fatigue, was first introduced in the early 1980s. The filaments are very slick chemically and did not lend themselves to being laminated to Mylar film until the manufacturer, Allied Signal, began to etch the yarn chemically prior to bonding. This second generation Spectra 1000 has proved more durable than its Kevlar counterpart. Another material is Vectran. Developed by Hoescht Celanese in the early 1990s to compete with Kevlar, it is just as expensive and sensitive to UV degradation, but has a far greater resistance to flex fatigue and is the principal material Hood Sails use to produce the upwind sails for the Challenge Round the World race yachts.

Quite apart from these developments in advanced materials, sail designers also learned to harness the results of computer stress analysis programmes to develop bespoke systems to produce laminated weaves designed to counter the contoured stress lines within each sail. Initially, sailmakers orientated the panels of cloth in line with the stresses before Sobstadt Sails came up with the concept of aligning continuous filaments of Kevlar, and Dacron/polyester across each horizontal panel and sandwiching them between layers of Mylar. North Sails then took this idea to its logical conclusion by building a massive adjustable sail mould and matching the filaments to the stress diagrams across the entire height of the sail to produce their 3DL racing sails. This technology and the quite separate 'Cuban' super-strength carbon filament cloth developed by Bill Koch's successful America[3] defence syndicate, also stemmed from the America's Cup.

These, and other advances in sail technology, make it essential for crews to have a basic understanding of cloth weaves and constructions in order to get the best performance from what are now high technology sails.

Weaving process

The individual strands are first twisted, either singly or in multiples, to form the exact weight or decitex of yarn required to make the warp or longitudinal threads of the cloth. Once spun onto reels, the filaments are steam-set before being passed through a weaving agent which binds them together and lubricates the threads in readiness for the next stage – weaving.

Much of today's sailcloth is of plain weave – a somewhat ambiguous term, as cloth manufacturers say it is the most difficult to perfect! To the casual eye, one piece of sailcloth looks very much like another, but many variations have been developed to suit specific sail designs, which can radically alter the stretch and recovery characteristics of the finished material. With high-aspect horizontal panelled mainsails, where strength in the vertical is of greatest importance, the weft or horizontal weave is considerably stronger than the warp. With a low aspect mainsail, where leech tension is less critical, the longer foot calls for greater strength in the warp. Various weaves have also been developed specifically for

The plain weave chosen for much of today's sailcloth construction with strength ratios between weft and warp set fairly close.

we refer to as 'crimp'. Radial panel layouts attempt to mimic the various load paths that emanate from the corners and disperse into the body of the sail, but there is no perfect thread alignment because small changes in trim change these load paths significantly. Radial sails, whether they be spinnakers or laminated upwind sails, need to be panelled with the warp running down the centre of each panel or 'gore' in order keep the bias of the fabric, scrim or taffeta, equalized on each side and thus retain their shape. The drawback to this is the wastage of cloth, for radial sails require 30% more yardage than cross - cut sails.'

Sailmakers test each batch of sailcloth for stability on an Instron test rig to determine individual stretch characteristics. They then try to match these characteristics to existing supplies to maintain uniformity and overcome the problems of reproducing accurate shapes from different rolls of material. Both Hood and North take this search for quality and control a step further by developing and manufacturing much of the specialist sailcloths themselves, including the Mylar laminated fabrics and Kevlar/Vectran weaves. This not only allows them to design and manufacture fabrics specifically for sailmaking, instead of using cloth developed for more general use, but also provides them with a high degree of quality control, which is not always available from commercial suppliers.

Laminated fabrics should be chosen ahead of standard cloth only where they provide a large performance differential without compromising utility. A film laminated No 1 genoa will hold its shape better than a similar woven sail. It is lighter and can be carried over a wider wind range. However, this gap narrows as cloth weight increases, to the point where bulkiness and the risk of wear and tear

headsails. With most overlapping genoas, the strength ratios between weft and warp are set fairly close, but high-aspect headsails with horizontal panels require a stronger weft to compensate for the extra loadings on the leech.

Ever since Alan Bond's *Australia II* won the America's Cup using radial panelled main and headsails, the common belief has been that these sails cut from warp orientated cloth are more 'hi-tech' than their cross-cut counterparts. Tim Woodhouse, the head of Hood Sails, begs to differ, saying that any sail made from woven cloth should be cross cut in panel configuration. 'The reason for this is elementary. The fill yarns go across the loom in a straight line and it is the warp yarns which are lifted and then lowered with each pass of sequential fill yarns. The mechanics require that the warp yarns travel around each fill yarn, causing what

more than negates any performance advantage these film laminates provide. Yet there is no doubt that these fabrics have revolutionised sail design and construction. Sailmakers have had to adapt their craft considerably to harness the film's strengths as well as to minimise its weaknesses. Where maximum load on a sail once demanded 8oz cloth, the entire sail was made from that material, but with the aid of computer analysis, sailmakers can now produce composite sails made up from any number of materials, each one calculated to cope with local stresses. Kevlar has 6 times the stretch resistance of polyester, PBO (para-phenylene benzo-bisoxazole) about 8 times, and carbon almost 50 times. This can result in a 30% weight saving over Dacron which is important when you consider that a 25lb (11.34kg) weight at the top of a 75ft (22.86m) mast is equivalent to having a man stationed permanently on the bow, in terms of the extra pitching moment!

However, there is a price to pay for this weight saving, for all share a common failing – poor flex fatigue characteristics. A second problem is delamination. This occurs when the glue joint fails or a sail is flexed and folded in a specific area, such as the end of a batten or around the outside radius of reinforcements. Polyester laminates also become stiff and brittle from UV degradation and no repair will increase the life span. This makes them difficult to justify for anything other than short-life racing, for laminate sails should neither be reefed, roller furled nor trodden on!

Sail shape and setting

There was a time when cruising sails were bent on the rig at the start of a season and their shape simply adjusted by sheet, halyard, outhaul and vang. Today, even the most basic cruising rigs are equipped with

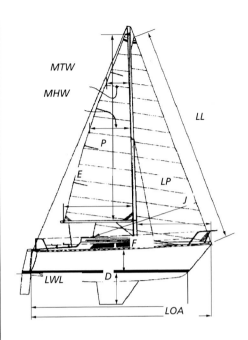

Standard measurement points and connotations on hull and rig.

flattening reefs, backstay adjuster, heavy multi-purchase or hydraulic boom vang, mainsail traveller, and variable position headsail sheeting positions. More sophisticated yachts have push-button genoa furling, in-boom or in-mast mainsail reefing, cunningham controls, and in some cases, fully battened mains. This is because the modern yacht is both lighter and so much more responsive than models that are merely a decade old. Even the smallest tweaks will register immediately on the speedo or VMG (velocity made good) dials, and crews need to have a far greater understanding of sails and their setting in order to get the most out of their boats. There is nothing more satisfying than being on a well sailed yacht. By involving all the crew in improving speed or distance targets, this keeps boredom at bay, and can have a positive effect on morale on long voyages, especially when a little competition is introduced between watches!

Mainsails

Unlike headsails and spinnakers, which are all designed to provide an optimum performance over a relatively small wind range, the universal mainsail must perform equally well in light breeze or full gale, to windward or running. This conflicting requirement for a flat sail with a chord/depth ratio of around 8:1 for windward work, and a fuller bellied aerofoil shape close to a 14:1 ratio when reaching, first led to the development of flexible rigs. Other adjustments, however, including the cunningham, flattener, boom vang, halyard, sheet and traveller, all play an important part in providing infinite variations to suit all conditions.

The mainsail cannot be discussed alone however, for when sailing upwind or reaching, it relies on the interaction with the headsail to improve the airflow over it. Without a headsail the boat cannot point high into the wind. Under mainsail alone the sudden deflection of airflow around the mast produces a large pressure drop on the lee side of the sail, causing an early separation of airflow, which leads to stalling. When a second aerofoil is introduced ahead of the mainsail, the airflow is smoothed out, reducing the pressure differential dramatically, with the result that laminar flow is encouraged over a much greater percentage of the sail, improving efficiency and delaying stall.

Shape and setting

Chord depth: Most mainsails are cut with a deeper draft in the upper two thirds of the sail to produce a more powerful shape, which takes advantage of the lowering drag co-efficient over these narrowing sail sections. This variation in vertical depth distribution should be maintained in all but the heaviest conditions when the heeling force aloft has to be reduced by increasing mast bend to flatten the sail.

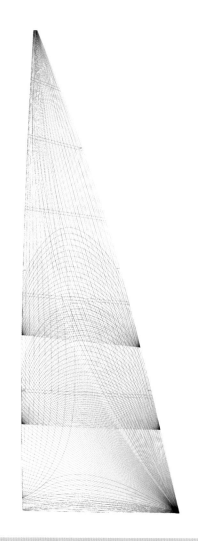

A stress map showing the characteristic loads on a mainsail.

Twist: As a general rule, the wind is stronger at masthead than at deck level and by allowing the leech to open, mainsail shape is twisted to match the changes in apparent wind which free progressively up the height of the sail. When the sail luffs evenly from head to tack and the tell-tales attached to the leech at the end of the batten pockets all stream aft, the main is invariably set with the correct amount of twist, but where there are no tell-tales to act as a guide, try to ensure that the top

A yacht under mainsail alone cannot point as high as one under main and genoa due to the sudden deflection of airflow around the mast which produces a large pressure drop on the lee side of the sail.

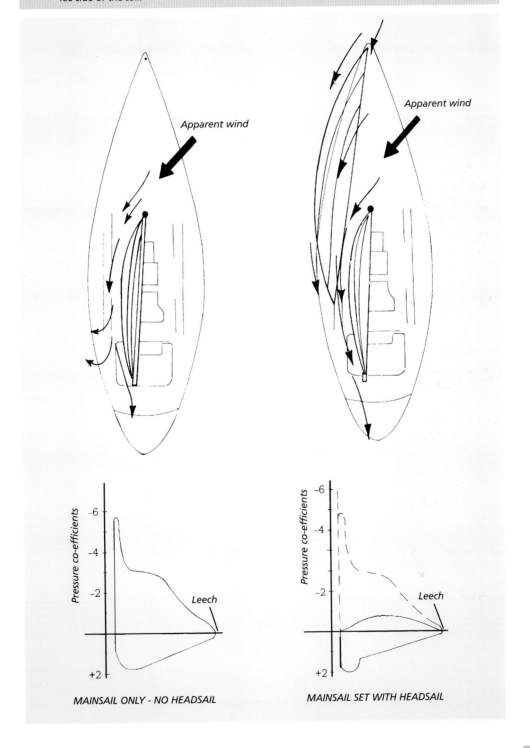

Apparent wind

Apparent wind

Pressure co-efficients

Leech

MAINSAIL ONLY - NO HEADSAIL

Pressure co-efficients

Leech

MAINSAIL SET WITH HEADSAIL

batten always runs parallel to the boom. An open leech encourages the air to flow off the sail, reducing the heeling force in the wind and thus weather helm, while a closed leech increases drag and the pivoting movement the mainsail has on the boat. In light conditions, choppy waters or immediately after tacking, it pays to exaggerate twist and encourage laminar flow in order to foot faster, but in medium air and flat water, a tighter leech will improve pointing ability. Twist should also be encouraged in heavy weather in order to de-power the rig and reduce heeling.

The mainsail

Shape controls

Mast bend: Sailing upwind in strong conditions, the mainsail should have an optimum chord depth of 8:1, which calls for considerable mast bend to flatten the luff over the upper two thirds of the sail, an increase in curvature that simultaneously moves the point of maximum draft further forward and opens the leech. Light conditions also call for a flattened entry to the sail in order to encourage laminar flow, so pre-bend is often required in the rig to provide an optimum chord/depth ratio of around 10:1. In moderate airs, when maximum fullness is required and the chord/depth ratio is increased to 14:1, the mast may require only a small amount of bend to take up luff round. Many mainsails now have a set of narrow guidelines, set 2-4in (5-10 cm) apart, close to the bolt rope at intervals up the luff so that the correct amount of mast bend can be set simply by sighting up the mast from tack to head.

Shelf foot: This tapered panel of cloth, sewn to the foot of the sail, provides the correct degree of shaping to the lower part of the sail as the outhaul is eased in light conditions. As winds increase to above 5 knots apparent, so outhaul tension is increased to close the shelf and produce a flatter shape for windward work.

Flattening reef: A second cringle in the leech, a short way up from the outhaul, provides a flattening reef for this lower part of the mainsail when the yacht first becomes overpressed upwind.

Cunningham hole: Changes in mast bend and foot tension tend to stretch the mainsail fabric, drawing the point of maximum draft aft of its optimum position. Tension on the cunningham pulls the draft forward and opens the leech slightly, reducing weather helm. In moderate to strong conditions it is often pulled down by its maximum amount to return the draft of the sail to a point between 45% and 50% of sail cord, as well as to take out the creases running perpendicular from the clew, caused by the mast bend.

Battens and leech cord: In heavy weather, a stiff top batten is required to control leech curvature, but in light airs a soft batten promotes shape in the sail without creating a hard edge at the leading edge of the batten pocket, so it always pays to carry a choice on board. Large mainsails will require extra stiff battens in the lower pockets to prevent the leech from flogging under the weight of reefing lines.

The leech chord, which to simplify control on some yachts, is led from the head of the sail down the luff to a small purchase block close to the gooseneck, should be tensioned just enough to eliminate flutter. If this results in a slight hook in the leech, this is less significant than having it shaking which, when left unchecked, eventually destroys the cloth along the leech.

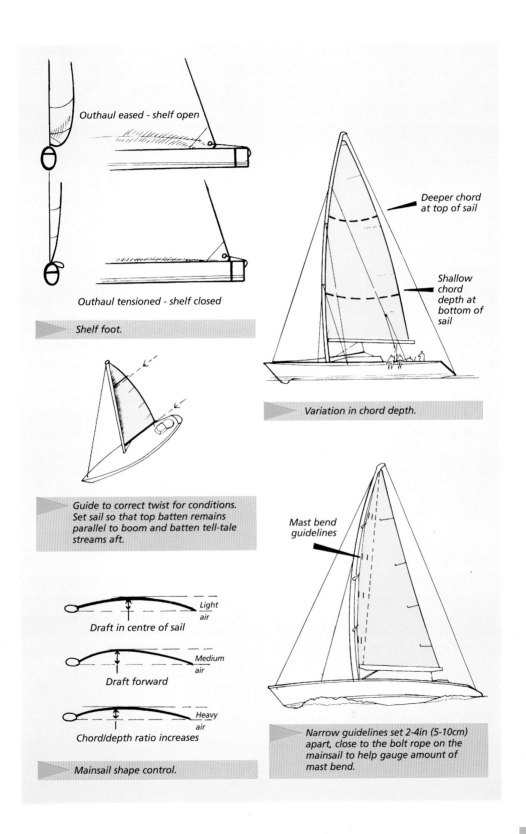

Outhaul eased - shelf open

Outhaul tensioned - shelf closed

Shelf foot.

Deeper chord at top of sail

Shallow chord depth at bottom of sail

Variation in chord depth.

Guide to correct twist for conditions. Set sail so that top batten remains parallel to boom and batten tell-tale streams aft.

Mast bend guidelines

Light air

Draft in centre of sail

Medium air

Draft forward

Heavy air

Chord/depth ratio increases

Mainsail shape control.

Narrow guidelines set 2-4in (5-10cm) apart, close to the bolt rope on the mainsail to help gauge amount of mast bend.

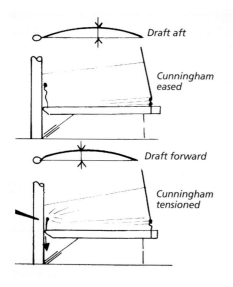

Draft aft

Cunningham eased

Draft forward

Cunningham tensioned

Cunningham control.

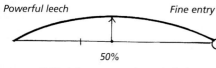

Draft set aft – 5 knots apparent wind

Powerful leech

Fine entry

50%

Critical shape – very close-winded

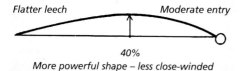

Draft set mid-way – 12 knots apparent wind

Flatter leech

Moderate entry

40%

More powerful shape – less close-winded

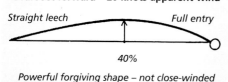

Draft set forward – 20 knots apparent wind

Straight leech

Full entry

40%

Powerful forgiving shape – not close-winded

Sail shape and effect of draft.

Traveller control and sheet tension: On many yachts traveller geometry automatically affects sheet tension whenever adjustment is made but, ideally, one should not affect the other. Changes in mainsheet tension primarily affect the degree of twist set in the sail but any adjustment also affects the width of slot between main and genoa as well as the degree of balance on the helm. The traveller should merely control the angle of the sail in relation to the centreline, but in light weather it often pays to draw the traveller car to windward to reduce tension on the sheet and keep the leech open.

Trimming: The sheet trimmer's job is to fine-tune the sheet traveller and mainsheet to get that top batten tell-tail to stream aft. Should it curl round on the leeward side, then the airflow is stalling out and tension on the leech needs to be eased, though there are times – like trying to fetch up to a mark or climb to weather of another yacht – when the increased pointing ability that a tight leech provides can be beneficial.

Most yachts require between 3°-5° of weather helm to be correctly balanced. Upwind in heavy weather on lightweight daysailers, where it rarely pays to reef the mainsail in wind strengths below Force 5, either the helmsman, or one of the crew, must play the sheet continually. He must rely on vang and backstay tension to maintain control over the leech, and pull the sail in and out like a barn door to maintain this balance and keep the boat sailing fast and upright. On larger yachts, less affected by motion through waves and short gusts, it is often sufficient to play the traveller in and out only when major alterations are required, and to adjust the windward runners to fine tune the amount of power generated by the sail. Only play the mainsheet in extreme conditions because any slackening in tension on the sheet increases fullness within the sail, which on fractionally rigged yachts in particular, can become a devil's-own job to pull back in again.

Sailing downwind: Once round the weather mark, tension in the backstay, runners and babystay is reduced to straighten the mast and increase the chord/depth ratio within the mainsail to 14:1. Tension on the cunningham is also reduced to maintain the position of maximum draft at around 50% of the chord length. The mainsheet now controls the overall angle of the sail and is eased until the luff is on the point of lifting. The leech is entirely controlled by boom vang tension. Where a hydraulic vang is fitted, the golden rule when hardening up from a run is always to take up on the pump before pulling in on the sheet, since the pressure exerted by the sheet on the end of the boom can be enough to bend the ram.

Genoas

Upwind, the genoa becomes the powerhouse, generating up to 90% of a yacht's forward drive, while the mainsail merely acts as a balancing rudder to the airflow. So the choice of headsail, and setting it to match the prevailing conditions is critical. With the exception of some Mylar laminated sails, genoas are designed to stretch so that their draft and fullness can be changed to match the apparent wind over a limited range of speed and angles. As wind speed increases so sail shape is progressively flattened, moving the point of maximum draft forward to maintain maximum forward drive. These changes are controlled by halyard, sheet and backstay tension.

No headsail can cope efficiently with wind speeds from 0-30 knots or wind angles from 30°-110°. This induced sailmakers to produce any number of sail designs, each one covering a relatively small wind speed/angle band. Many overlap each other in this respect and current sail limitation rules are often a governing factor. Therefore, the choice of headsails centres around expected sailing conditions while, at the same time, providing coverage throughout the wind range.

Vertical v horizontal cut: Sailmakers have experimented with vertical panelled sails for many years in an effort to lessen leech stretch, but it was not until the development of warp orientated Mylar laminated Kevlar cloth in the early 1980s, that the problem was finally cracked. The breakthrough came during the build up to the 1983 America's Cup with sail designer Tom Schnackenberg's computer work for Alan Bonds successful *Australia II* campaign. Schnackenberg had already developed a series of computer pro-grammes for generating panel shapes for North Sails and remained closely involved in later analysis work carried out by Danish engineer Michael Richelsen into mapping the stress patterns and load lines that build up in a sail. This showed exactly how the major stresses radiate from the head and clew then run almost parallel to the leech through the mid part of the sail.

Kevlar cloth is only Kevlar in one direction. Either the fill or weft yarns running across the panel or the warp yarns running the length of the cloth are of this golden yarn; the other is invariably a Dacron variant. Schnackenberg reasoned that if he could orientate the Kelvar yarns or warp cloth exactly in line with the major stresses he could build lighter and stronger sails that would hold their shape better than the horizontal cut sails. The idea reduced distortion but provided a valuable 15-20% weight saving.

Vertical
Cut

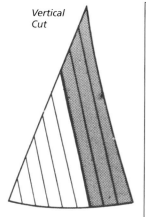

Australia II
type Cut

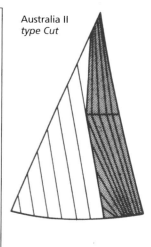

Spider
Cut

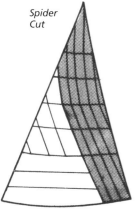

Australia II
heavy
weather
tri-radial

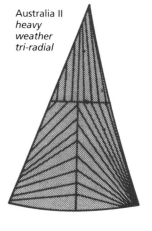

Fan
Cut

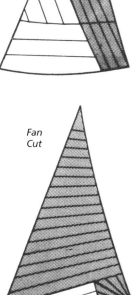

*The most significant sailmaking development for
many years came with computer analysis of the
stresses that build up in a genoa. This allows
sailmakers to design panel layouts aligned with
those stresses to minimise distortion and lessen
the overall weight of the sails.*

C-Cut

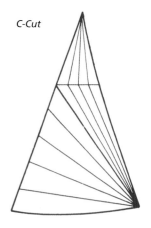

Australia II's vertical cut sails with their rocked panels and radial corners performed better on three important counts. First, warp orientated cloth offers a 10-20% weight saving over similar fill orientated fabric because, unlike a fill thread, the warp can be pre-stressed during the weaving and processing. This had the effect of reducing weight aloft and thus the healing moment, as well as easing handling, which improved tacking times. Secondly, however strong the seaming, crosscut Kevlar sails suffer 15-20% greater stretch along the leech because of the elasticity in the Dacron stitching which was negating much of the advantage of using Kevlar. Finally, the radial corners Schnackenberg built into *Australia II's* sails distributed the loadings into the body of the sail more evenly than the standard triangular patches and were also lighter and more pliable into the bargain, making tacking all the easier.

The lessons learned during that historic summer in Newport had a direct and immediate effect on yacht racing in general, as lofts right across the world feverishly developed their own versions of Schnackenberg's distinctive sails. For their part, North Sail designers came up with a consensus of what they had developed by producing their bi-radial C-Cut genoa and mainsail designs which had just one horizontal seam, before moving on to develop their one-piece moulded 3DL manufacturing process.

Reefable headsails: These have long been a legitimate way to increase the sail wardrobe without infringing class limitation. A reefable heavy No.1 genoa for example can double as a No.2 and allow for an extra light weather headsail to be carried. Headsails above No.2 are not suitable for reefing. On yachts of 50ft (15m) or more where the limitation rules are often less discriminatory, these compromise reefs should be avoided in all but the smallest sails. This is because the position of the second clew cannot always provide effective control over leech flutter. The option is also governed by the amount of cloth that can be furled into the foot of the sail.

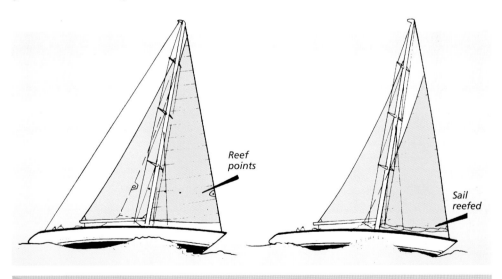

The reefable headsail – two for the price of one and a legitimate way to circumvent the sail limitation rules governing sail inventories on small yachts.

Drifter.

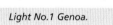

Light No.1 Genoa.

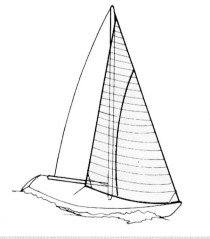

No.2 Genoa.

Drifter: Made up to maximum dimensions from the lightest cloth, this sail is intended to get the boat moving and build up apparent wind in fickle conditions.

Range:	Dacron, 0-5 knots
	Mylar, 0-8 knots
Wind angle:	30°-50°

Light No.1 genoa: A full cut genoa designed to generate maximum power in light conditions. An effective sail in both smooth and choppy water, it is often cut with a flat entry to ensure good pointing.

Range:	Dacron, 4-12 knots
	Mylar, 4-14 knots
Wind angle:	28°-50°

Medium No.1 genoa: Cut flatter than the light No.1, with the point of maximum draft placed further forward, this sail is often cut with a very fine entry, but shape can be adjusted to power the yacht through a swell.

Range:	Dacron, 12-18 knots
	Mylar, 9-22 knots
Wind angle:	28°–50°

Heavy No.1 genoa: Cut flatter than the medium No. 1 with more leech hollow to reduce heeling, this sail is normally specified for yachts over 40ft with enough inherent stability to allow a full LP genoa.

Range:	Dacron, 18-24 knots
	Mylar, 14-25 knots
Wind angle:	28°-55°

No.2 genoa: This often full-hoist sail has its overlap reduced to between 130% and 145%. The sail is cut to the same shape as a heavy No. 1, though some sailmakers also produce hybrid No.2 and 3 genoas, using heavier strength material in the foot and head to improve their wind range.

Range:	Dacron, 22-28 knots
	Mylar, 20-30 knots
Wind angle:	35°-55°

No.3 genoa: A high aspect sail generates less drag than a low aspect design of similar area, so rather than cut down on hoist, most No.3 genoas are narrowed at the foot to between 89-100% LP. Only on racing boats prone to lee helm or long-keeled cruisers is a low aspect sail favoured.

Range: Dacron, 26-30 knots
            Mylar, 22-35 knots
Wind angle: 22°-45°

No.4 working jib: Intended primarily for cruising yachts, this full sail cut with a 90% hoist and 90-105% overlap, often has a high clew to keep the foot out of the water and aid visibility. An ideal cruising sail in moderate/strong conditions.

Range: Dacron, max 40 knots
Wind angle: 28°-90°

No.4/5 genoa: The size of these heavy weather headsails is governed by the stability of an individual yacht, but generally speaking they will have 90% hoist and 85% overlap. It is important that these sails are cut and set, with some shape to provide the power in extreme conditions to lift the yacht over waves, otherwise they merely push the yacht to leeward reducing VMG performance dramatically.

Range: Dacron, 40 knots +
Wind angle: All

Storm jib: Made up from orange coloured material to aid search and rescue operations, this headsail, which is often set in tandem with a tri-sail, is compulsory equipment in ocean races.

Range: Dacron, 40 knots +
Wind Angle: All

Reacher: A powerful full-cut sail with a rounded leading edge for maximum drive in close reaching conditions. Like most reachers, this sheets to the transom to provide maximum width of slot to allow a

No.4 Working Jib.

No.3 Genoa.

No.4 Genoa.

staysail to be flown inside. Because of the inherent fullness shaped into reaching sails, they require more headstay tension than a genoa would when set on a close reach. Once the sail's maximum wind strength has been reached, it is often best to change down to a reefed No.2 genoa sheeted out to the leeward rail, unless a blast reacher is carried.

Range: Dacron, 6-22 knots
Wind angle: 40°-85°

Blast reacher: A smaller full-hoist reacher cut with a short overlap to reduce the excessive drag and healing force created in heavy air by large overlap sails. Often equipped with reefing points, this sail has a lower clew point than most reachers and sheets forward of the transom to provide a low centre of effort and less heel. The blast reacher can also be used to good effect as a poled running sail when conditions are too strong for a spinnaker.

Range: Dacron, 18-35 knots
Wind angle: 45°-85°

Cross-cut furling genoa: This is the ideal multi-purpose genoa for cruising and short-handed racing. It is attached to a roller furling headstay which is usually controlled with a continuous line led back to the cockpit. Purpose-made sails are usually made with a a foam luff insert to maintain the correct shape when the sail is set partially furled or reefed. The sail remains rolled up on the headstay when not in use and has a UV resistant stripe down the trailing edge to protect the sail from uv. degradation when fully furled.

Range: Dacron, 4-30 knots
Wind angle: 28°–50°

Multi-purpose genoa (MPG): This sail is available in two versions - a light air b-radial design made from spinnaker nylon for use in wind strengths up to 12 knots,

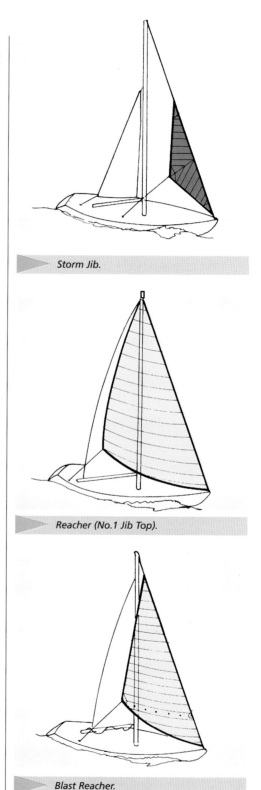

Storm Jib.

Reacher (No.1 Jib Top).

Blast Reacher.

Cross-cut Furling Genoa.

Light air MPG.

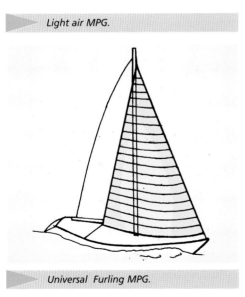
Universal Furling MPG.

and as a 'bullet proof' universal furling genoa. The latter is constructed from 3.4oz cloth with a second ply around all three edges to insure against damage, should the furling mechanism fail. This sail became one of Dee Caffari's main armaments during her solo non-stop record chasing circumnavigation in the 72ft (21.95m) Challenge yacht *Aviva*. The main benefit of this sail is it's wide wind range, and ability to be reefed easily, using the furling system to reduce or expand sail area.

Light air MPG:
Range: 1.5oz Dacron, 0-12 knots

Universal furling MPG:
Range: 2.2oz Dacron, 10-35 knots

Trim and setting
The four variables affecting headsail trim are draft, camber, luff sag and twist. These are controlled by fine-tuning halyard, sheet, runners and backstay tension, (together with sheet lead positioning) to produce an optimum shape to match wind and sea conditions. Many find the subject totally mystifying, but with the help of telltales, shape stripes, trim lines and calibration marks on tracks and halyards, the task is equal to any sailor once the fundamentals have been grasped.

Before discussing the mechanics of headsail shape, it is important to diagnose what optimum shape is. The prime objective is to produce a uniform slot between genoa and mainsail, both sails having the same degree of twist to form a perfect venturi that will maintain laminar flow across the whole sail plan. The second objective is to ensure that the genoa telltails lift and fall evenly up the entire length of the luff, while the third, and possibly most mystifying objective, is to match headsail camber to the prevailing conditions.

Wind tunnel research has shown that it is the shape of camber, and not merely the position of maximum draft, that plays the most significant part in producing forward drive. Correct shape, particularly over the leading third of the sail, can increase a sail's performance by a startling 50%, while the position of maximum draft has only a 10% effect.

In ideal beating conditions – light to medium winds and flat water – a headsail with a flat entry and maximum draft set between 45% and 47% aft from the luff, will enhance pointing ability without loss of speed. The trade-off, however, is that the performance band is narrow, placing a high priority on steering and trimming skills to keep the yacht in the 'groove'. A rounder entry and a draft position between 40-45% produces a more forgiving sail shape. While not providing the same high pointing ability, it does offer a wider performance groove than the flat entry sail, making it a better match for choppy, unstable conditions – or an inexperienced hand on the helm.

Setting a headsail to the required shape is akin to tying a crown knot in the end of a rope - pull one strand excessively and the other two fall out of balance. Each has to be pulled bit by bit to form a perfect knot. Like those three strands, halyard, backstay and sheet tension interact with each other to affect the shape of the headsail. Sheet, runners and backstay tension affect the twist and camber of a sail, while halyard tension controls the position of maximum draft.

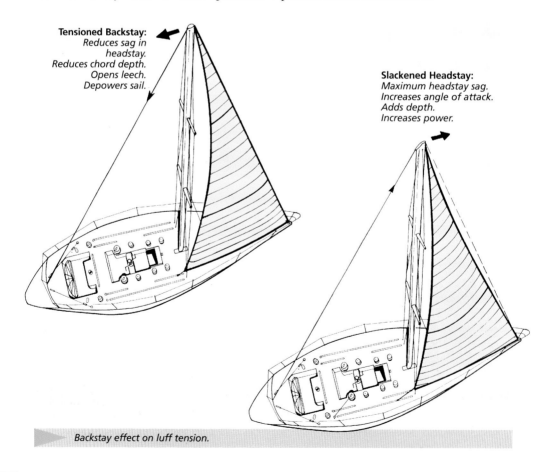

Tensioned Backstay:
Reduces sag in headstay.
Reduces chord depth.
Opens leech.
Depowers sail.

Slackened Headstay:
Maximum headstay sag.
Increases angle of attack.
Adds depth.
Increases power.

Backstay effect on luff tension.

Halyard tension: This dictates the position of maximum draft by balancing the stretch that takes place along the leech of the genoa as the wind increases. Greater tension pulls the draft forward, less tension allows it to move aft. Low stretch Mylar sails have a critical tolerance, much smaller than Dacron sails, and too much tension can cause them to blow out. It is essential to mark the halyards with indelible ink or seizing so that tension, once found correct for a set of conditions, can quickly be repeated. Halyards can be marked close to where they emerge from the lower mast and measured against a calibration strip on the side of the section.

Backstay tension: This controls headstay sag on a masthead rig and has a direct effect on the amount of camber and twist set in the mainsail. As an alternative to the backstay adjuster, some yachts are fitted with a load cell to provide the afterguard with a true pressure reading instead of interpolating from the backstay reading. The pressure on a hydraulic backstay is registered on the control dial but a calibrated codline running between backstay terminal and adjuster provides a visual alternative to showing the amount of tension applied.

A rounded leading edge to the genoa is required in light airs or choppy conditions to make the yacht foot faster. This is achieved by easing the backstay pressure to around 25% of maximum to introduce some sag in the headstay. Remember though that in gusty conditions each puff increases sag, and thus luff round, just when a flatter shape would be preferable, so have a crewman stationed near to the hydraulic pump to increase tension wherever a gust looks imminent. As wind strength builds up, so pressure on the forestay must be increased to match, for

Heeling force

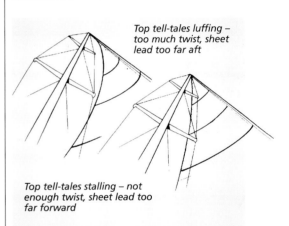

Top tell-tales luffing – too much twist, sheet lead too far aft

Top tell-tales stalling – not enough twist, sheet lead too far forward

excessive sag, which allows the luff to curl to leeward, limits sail twist and increases the heeling force in the sail.

Runners and checkstay tension: Running backstays are common enough on fractional rigs where they provide essential control over headstay sag and mast bend, but they are also utilised on masthead boats, for the extra support they provide can allow a smaller mast section to be chosen. Sailing to windward in moderate conditions, maximum tension is applied to the runners to minimize headstay sag, but in choppy conditions, tension is eased to allow some sag in order to give the genoa a fuller, more powerful shape. It is this constant adjustment of backstay and

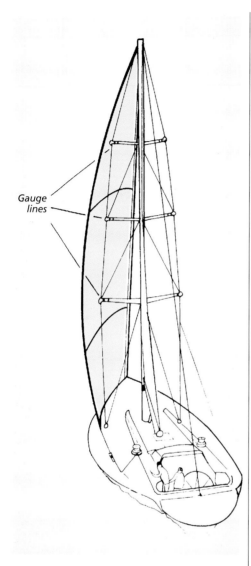

Gauge
lines

the sheeting angle can improve the venturi effect and thus efficiency in light to moderate conditions. The rub however, is that this rotates the heeling force closer abeam as well as narrowing the performance groove, thus making the genoa more prone to stalling and less able to provide the acceleration to drive the yacht through a slop effectively.

A narrow sheeting angle – between 7°-8° degrees from the centreline – will improve pointing ability in light to moderate winds and smooth water but this should be widened to 9°-10° when speed through the water takes priority, ie:

- when winds are either very light or strong
- seas are choppy
- the genoa is set at the top of the range
- the helmsman is inexperienced

In gusty conditions, the sheeting angle may need to be widened with a barber-haul sheet led to a foot block on the outside track in tune with any increase in apparent wind.

Each headsail has an optimum fore-and aft-sheet lead angle, and during initial sail trials, track positions and halyard tensions should be noted for easy reference when the sail is recalled. However, variations in halyard tension and more significantly, alterations in course to the wind, call for changes in foot block position whenever the sheet is eased, for the lead must be pulled forward to maintain the same sheet angle in order to control twist. Hood was one of the first sailmakers to simplify this problem by marking trim lines on their genoas, close to the clew, to act as an alignment guide. These are marked either when the sail is made, or when set correctly during sailing trials. When there are no trim lines to act as a guide, the correct sheet angle can be determined by sailing to weather with the headsail pinned in hard and watching the luff break. If the top tell-tales break first, the lead is too far

runner tension that provides the throttle control on the rig, giving the afterguard the ability to quickly change sail shape to suit a wide range of sail conditions.

Sheet lead position: This has a direct bearing on both width of slot and the degree of twist set into a sail. Narrowing

The benefit of the cutter rig shown here as Group 4 Securitas battles to windward in a Force 9 gale. The staysail not only improves the venturi effect between the genoa and mainsail, but keeps sail area low down to minimise heeling.

aft, and too far forward if the lower ones are first to stall. Only when all the tell-tales mirror the pressure on the luff is the sheet angle correct.

Sheet tension: This affects camber and twist. By pulling the sheet in hard, twist, depth of camber and sheeting angle are all reduced, improving pointing ability in flat-water conditions. Easing the sheet produces a more powerful shape, which helps the yacht accelerate after a tack and increases drive in light airs or choppy conditions. Upwind, the genoa sheet has to be played continually to match changes in wind velocity and preserve optimum sail shape. The trimmer's primary task is to prevent gusts and lulls from distorting shape but he must also work in synchronisation with the helmsman, easing the sail slightly then slowly pulling it in again whenever the boat bears away over a wave, or the bow is headed up slowly to take advantage of a lift.

The best way to maintain correct trim is to monitor the gap between headsail and spreader tips – a task some crews find is helped when two taped gauge lines are set 3in (8cm) apart at the end of each spreader to sight the leech curve. Spreader length and position varies from one yacht to another so there can be no hard and fast guide to sheet tension, but a No.1 genoa sheeted to within an inch of the top spreader in high pointing conditions may need to be eased by 8-9in (20-23cm) before being set correctly.

Changing down
Each headsail has a set wind range prescribed by the sailmaker, but some yachts lacking stability often become overpowered before those limits are reached. VMG takes a severe knock when a yacht is over-pressed and the call to reef or change down should always be made

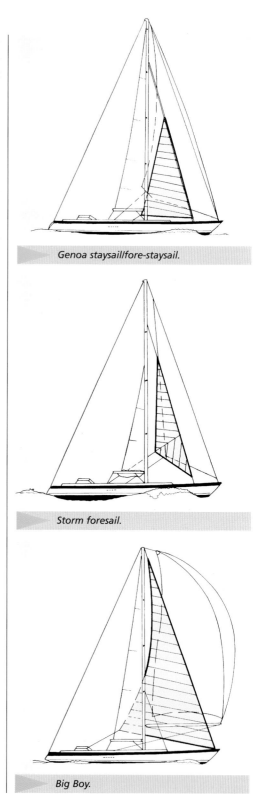

Genoa staysail/fore-staysail.

Storm foresail.

Big Boy.

before heel exceeds 25° or 20° on yachts with extreme girth.

On small lightweight fractionally-rigged daysailers, which are invariably raced over short legs and have a restricted wardrobe anyway, it pays to work through the headsail changes before setting a reef in the main. Less time is lost playing the traveller to keep the boat in balance upwind during gusty conditions, than taking crew weight off the weather rail to set a reef and shake it out again. Apart from taking in the flattening reef, this rule often holds true on larger yachts whenever racing around short inshore courses. Each new leg invariably requires a change of headsail or spinnaker, and in the confusion of rounding a mark in the midst of a large fleet, a full hoist mainsail in all but extreme conditions leaves one less set of adjustments to worry about. Only on long offshore legs does sail plan efficiency outweigh crew efficiency. When the call for sail changes is less frequent, more time can be devoted to perfecting balance by reefing the mainsail and hoisting larger genoas. Each yacht has its own optimum sail reduction scale which your sailmaker or designer should be able to provide.

Staysails

The staysail is designed to regain the slot effect lost between headsail/spinnaker and mainsail, once sheets are eased. These sails, which require attached airflow to be effective, can be carried from 50°-150° apparent and work best in moderate conditions. On anything broader, the staysail becomes blanketed by the mainsail, and also affects the airflow around the spinnaker. Closer to wind, however, the double-head rig – genoa or reacher with a staysail set inside – often proves to be the fastest combination when the apparent wind is between 50°-70° and is flown in preference to a close reaching spinnaker.

Types

Genoa staysail: Originally developed for use with a reacher or genoa, this staysail's short 70% hoist and 80-100% LP makes it an ideal spinnaker staysail for strong close reaching conditions. On level rated yachts with their limited sail inventories a 'Big Boy' with reefing points along luff and leech to create a low aspect staysail, offers a useful compromise.

Wind range:	5-25 knots
Wind angle:	55°-90°

Fore-staysail: With its 65% hoist and 70% LP, the fore-staysail is similar to the genoa staysail except that it is attached to the inner forestay, rather than remaining free-luffed. The sail is set inside a reacher or high clewed genoa in close reaching conditions.

Wind range:	5-25 knots
Wind angle:	45°-120°

Storm-foresail: This specialist sail with its short 60% hoist and minimum LP is designed to be set in conjunction with a jib top in strong conditions.

Wind range:	35 knots +
Wind angle:	All

Big Boy: Designed for setting inside a spinnaker when beam or broad reaching, the Big Boy, Lazy Boy or tall spinnaker staysail, as some sailmakers label it, has a full hoist and an LP of between 85 and 120%. The sail is cut with a high clew to provide the maximum overlap on the mainsail, and is sheeted through the end of the boom.

Wind range:	0-15 knots
Wind angle:	80°-120°

Daisy staysail: Designed specifically for light airs and wide apparent wind angles, this specialist staysail is full in shape and can be cut with a high clew for boom-end

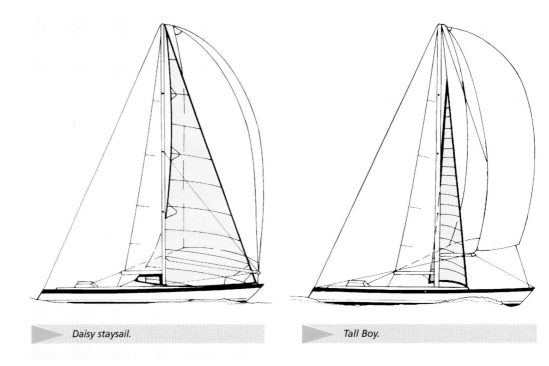

Daisy staysail.

Tall Boy.

sheeting, or made to sweep the deck and take advantage of the end plate effect that this provides. It has a full hoist and 80-85% LP, is made from the lightest hard finish spinnaker cloth or Mylar and must be handled with the greatest of care (hauled down using the flat of the hand and not grasped with enthusiasm) otherwise it tears.

Wind range: 0-12 knots
Wind angle: 60°-120°

Tall Boy: Beyond 120° apparent, normal staysails become ineffective, but a narrow Tall Boy made from light spinnaker material and set across the deck from the weather side just forward of the mast, adds to the projected area of the mainsail when running, as well as improving the airflow across the leeside. The sail, which generally has a $^7/_8$ hoist and a width equal to the yacht's beam, is sometimes made of

stronger cloth to double as a windward staysail on boats rigged without forward lower shrouds.

Wind range: 5-20 knots
Wind angle: 45°-60° or 130°-150°

Mizzen genoa: This sail is the ketch-rigged yacht's secret weapon when sailing against sloops. Tacked down amidships and hoisted free-luffed to the mizzen mast, this sail fills the slot between main and mizzen improving the venturi effect and laminar flow. It can be set from as little as 55° apparent wind and up to Force 5 in strength, and can add a knot or more to boat speed.

Wind range: All
Wind angle: 55°-90°

Mizzen staysail: The mizzen staysail, which is hoisted free-luffed, sheets to the mizzen boom and, like forward staysails, is tacked either to the centreline or weather

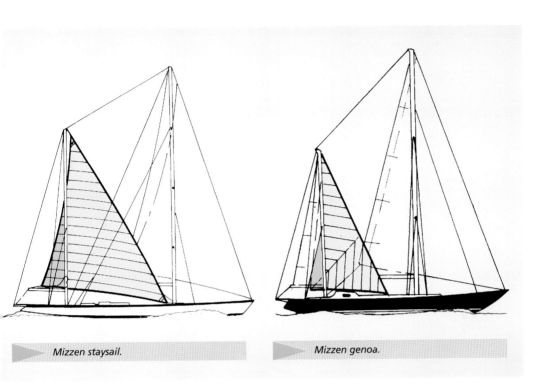

Mizzen staysail.

Mizzen genoa.

rail according to the apparent wind angle. On well-balanced ketches, a heavy weather mizzen staysail can prove beneficial provided that it does not add greatly to weather helm.

Wind range: All
Wind angle: 70°-130°

Trimming

Genoa staysails: A double-head rig is most effective between apparent wind angles of 50°-75°, when the wind is between 10 and 20 knots and sea conditions are smooth. Below this wind speed, the airflow is likely to stall in the slot, and in stronger conditions, trim and steering can become unsettled. These sails perform best set inside a reacher whose high clew and stern sheeting provide a wide slot and better control over twist than can be achieved with a genoa sheeted down to the rail.

By setting the genoa/reacher trim first, the staysail and mainsail can be set to mirror headsail twist and form two evenly spaced parallel slots between headsail and main. To achieve this, however, the staysail sheet lead may require a barberhaul arrangement made up from sail ties or spare line across the deck to achieve the correct lead position. Like the genoa, the staysail requires laminar flow to be effective and must be kept on the point of luffing with a crewman playing the sheet continually, otherwise the airflow will stall.

Spinnaker staysails: These staysails, designed to improve the slot effect between spinnaker and mainsail can be carried as close as 65° apparent, but only if conditions are ideal – flat seas and a wind between 10 and 18 knots apparent. Below that wind speed, the sail merely interferes with the flow across the spinnaker. Above

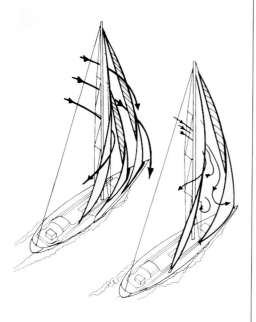

Staysail setting.

20 knots, the sail can cause excessive heeling and handling problems. However, in gusty conditions a good sheet hand freeing the staysail sheet in the puffs to avoid broaching, then trimming in again during the lulls when the boat would otherwise be underpowered, can help the yacht pull away from her opposition.

With apparent wind closer than a beam reach, the staysail needs to be tacked down on the centreline and is only moved out to the weather rail on broader courses once the spinnaker pole has been squared off enough to allow this. The fore-and-aft position of the tack is determined by the apparent angle and amount of wind. On a close reach in moderate to fresh winds for instance, the sail can be tacked as close as a quarter of the distance from bow to mast because the spinnaker will be lifting clear.

When conditions are more marginal or the course broad, the sail needs to be tacked to the weather rail approximately a third of the distance from the bow, in order to let the spinnaker breathe. When close reaching, the staysail sheet is led to the leeward rail or temporary foot block barberhauled inboard to provide the correct twist and foot shape, or through the end of the boom on wider points of sail. This wider sheeting base may require the staysail tack being raised on a pennant to regain the correct twist and foot shape. The staysail's luff tell-tales determine the correct fore-and-aft sheet lead position and should just luff slightly at the top of the sail to maintain an open leech so that air is not sucked away from the spinnaker. When trimming, the staysail sheet hand must take his cue from the spinnaker trimmer, easing his sheet immediately when adjustment in chute trim is called for. This is especially important whenever the spinnaker collapses, for the suction of air across the staysail starves the chute and makes it hard to set again.

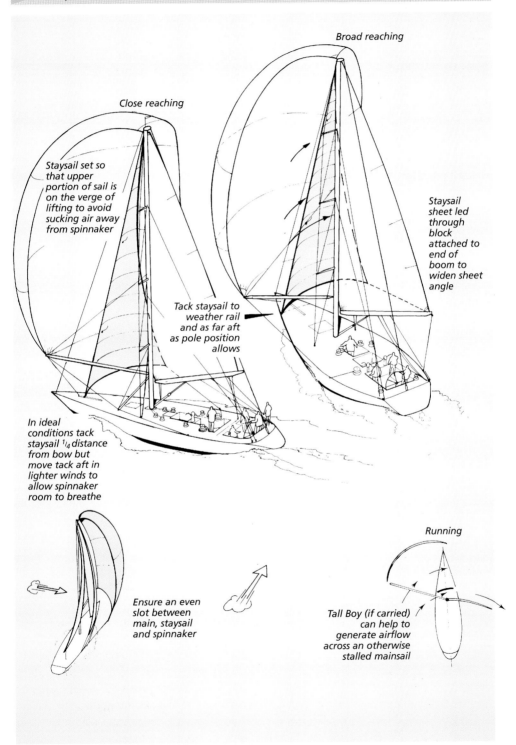

Broad reaching

Close reaching

Staysail set so that upper portion of sail is on the verge of lifting to avoid sucking air away from spinnaker

Staysail sheet led through block attached to end of boom to widen sheet angle

Tack staysail to weather rail and as far aft as pole position allows

In ideal conditions tack staysail ¹/₄ distance from bow but move tack aft in lighter winds to allow spinnaker room to breathe

Ensure an even slot between main, staysail and spinnaker

Running

Tall Boy (if carried) can help to generate airflow across an otherwise stalled mainsail

Running dead downwind, the Tall Boy, if allowed within class rules, can be brought into play. This is tacked to the weather rail just forward of the mast and, as part of improving flow across an otherwise stalled mainsail, can help to steady the yacht's rolling motion.

Spinnakers

Tri-radial, cross-cut, floater, flanker, star-cut, tri-star, jumbo – the various spinnaker types can be as puzzling to the raw deckhand as their setting. There is no other sail that causes such confusion – panic even – than the spinnaker. Yet, once mastered, there is nothing to match a brisk spinnaker leg for sheer excitement. Surfing with spinnaker set, the difference between wellbeing and wipe-out is balanced on a knife-edge. Helmsman and trimmer must work as one. If either is slow to anticipate the other, or waves and wind, then a broach is almost inevitable. Get it right though, and the boat comes alive, the roar from the spray becomes deafening and adrenaline works overtime. There is no greater excitement.

Getting the most from a spinnaker in light or heavy conditions takes practice and more practice. There is no excuse for a wine-glass set or worse, a spinnaker wrap around the headstay, but it happens in the best of circles and invariably through a loss of concentration or lack of foresight on the part of the afterguard that leads to a harassed hoist or dousing. The secret to successful spinnaker handling is early preparation and smooth, unhurried execution. Nowhere is that old saying, 'More haste – less speed' more apt than when setting a chute.

Design

Spinnaker shape results from a mixture of higher mathematics and the sailmaker's art of compromise and experience. With pole height and spinnaker width often limited by class rules, it is not possible to design a spinnaker with a uniform cord/depth ratio. For this reason, the lower panels are cut with greater fullness and serve as a base for the correct shaping through the middle sections of the sail, where shape is less restricted by the sheeting platform. The head is also a compromise in design, for while the computer shows up the benefits of producing a spinnaker with a head angle of 150°, experience dictates that this does not set effectively in anything but the most stable environment. Thus, head angles are reduced to around 120° on a floater and maxi-sized tri-radial, and brought down to 75° on star-cuts and flankers.

Experience also shows that a flat eclipse with a chord/depth ratio varying between 4:1 and 7:1 is the optimum shape for a general purpose spinnaker, for this presents the greatest projected area for running and can be transformed into a smooth aerofoil shape for reaching simply by lowering the pole to increase luff tension. To aid directional stability and sheet control, the sailmaker also adds a little extra round to the leeches, which encourages the luff to fold early and help the crew to maintain optimum trim.

The ideal chord/depth ratio varies according to the wind angles and the conditions for which the spinnaker is designed. A running sail is normally shaped to a 4:1 ratio while a general-purpose tri-radial has a 5:1 ratio and flanker and star-cut takes up a flatter 7:1 shape. Likewise, head shaping can vary. The profile of a tri-radial is cut with an L/D ratio of 5.89:1; with reaching spinnakers it is 6.25:1 and flankers are flattest of all with a 7:1 ratio.

In theory at least, the spinnaker can be designed to suit a wide variety of apparent wind angles simply by altering pole height and sheeting positions. Only extreme shapes or projected areas limit usage to

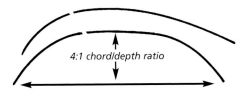

4:1 chord/depth ratio

Lowering the pole on a reach increases luff tension and promotes an aerofoil-shaped spinnaker.

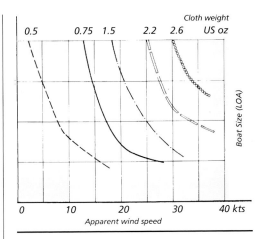

Wind range comparison between spinnaker cloth and boat size.

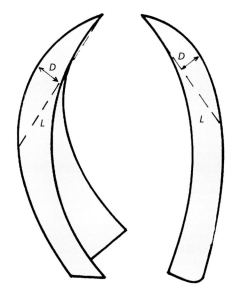

The differences in head shape of reaching and running spinnakers. The running spinnaker will have a chord/depth ratio of 4:1, and be elliptical in shape to give the greatest projection. A reaching or general purpose spinnaker requires a flatter chord/depth ratio of between 6.25: and 7:1.

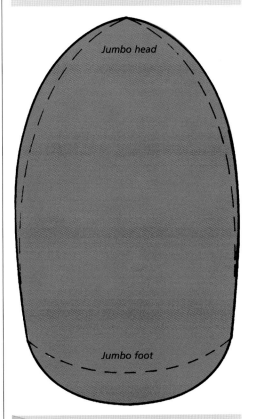

Big is not always best. Jumbo spinnakers may offer the greatest projected area when running but are difficult to control when reaching. The wide shoulders collapse early, trapping dead air in the large foot.

small wind angles. Large spinnakers, for instance, are not always the best choice, especially on lightweight designs, which must be sailed upright to perform. This lesson was learned first in fast planing dinghy classes like the Fireball, 470 and 505 where a smaller spinnaker provided a better interaction between jib and mainsail to produce more power and less leeway than the maxi-sized chutes, particularly when reaching. The small spinnaker provides the same benefits for larger yachts and, with head angles narrowed to 75°, their flatter shape and shorter hoist allows a staysail to be set inside, even on quite tight reaches, which more than compensates for any loss in area.

The jumbo foot and head, two other aspects of spinnaker design, wax and wane in popularity. The jumbo head provides extra projected area aloft which is useful when running downwind, but the sail has to be over-trimmed to keep it from collapsing, and the excessive shoulders make it next to impossible to support when reaching. The jumbo foot works well in apparent winds above 15 knots but below that, the extra cloth tends to weight the sail down as well as trap dead air. This is particularly the case on reaching legs, when the foot tends to curl up and choke the slot.

Spinnaker types

Cross-cut: The cross-cut spinnaker, developed in 1951 by Ted Hood, was a first step towards solving the problems of stretch inherent with all early designs where the panels of cloth ran parallel to the luff tapes. The design proved to be a good running sail and was copied by sailmakers the world over, but its reaching ability was still limited by the bias stretch within each panel of cloth, which increased fullness, particularly in the middle of the sail just where it needs to be flattest.

Weight	Wind range	Wind angle
0.75 oz	5-10 knots	120°-180°

Radial head: The need for better shape control to improve the spinnaker's reaching capabilities led to the development of the radial head, where the upper panels, all radiate from the head, which reduces bias stretch considerably. The sail's simple construction is still

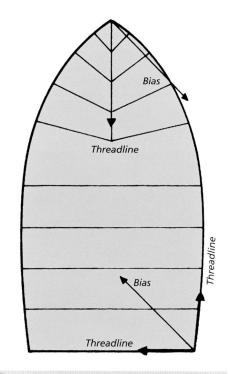

Cross-cut.

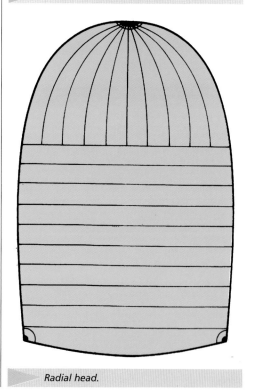

Radial head.

perfectly adequate for dinghies and small keelboats, since strain levels never result in excessive distortion within the lower panels. The sail also remains an economical running sail for larger yachts.

Weight	Wind range	Wind angle
0.5 oz	0-5 knots	90°-180°
0.75 oz	5-10 knots	90°-180°
1.5 oz	6-16 knots	90°-180°

Star-cut: Following the success of the radial head spinnaker, cutting the other panels to radiate from the clews was the natural development to solving the problem of bias stretch across the rest of the sail. This design, originated by Bruce Banks, was one of the few worthwhile innovations to stem from the British 12 Metre yacht *Sovereign*, during her hapless campaign to win the America's Cup in 1964. Far from stretching as the strain increases, the three radial corners tend to pull on the centre of the sail and flatten it, and will maintain this shape even when close reaching. The star-cut is invariably made from strong cloth, heavily reinforced at the clews and can double as a No.3 running spinnaker in heavy weather.
Wind angle 60°-90°

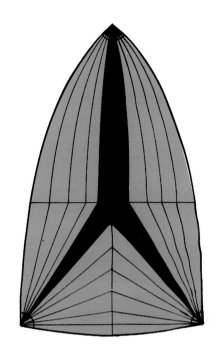

Star cut/super star cut/floating star.

Floating star: Made from the lightest of materials, this specialist sail is designed for light reaching conditions, but is also used as a regular ghosting spinnaker when the slop left after a storm makes a regular sized floater impossible to set. It is invariably cut with a flat head and narrow shoulders to simplify setting in choppy conditions. This lightweight sail is susceptible to blowing out if subjected to too much pressure, so while the trimmer concentrates on keeping the sail filled, another crewman needs to keep a eye on the anomometer.

Weight	Wind range	Wind angle
0.5 oz	0-5 knots	60°-180°
1 oz	0-10 knots	55°-75°

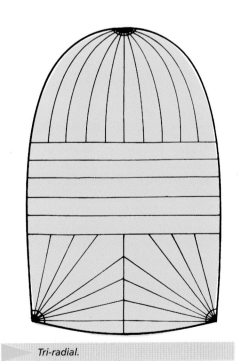

Tri-radial.

Tri-radial: Essentially a star-cut with several horizontal panels across the middle to provide greater fullness, this design has proved to be the best multi-purpose spinnaker for all but the smallest keel boats where the radial head remains adequate. The full lifting head, round forgiving leeches, elliptical centre sections and gently contoured foot make the tri-radial spinnaker adaptable for a wide range of apparent wind angles and will not distort even when close reaching.

Weight	Wind range	Wind angle
0.75 oz	5-10 knots	60-180°
1.5 oz	5-16 knots	60-180°
2.2 oz	14-23 knots	85-170°
3 oz	18-30 knots	85-170°

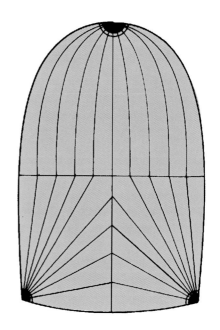

Mylar tri-radial.

Mylar tri-radial: The need to maintain spinnaker shaping throughout the wind range eventually led sailcloth manufacturers to develop a Mylar-backed lightweight scrim to solve the problems of bias stretch. This was used initially for making floaters, but as adhesive technology advanced to provide a stronger bond along the seams, heavier spinnakers have been made. These sails are generally all-purpose, and cut to a tri-radial pattern.

Weight	Wind range	Wind angle
1 oz	0-14 knots	60-180°

Spider Cut: Computer stress analysis programmes gave designers at Sobstadt Sails the idea of orientating the centre panels of their tri-radial spinnakers to align the warp threads with the stress lines. This resulted in a patchwork of panels across the centre and solved the problems of bias stretch in the main body of the sail.

Weight	Wind range	Wind angle
0.75 oz	5-10 knots	60-180°
1.5 oz	5-16 knots	60-180°
2.2 oz	14-23 knots	85-170°

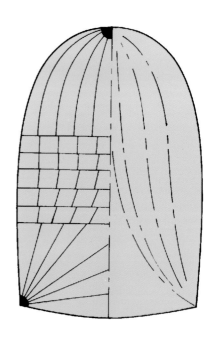

Spider Cut showing stress lines.

Super flanker: This sail is smaller than the regular flanker, and can be carried in greater wind strengths without producing excessive heel. Flown with the head eased some 3ft (1m) from the mast, and with the pole set high on fractional rigged yachts, it sets well out from the boat, allowing a staysail to be set at closer angles to the wind than most reaching spinnakers. The shoulders are narrower than a regular flanker and prevent the leech from hooking to weather and stalling the slot. The sail also doubles as a storm spinnaker.

Weight	Wind range	Wind angle
2.2 oz	23-30 knots	50-170°
3 oz	28-40 knots	50-170°

Floater: The floater, a name derived from the fact that the material is light enough to float, was developed by Hood for use onboard *Intrepid* during the 1967 America's Cup trials. It pulled her out from more than one hole in wind that left rivals dead in the water. The sail, which is light enough to fill in the most limp conditions, can be made up from 0.3oz Mylar laminate, though there are many who prefer a slightly heavier nylon, which is more forgiving cloth that is easier to trim in a fluctuating breeze.

Weight	Wind range	Wind angle
0.5 oz	0-5 knots	60-180°

Storm spinnaker: This small spinnaker, designed for ocean passages, has narrow shoulders and a maximum width along the foot. Used only in heavy running conditions, the sail has a short hoist to keep the centre of effort as low as possible, and because of its small area, it is sometimes sheeted inside the forestay. The sail is made up from a heavy cloth – 2.2 oz minimum, and often a two-ply construction.

Weight	Wind range	Wind angle
2.2 oz (two ply)	35 knots +	90-180°
3 oz (single ply)	35 knots +	90-180°

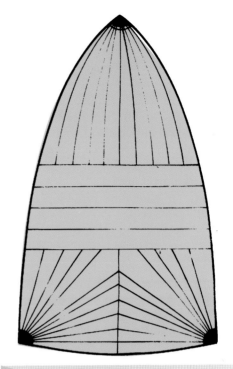

Super flanker.

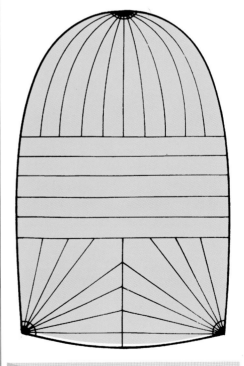

Floater (tri-radial).

Chicken chute: Even smaller than a storm spinnaker, this 'pocket handkerchief' was developed by Hood for brown trouser days in the Southern Ocean when conditions become too rough to hoist anything bigger. The head is attached to both spinnaker halyards and a downhaul is led to a foot block at the bow to stop the sail from oscillating. This aptly named sail generates more lift than two poled out jibs and keeps the bow from burying.

Weight	Wind range	Wind angle
2.2 oz (two ply)	35 knots +	130-180°
3 oz (single ply)	35 knots	130-180°

Asymmetric spinnaker/cruising chute/MPS: Originally developed by Hood Sails back in the early 1970s, the first models were fashioned from old spinnakers to provide short-handed crews delivering race yachts from one regatta to the next with a running/reaching sail without the need to

Storm spinnaker.

set up the spinnaker pole. The MPS (multi-purpose sail) is hoisted and set like a headsail, and has become a favourite on cruising yachts. It can also be supplied with a sock which takes out all the hassle of hoisting and lowering such a wide acreage of sail. The MPS is available in various weights from Floater to a heavy weather reacher, but for general purpose cruising, 1.5 or 2.2 oz cloth is optimum.

Hood asymmetric sails are constructed with a second ply of cloth on the first five panels of the luff and the last three panels of the leech to act as a shock absorber when the load is taken up on the corners and luff, and to extend the life of the sail. This extra strengthening also provides a greater measure of protection should the sail fill before the sock is fully retracted.

Weight	Wind range	Wind angle
1.5 oz	5-16 knots	60-140°
2.2 oz	14-23 knots +	70-140°

Chicken chute.

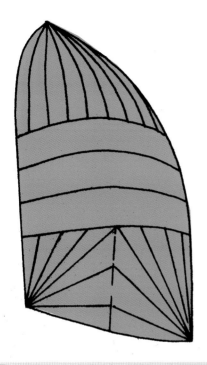

Asymmetric spinnaker/cruising Chute/MPS.

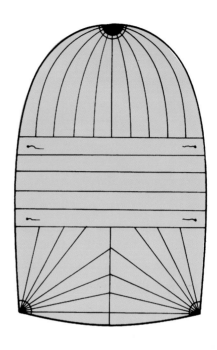
Tell-tales help determine correct pole height..

Spinnaker trim

The key to better spinnaker control and performance is concentration, constant attention and co-ordination between trimmer and helmsman. The sheet must be trimmed continually, not only to keep the luff tape on the point of curling, but also to balance the pressure on the helm. The helmsman's task is to steer a smooth course, maintaining airflow across the spinnaker, tacking downwind if necessary.

Reaching: That old saying 'Keep the clews level' was the golden rule to setting the old cross-cut spinnakers which distort badly when reaching. With modern stretch-free tri-radial designs, the clews remain level whether the spinnaker is set well or not, and the crew must take a keener interest in the more important aspects of shape and draft position to gain the best performance. One successful method of monitoring correct pole height is to attach tell-tales to the luffs of the chute at one third and two-third heights approximately 1in (0.3m) inside the tapes. Then, if the upper luff tell-tale stalls first, the pole is too high, and too low when the bottom luff begins to flutter. These provide an accurate guide on all points except running downwind, when the sail is merely catching the air and little flow is generated.

When the wind fluctuates in strength and direction, pole height and position need to be adjusted just as much as the sheet. When wind speed drops there must be someone on hand to ease the pole topping lift if the head looks like folding, for the sail will be generating less lift. Conversely, when the wind increases, the pole must be raised otherwise the lower portion of the sail will luff first. As the wind direction alters, crew should not only trim the sheet, but play the pole as well, easing

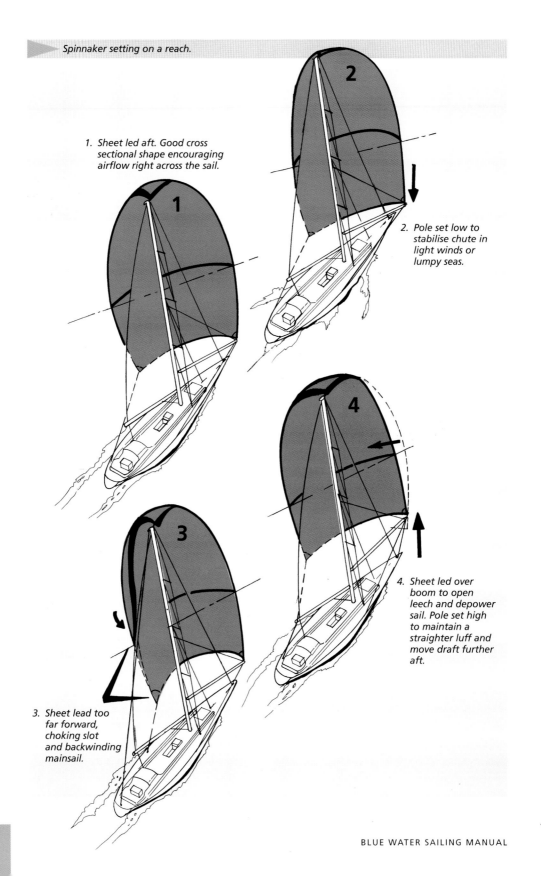

1. Sheet led aft. Good cross sectional shape encouraging airflow right across the sail.

2. Pole set low to stabilise chute in light winds or lumpy seas.

3. Sheet lead too far forward, choking slot and backwinding mainsail.

4. Sheet led over boom to open leech and depower sail. Pole set high to maintain a straighter luff and move draft further aft.

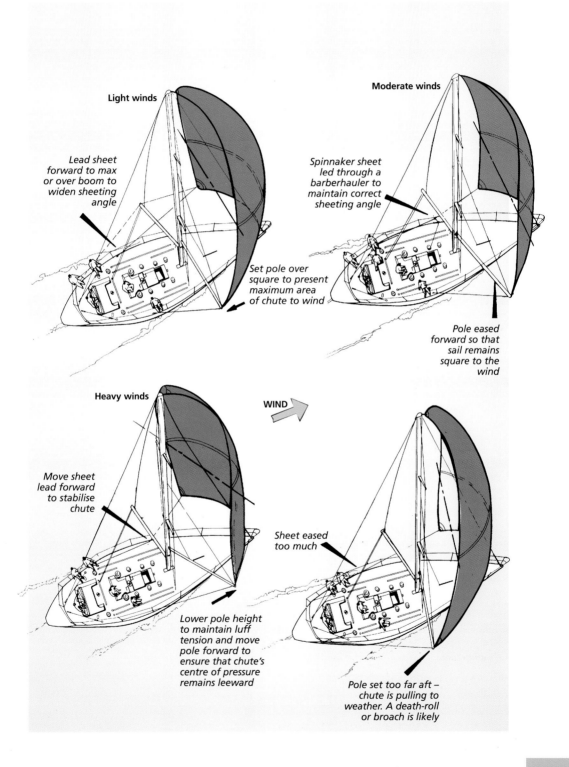

Light winds

Lead sheet forward to max or over boom to widen sheeting angle

Set pole over square to present maximum area of chute to wind

Moderate winds

Spinnaker sheet led through a barberhauler to maintain correct sheeting angle

Pole eased forward so that sail remains square to the wind

Heavy winds

Move sheet lead forward to stabilise chute

Lower pole height to maintain luff tension and move pole forward to ensure that chute's centre of pressure remains leeward

WIND

Sheet eased too much

Pole set too far aft – chute is pulling to weather. A death-roll or broach is likely

it forward should the luff begin to curl so that the sail is continually being rotated around the bow to present the most effective shape to the wind. These are the conditions when concentration provides so many gains.

In general, the aim is to keep the spinnaker luff vertical and at right angles to the pole, which sometimes calls for the spar to be set over-square. On a tight reach in light airs for instance, a pole set a few degrees away from the forestay brings the chute out from under the staysail, giving both more room to breathe. On very shy reaches (55°-60° apparent) the pole has to be set 30° or more over-square, simply because its swing is limited by the forestay, but these flat spinnakers are designed for this, and the pole should continue to be set to weather even when the wind is abeam.

Running: When running dead downwind or, more preferably, tacking downwind at angles of 85° or more to generate some flow across the spinnaker, the object is to project the greatest area of sail to the wind. With a masthead rig, it is possible to lead the sheet over the boom; this not only provides the widest sheeting base, but also tends to de-power the foot in heavy weather. With a fractional rig however, this sheeting arrangement is not always practical. It restricts the proportionately longer boom and has to be sheeted forward to B max – the widest part of the deck. In strong conditions, a forward sheeting position using a barberhauler or choker line tacked down to the chain plates, does help to stabilise an oscillating spinnaker, as well as induce greater fullness into the bottom of the sail.

Draft is also influenced by the angle of the pole. Over-squaring the spar in light to moderate winds will flatten out the lower panels to present the widest projected area, but in heavy weather it is better to

have the pole less than square to ensure that the centre of pressure remains to leeward to avoid the likelihood of a death roll. In light to moderate conditions, easing the halyard 8-9in (23-38cms) depending on size of rig, will allow the sail to set further forward in clearer air.

Trimming asymmetric/MPS sails: The optimum apparent wind angle for the asymmetrical spinnaker or MPS is from 60° to 140°, depending on wind speed. The sail has a very round luff and much flatter leech, designed to set with about 25° of twist to take account of the wind

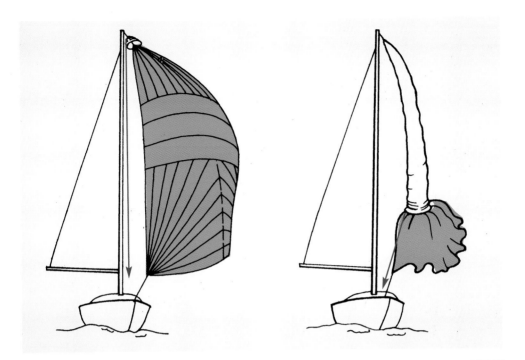

The MPS cruising chute is an ideal down wind sail for sailing short-handed and for those who do not wish to be bothered with all the paraphanalia of spinnaker and jockey poles, foreguys, and lazy sheets and guys. They are also very easy to hoist and recover, especially when a spinnaker sock is employed. Simply hoist the sock with the MPS inside up on the spinnaker halyard, then pull down on the sock control line to concertina it at the head of the sail. When it comes to dousing the sail, you simply haul down on the control line attached to the mouth of the sock to envelope the sail, then lower the halyard. Beware of pulling too hard. If the sock becomes choked with cloth, too much tension can tear the sail. The simple solution is the pull the sock back up to clear the sail, then hold the luff of the sail tight as the mouth is drawn down again.

gradient or increase in wind speed at the masthead. This sail is ideal for reaching, for the sail's asymmetry and twist produces more speed and less heel than a symmetrical spinnaker would in the same conditions.

When close reaching, the tack should be set within a metre from the bow to stabilise the sail, but the further aft the wind goes, the more the tack strop can be eased to allow the sail to set further in front of the boat. As a rule of thumb, the tack strop should be approximately $1/3$rd the length of sheet played out.

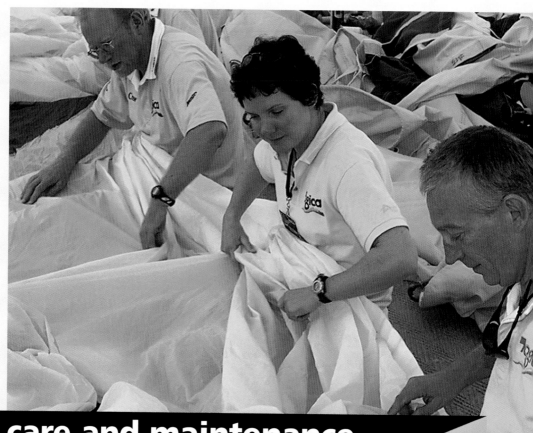

care and maintenance of sailcloth

3

The old adage 'A stitch in time saves nine' could never be more true than with sails. Good sail husbandry will enhance their life considerably. Here we advise how to protect them, make instant repairs and remove stubborn stains.

Stains

Whilst badly marked coloured sails may require the attention of an experienced finisher or dry cleaner, most stains can be removed from white sailcloth using everyday cleaning materials, or chemicals available from the chemist.

Blood

Soak the stained portion in cold water containing half a cupful of ammonia to 2.5 litres of water. If residual stains are still present after this treatment, damp the stain with a 1% solution of pepsin in water, acidified with a few drops of diluted hydrochloric acid. Allow to stand without drying out for 30 minutes, and then rinse thoroughly with fresh water.

Mildew

Scrub lightly with a dry stiff brush to remove as much of the mould growth as possible and then soak the stained portion for 2 hours in a cold solution of bleach (sodium hypochlorite) at a strength of approximately 1% available chlorine. A proprietary brand of bleach, such as Bleach, may be used in the proportion 1 part bleach to 10 parts water. Wash thoroughly in fresh water and repeat the treatment if necessary. Any residual smell of chlorine, after the final washing, may be removed by immersing for a few minutes in a 1% solution of sodium thiosulphate. Finally, rinse with fresh water.

Oil, grease and waxes

Small stains of this nature can be removed by dabbing with trichloroethylene or by the use of proprietary stain removers. Heavy staining is best removed by brushing on a mixture of detergent and solvent. This can be prepared by dissolving 1 part of Lissapol NX in 2 parts of toluene. Alternatively, a proprietary brand such as Polyclens paintbrush cleaning fluid may be used. These 'solvent/detergent' mixtures should be brushed well into the fabric, left for about 15 minutes and then washed off with warm water. A well ventilated place should be selected for carrying out this treatment, and precautions should be taken if the solvents are inflammable.

These treatments will remove oils, greases, petroleum jelly and most lubricating mixtures, but they will not remove stains caused by the fine metallic particles often associated with lubricants. These stains can be removed after the oil or grease has been eliminated.

Metallic stains

Stains caused by metals in the form of rust, verdigris or finely divided particles, can be removed by either of the following methods. Do not allow the solution to come into contact with galvanised iron or copper.

1. Immerse the stained portion in a 5% solution of oxalic acid (dissolved in hot water). The hands and the fabrics should be washed very thoroughly after using oxalic acid solutions, as this chemical is poisonous.
2. Immerse the stained portion in a warm solution containing 2 parts of concentrated hydrochloric acid per 100 parts of water. Wash off thoroughly with water.

Pitch and tar

Organic solvents such as perchloro-ethylene, trichloroethylene, trichloro-ethane (Genklene), solvent naptha or white spirit may be dabbed on to the stain to effect removal. Again care should be taken to work in a well ventilated position, and due precaution should be observed when using inflammable solvents.

Paint and varnish

Dab the stain first with trichloroethylene and then with a mixture of equal parts of acetone and amylacetate. Shellac varnish is easily removed with alcohol or methylated spirit. Paint strippers based on alkalis should not be used.

Storage

All sails should be folded or rolled in a manner which avoids sharp creases. Sails made from polyester fibre should be stored under well-ventilated, clean conditions and dampness, which may encourage the growth of mildew, should be avoided as far as possible. While mildew growths do not affect the strength of fabrics, they can cause stains, which are unsightly and not readily removed.

Mylar laminated sails

This material has now been in continuous development for several years during which early problems of sailcloth selection, delamination, sail handling and sailmaking techniques have advanced to a high level of acceptability. However, careful attention when setting and handling Mylar film sails is still required.

Folding the sail

Use the normal method of flaking down the sail on deck along the line of luff. Fold loosely and store in an ample sized sausage bag. With very heavy sails it may be necessary to roll the sail from the foot upward.

Stowing below

Avoid cramming the sails into a restricted space or sitting or walking over them below deck. This forms the hard, almost permanent, creases which tend to lead to localised delamination.

Using the sails

Before hoisting the sail for the first time, make sure that spreader ends, cotter pins, turnbuckles and swaged ends have all been well wrapped with tape to avoid any sharp corners in the rigging. It is recommended that spreader ends be wrapped with a soft cloth or leather before taping over.

Spreader patches

The first time of hoisting, it is recommended that the position of the spreader ends be marked on the sail and an adequate area of self-adhesive sticky-back or insignia cloth cut and applied to the areas to provide additional protection for the sail. Always retain additional material, for mending any small holes or slight tears that may occur from time to time in the film component of the sailcloth.

Running in a new sail

Although the components from which these sails have been made have extremely low stretch properties, it is recommended that they are set in wind strengths well below maximum for the first two hours of their life. When reaching, avoid reefing or turning up hard on the wind during this initial period. This running-in period will then allow the components to bed down evenly to ensure optimum performance and extended life.

Halyard tension and sheet lead

Film sails are generally more sensitive to halyard tension than woven sails. Each sail has a set shape built into it and only moderate halyard tension is required. Optimum sheet lead is usually one position forward for an equivalent sized Dacron/polyester sail.

Using the sail

It is important to adhere strictly to the recommended maximum windspeed advised by the sailmaker. It is good practice to mark this maximum wind speed on the outside of the sailbag as well as on the clew of the sail. When tacking, avoid hanging on to the sheet until the sail is aback, for the sail will be stretched over the spreader ends, increasing the possibility of snagging or tearing the film laminate on the rigging.

Never leave the sails flogging; any unnecessary fluttering puts a greater stress on the adhesive materials used in the manufacture. On large yachts, a tacking line attached to a grommet in the

Handle with care! Sails are easily torn with heavy handling. Use the flat of your hands when dousing the sail rather than pulling on the cloth.

centre of the foot of the sail is recommended. This not only reduces wear and tear of the sail but speeds up the tacking procedure.

UV (sunlight) resistance

Although these laminate materials offer good resistance to sunlight, it is recommended that the sails be stowed below when not in use. Avoid leaving sails flaked out on the deck or over the boom for extended periods of time without first placing a cover over them.

Repairs

It is important to maintain the polyester film intact. This is best achieved by applying a generous area of sticky-back or self-adhesive insignia tape over the damaged area.

Washing and cleaning

Always rinse the sails with fresh water after sailing to remove salty particles. Localised stains can be removed using mild washing conditions and luke warm water. Never attempt to launder a Mylar sail.

rigs: strength and design   4

Rigs have changed dramatically over the past decade. Not only are spar sections now smaller, often lighter and certainly more flexible, but the supporting rigging, at one time adjusted once at the start of the season, is now a forest of solid rod or aramid fibre offering the ability to make continual adjustment to suit even the smallest changes in trim or conditions.

The belt and braces approach to rigging has been superseded by a technical age of efficiency and less windage. The rub is that this advance has also led to many more breakages caused by badly fitted rigging or inexperience on the part of crews, for the low profile spider-web rigs that have evolved are neither fail nor foolproof.

In the 1970s, wooden spars may have been superseded by alloy extrusions, but masts were still relatively short, designed to stand absolutely straight both athwartships and fore-and-aft, and chainplates remained at or near the rail to provide the broadest support. Boats under 39ft (13m) needed no more than single spreader support, together with forward and after lower shrouds, while large yachts relied on a double spreader configuration. Backstays were tensioned with a turnbuckle wheel on a screw to loads that never exceeded 15% of breaking strength, and other stays had equal margins of safety.

Today yachts have taller masts designed to bend fore-and-aft to adjust sail shape, chainplate bases are narrower and 3 to 5 spreader rigs have become a common sight. Hydraulics now control not only backstay and vang, but mast rams, inner forestays and outhaul at pressures near to 50% breaking loads. Closer chainplate bases and taller, slimmer spars have dictated the need for solid rod shrouds. The decreased stretch these provide over 1x19 wire have proved vitally important in controlling both athwartships and fore-and-aft movement of the mast. New fitting systems also had to be devised, since the original swage terminals used successfully on 1x19 wire did not last long at these higher stresses.

There was another problem too. Back in the early 1970s standing rigging was just that. The mast did not bend, so lead angles at shroud and chainplates remained constant. Today's bendy spar causes changes to these shroud lead angles at spreader tips, tangs and chainplates every time an adjustment is made – and each change is invariably made when the shrouds are carrying a high tensile load. 'Standing rigging' is, in essence, no longer standing rigging. It is being adjusted constantly by changes in mast bend, backstay loads and inner forestay or babystay adjustments.

Metal fatigue

To understand how these changes in stress and constant adjustment affect rigging life and fitting design, it is important to understand the basic causes of metal fatigue. Metals fail for various reasons including corrosion, overload and fatigue. In the case of a tensile failure (overload) the metal is loaded beyond its ultimate strength. For example, if a shroud with a breaking strength of 8,000lb is suddenly loaded to 10,000lb, it will break. However, provided the designer did his sums right, rigging rarely fails due to simple tensile overload unless the yacht suffers a major capsize.

Fatigue failure, on the other hand, results from repeated stress cycles below the metal's ultimate tensile strength due to applied tensile or bending loads. Most people are not strong enough to break a wire paper clip merely by pulling it apart (tensile failure), but bend the wire back and forth and it will break quite easily (fatigue failure). It would also break if the wire is repeatedly loaded and unloaded at something less than the ultimate tensile strength, assuming the applied stress is above its so-called 'endurance limit'.

The number of cycles to failure is dependent on the applied stress. Consider transverse rigging. On each tack the windward shrouds are loaded and the leeward shrouds go slack. If this cyclical loading results in a rigging failure after 1000 tacks, the stress level is clearly

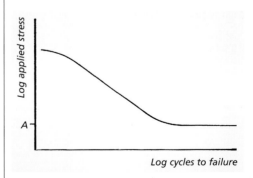

Fatigue failure. If a load exceeds the endurance limit (load A) the part will fail after a certain number of bending cycles.

unacceptable. If, on the other hand, the stress is below the endurance limit, we may be sacrificing windage and weight aloft due to oversized shrouds. The applied stress is kept reasonable by using adequate safety margins in design and by increasing rigging size as loads increase. Typically, shroud tensile loads are designed with a safety margin of three for long distance events like the Global Challenge races, and two for rounds-the-buoys competition.

However, the bending stress at points of attachment under high tensile load, must also be taken into account since these changes add to the applied tensile stress, lowering fatigue life dramatically. To prevent high bending stresses, mast tangs, shroud terminals and spreader tip configurations must be very carefully designed. The terminals and attachment points, originally developed for a stiff rig, are invariably inappropriate for the bendy mast and have caused many dismastings.

One example is the 'bare ball' tang; a simple stainless ball captured on the end of a rod, developed originally during the days of stiff rigs. This provided enough freedom of movement on the leeward side to prevent fatigue problems when it was slack, but could not cope when the lead angle changed under high tensile load, for the rotational force required to turn the ball in its seat created a bending stress too. If the lead angle repeatedly changes by more than about 1°, fatigue failure is always likely to occur where the rod emerges from the ball.

Bending stress calculations, backed up by experience, provide clear guidelines to rig specifications and their installation, the most important being that misalignment at rigging attachment points must never exceed 1°. The tolerance is small but the price for flouting this rule is invariably higher than mere shroud failure. One lower intermediate shroud on *Ceramco New*

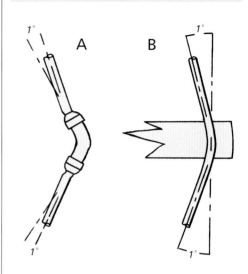

A: Overbent spreader bend showing maximum of 1° each end.

B: 1° misalignment of non pre-bent rod at spreader tip.

Rod Size	Diameter (in)	Guide Tube Bend Radius
-3	0.143	41
-4	0.172	50
-6	0.198	57
-8	0.225	64
-10	0.250	72
-12	0.281	80
-17	0.330	94
-22	0.375	107
-30	0.437	125
-40	0.500	143
-48	0.562	161
-60	0.660	172

The length of the guide tube required for a given shroud angle change is given by equations (1A & 1B).

L = 0.175 RO
L = 0.175 R (0-2)
L = Tube length (inches)
R = Tube bend radius (inches)
O = Total angle change of shroud at spreader (degrees)

For example, for a four degree (4°) bend with -10 rod, from equation 1A,
L = 0.075 (72") (4°) = 5".

Alternatively, from equation 1B,
L = 0.175 (72") (4°-2°) = 2.5".

Guide to tube radius to limit bending stress to 50Kpsi.

Zealand was bent through 10° instead of 21° at the lower spreader tip, and when this eventually failed 4,500 miles from Cape Town during the first leg of the third Whitbread Round the World Race, it not only carried away the mast but all expectations Peter Blake and his crew had of winning the race.

Most rod is not dead straight when it is assembled. Rigging should be coiled for shipment with the rod's natural curvature. Coil size for shipment should be as great as possible. If coil size is kept longer than 200 x rod diameter, little or no permanent set will be induced in the rod. If the coil has to be smaller, this will introduce permanent curvature, and the rod must be straightened again before installation.

The Global Challenge fleet use 1x19 wire rigging rather than rod because any fatigue problems are visual, usually with one strand breaking at a time, which should be picked up during the weekly rig checks. The fact that wire rigging is heavier and bulkier than rod is immaterial when the yachts are equipped identically, though problems with breaking bottle screws during the first race did highlight the fact that when a one-design yacht suffers a failure, the same problem is likely to surface on others in the fleet too.

Mike Golding's *Group 4 Securitas* was the first to experience the lower tang failure on the bottle-screw holding her forestay, four days into the second stage of the British Steel Challenge around Cape Horn. Soon after, the same screws broke on four other yachts within the fleet, though mercifully, these failures led to only one dismasting – on *British Steel 2*. Initial suspicions laid the blame on fatigue failure, caused by restricted articulation where the bottle-screw tang was attached to the deck chain plate. *Group 4* hurriedly flew out a replacement bottle-screw for their yacht and brought back the broken fitting for analysis. But when the replacement screw given to *Group 4* also broke just 2,000 miles later, this raised more questions than answers. The biggest was how could such a basic fitting, designed with enormous margins of safety, fail in this way?

The answer lay in the manufacturing. The Challenge Business commissioned a series of tests on multiple screws. The results were damming. Not only did the laboratory report show up wide variations in the manufacturing process, but also considerable differences in the metallurgy of the forged steel components. This led the company to re-evaluate not only the

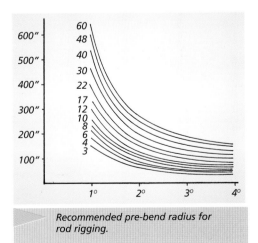

Recommended pre-bend radius for rod rigging.

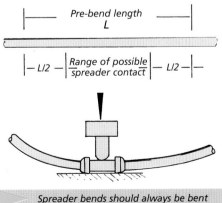

Spreader bends should always be bent in line with natural curvature of rod.

supply of fittings for their fleet of round-the-world yachts, but the basis by which each item is homologated.

All this was cold comfort to the crews still battling their way across the Roaring Forties. They resolved the immediate problem by changing the lower tang fitting with one taken from a bottle-screw holding a lesser-loaded lower shroud, and all the suspect fittings were replaced when the yachts reached Hobart, their second port of call.

Fractional rigs

One trend to evolve from the dinghy world is for sweptback spreaders on fractional rigs, which negate the requirement for runners, yet still provide sufficient support to carry masthead gennakers. Where these asymmetric spinnakers are carried, the designers incorporate forward jumpers or a stiffer, heavier, topmast, and rely on variable backstay loads to control forestay tension. On dinghies, 25°–30° of spreader sweep is common and forestay tension is obtained by pre-bending the rig, coupled with pressure on the mainsheet exerting tension up the leech of the sail to bend the top of the rig. This concept, with some small variations, has been taken offshore. Spreader sweep is generally not as high as 30°, so instead, the backstay has been called on to provide the additional force necessary to tension the forestay. As a consequence, narrow angled jumpers are used to support the topmast. Alternatively, a heavier mast section is specified to stop the backstay putting too much bend in the topmast when used to tension the forestay.

From the 1980s onwards, the chain plate base for masthead rigs was always set inboard to minimise the sheeting angle required for large overlapping headsails. These large headsails remain enshrined within many class rules, including the International America's Cup Class (IACC)

when it was brought in to replace the old 12 Metre rule back in the early 1990s. This provided a 6ft (3m) overlap of unmeasured genoa area in the leech of the sail to give crews something to do when tacking, and thus make for better television! This in turn led to the so-called 'inside-out' rigs with their banana spreaders, which allow these genoas to be set inside the standing rigging. This is achieved by having a short first spreader to allow the genoa to be sheeted inboard, coupled to a second full width spreader that curves aft like a banana to clear the leech, and a short third spreader that fits inside the sail overlap. This resulted in the cap shrouds running up from the gunwale straight to the second spreader without touching the first spreader at all.

On other yachts with wide chain plates, simply sweeping the spreaders aft and limiting the overlap to 115% will also accommodate the large genoa. Max-width chain plates can sometimes save far more weight than the shift from alloy to carbon. This is because weight in the rigging as well as the mast section can be reduced by as much as half. Pointing ability is maintained by sheeting the genoa inboard through the V1 stays, which still allow for considerable overlap.

Sweeping the spreaders aft is probably a misnomer. A better description might be swept diagonals because the diagonals provide an aft component that tensions the forestay and locks up the mast bend. This results in a very safe rig, for once the mast bend has been set up, it remains fairly constant.

A number of yachts with substantial sweep still use runners, probably because they give the crew a feeling of greater safety, though in many cases they are superfluous. If the rig is set up correctly, the runners do not have any effect on mast bend. Swept spreaders are fine for cruising yachts and those being sailed short-handed. Only on grand prix racing boats where crews often modify the mast bend/mainsail luff curve to suit the wind strength and seas conditions, are in-line spreaders the only way to go. For the vast majority, however, a swept spreader fractional rig makes common sense, particularly when matched with modern sails, which retain their shape over a wide wind range.

Carbon rigs

Carbon fibre masts can offer considerable weight savings over alloy spars, but there has been considerable confusion over their cost and performance. These savings in weight aloft are especially pronounced with large yachts, which generally have a

The layman's guide to spreader sweep and runners.

0-5°:	Might as well be in-line.
6-10°:	Don't bother. You have the worst of both worlds.
15°:	The rig will probably require checkstays.
20°:	Masthead rigs OK with no checkstays, though it may need runners.
25°:	Fractional rigs OK with no checkstays. Masthead rigs OK with no runners.
30°:	No runners required on either Fractional or Masthead rigs.

The Melges 24 sport keelboat has a typical fractional rig with swept back spreaders without runners.

relatively shallow draft and lower righting moment. Carbon rigs not only lower the pitching moment and improve the yacht's motion, but also allow designers the option of balancing this improved righting moment with corresponding reductions in draft and ballast.

On racing yachts, carbon spars offer greater stability and higher sail carrying capacity without increasing displacement or draft. Only on smaller yachts under 40ft (13m) where draft is ample and the standard of racing may not be at the highest level, does the cost/weight-effective option of carbon remain questionable for the moment.

Carbon spars are now standard spec on many 70ft (23m) + yachts, and as mast manufacturers get more experience with this material, it is easy to see carbon being specified as widely as aluminium on much smaller boats where performance and/or minimal motion are important factors within the design. Our comparison table between an alloy and carbon rig for a 60ft (20m) yacht designed for short-handed cruising, gives a good indication of the relative benefits and savings.

The comparative alloy mast section is 13.4in x 8in (340mm x 205mm). The yacht's masthead rig is supported by three swept back spreaders. The bare alloy mast section weighs 831lb (377kg) compared to 450lb (204kg) for the carbon version. The section weights are 928lb (421kg) and 547lb (248kg) respectively, which take account of additions such as conduits, fairing, paint, bonding glue, local doublers and boxes. Since some weight savings associated with carbon get diluted by the weight of additional items, it is worth considering using the cheapest carbon materials and invest these savings into titanium spreader tip cups, Kevlar runners and pultruded diagonals. These figures relate to the most common low modulus graded carbon.

For a yacht of this size, the mainsail alone weighs 176lb (80kg), so the total weight aloft, including mainsail, genoa, furler, battens, boom and spinnaker pole is substantially higher – 2535lb (1150kg) or more. Thus the 428lb (191kg) saving in the carbon rig represents 17% of the entire rig. When skippers go to the length of getting crew to cut their toothbrushes in half and

Comparison stats between alloy and carbon mast on a Warwick 60.

Rig components	Alloy weight	% of total in carbon	Carbon weight	% of total in carbon
Rods	147kg/324lb	19%	14.07kg/324lb	26%
Rod fittings	71.6kg/158lb	9%	71.6kg/158lb	13%
Spreaders	30.5kg/67lb	4%	15.7kg/35lb	3%
Spreader roots	27.8kg/61lb	4%	24.3kg/54lb	4%
Halyards	17.4kg/38lb	2%	17.4kg/38lb	3%
Section	420.7kg/927lb	55%	248.2kg/547lb	43%
Fittings	37.1kg/82lb	5%	37.1kg/82lb	6%
Wires	10.5kg/23lb	1%	10.5kg/23lb	2%
TOTAL RIG	**762.6kg/1681lb**	**100%**	**571.7kg/1260lb**	**100%**

leave even basic comforts ashore, this represents a considerable saving. Just as important, the cost difference between the two options amounted to just 19%.

What this weight saving means in terms of ballast varies with the design of the yacht, but in the case of our 60ft (18.28m) yacht, it allowed the designer to shed 2204lb (1,000kg) of ballast. That represents both a worthy saving and performance improvement, which, when scaled up to superyacht levels, can result in the reduction of several tonnes.

Another valuable weight saving can be made with the rigging. Rod rigging is a major element within the overall calculations which can be offset by the use of aramid fibre and other forms of non-metallic standing rigging, runners and check stays. Combine these weight savings with those afforded with titanium fittings, and the total rig package can be reduced substantially.

Polymer rigging

Nitronic 50 rod rigging with a breaking strain of 8,000lb (3628kg) offers a 16% weight saving and 20% reduction in windage over 1x19 wire, but invest in pultruded Aramid standing rigging and Vectran running backstays and the weight savings jump to 80%. Move up to PBO (polyphenylene benzobisoxazole) or Zylon (manufactured by the Japanese chemical company Toyobo) and you have a material that is 60% stronger than Vectran and suffers half the stretch. PBO's only weakness is UV and salt degradation which means that it has to be fully encapsulated but has nevertheless become common on America's Cup yachts, swing keel maxis, Volvo 70s, Open 60s and multihulls for backstays, checkstays, and Code Zero luff cables. It is very expensive, but as the market widens, so prices are likely to fall from mortgage to pocket book proportions.

Rope technology has also advanced considerably to the point where 12,000lb polymer cordage is now down to a size we would not have used to sheet a light-air spinnaker a decade ago. The longevity properties of Spectra, or Dyneema ropes as they are called in Europe, make this a particular favourite for halyards, sheets and control lines. Unlike Kevlar, it is not only impervious to flex fatigue and UV degradation but retains more of its breaking strength when turned around a halyard sheeve or turning block. Indeed, it is even used to connect standing rigging to shroud plates and as a lighter, stronger replacement to shackles.

Setting up a mast is a technical, but logical process. Making the rig safe is relatively easy, but tuning to maximise performance can be far more taxing. Here we explain the basic parameters for both masthead and fractional rigs.

The masthead rig

The masthead rig is the easiest to tune even when supported by triple spreaders and runners. The yacht designer can calculate both mast position and rake quite accurately, leaving the crew with the task of simply fine tuning it all during initial sailing trials to take account of the changing waterline as the yacht heels, and draft position of the sails. The weight on the helm provides the best clue to correct positioning and rake. Optimum weather helm is approximately 3° in moderate winds under full sail. If there is much less rudder angle than that, the yacht may exhibit lee helm in light airs, and, more than that, have uncontrollable weather helm in strong conditions. If the rudder angle is more than 5° above its neutral position, the mast will need to be moved forward (one notch at a time) and aft if there is little or no weight on the helm.

Mast rake invariably has a bearing on pointing ability. Sailmakers recommend an angle between 0.5° and 1° as a starting point. This is much less than a fractional rig requires where the optimum is often closer to 3° but is still a significant amount, representing almost 4ft (1.2m) of rake on a 75ft (23m) yacht. If the boat does not appear to be pointing high enough, try adding a little more rake. If this improves matters but also increases weather helm, then push the mast step forward a notch and shorten the forestay to maintain the same degree of rake.

Lateral support

Unlike fractional rigs, the masthead rig must remain in column even in the

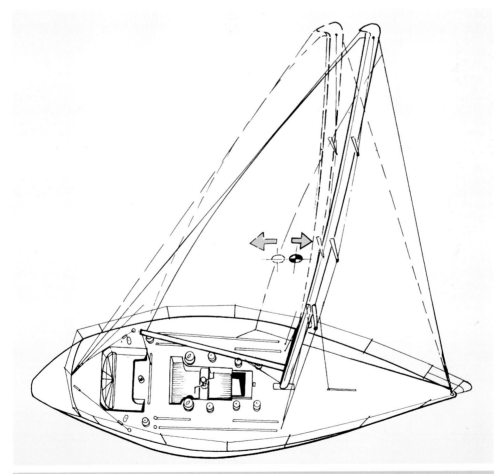

The centres of lateral resistance and effort acting on hull and sails move fore-and-aft several feet as the angle of heel and sail trim change, and are only brought back into balance by the rudder. If the rudder angle is excessive the mast will need to be moved forward - or aft when there is little or no weight on the helm.

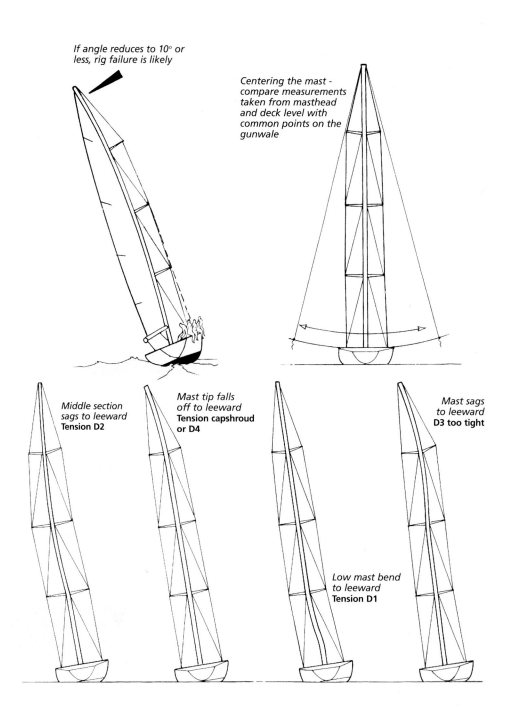

If angle reduces to 10° or less, rig failure is likely

Centering the mast - compare measurements taken from masthead and deck level with common points on the gunwale

Middle section sags to leeward **Tension D2**

Mast tip falls off to leeward **Tension capshroud or D4**

Mast sags to leeward **D3 too tight**

Low mast bend to leeward **Tension D1**

A masthead rigged Challenge yacht sailing under storm tri-sail and staysail, breasting Force 10 winds across the Pacific towards Wellington, New Zealand.

heaviest conditions. If the spar has any tendency to bend to leeward, this not only induces headstay sag just when a tight forestay is required to maintain a flat shape to the genoa, but can ultimately lead to failure if the angle between masthead and cap shroud falls below 10°. Beyond this critical angle, the leverage on the shroud can become strong enough to break either the rod or its supporting spreader.

Setting up the mast

With forestay length set to provide the required rake, the mast is first centred in the boat by comparing measurements taken on either side of the masthead and deck level to common points on the gunwale (not chain plates, which are not always so accurately placed) before wedging the sides of the spar with chocks at the partners to limit any side bend.

The shrouds are termed V for Vertical and D for Diagonal and numbered from deck level upwards. Hence Dl, D2, D3, D4 and Vl, V2, V3 on the triple spreader rig. Start by tensioning the lower rigging until it is hand tight, tensioning the D1s, which hold the lower mast in column in the high wind range first, before doing the same with the D2s and Vls if they are not one and the same. Once all the rigging screws are hand tight and holding the mast straight (checked by looking up the luff track), the rig can then be fine-tuned under full sail in 12-15 knot winds. Sail to windward on both tacks and make small changes to the leeward turnbuckles (one turn at a time) before tacking and checking the results. Common sense dictates what adjustments need to be made to pull a bending spar back into column. If the lower sections sag to leeward, the Dls need more tension. The same applies to the cap shrouds if the tip falls away. If side bend cannot be totally eradicated, even with very tight rigging, then spreader lengths may need to be increased. Remember though that all rigging, even rod, shows some initial stretch, so check the mast again after a few days' sailing and be prepared to re-tension the shrouds.

Pre-bend

Some fore-and-aft pre-bend within the rig is desirable, for it produces a more efficient shape across the middle sections of the sail, and mainsails are invariably shaped with some extra luff round to take account of this. The amount of pre-bend varies with the mast section and size of the boat but on a typical 59ft (18m) tall mast, a minimum 6in (15cm) of pre-bend, which may be extended to 8in (20cm) or more when conditions dictate the need for a flatter shape to the mainsail, is not uncommon. With masthead position and rake determined by forestay length, pre-bend is induced either by placing chocks in the partners behind the mast to push the section forward at deck level or by moving the step aft. On smaller yachts with deck stepped masts, the same can be achieved by cutting the base of the spar at an angle or shimming the aft edge.

Pre-bend is induced by placing chocks behind the mast at deck level, or with deck-stepped masts, cutting the base at an angle or shimming up the aft edge.

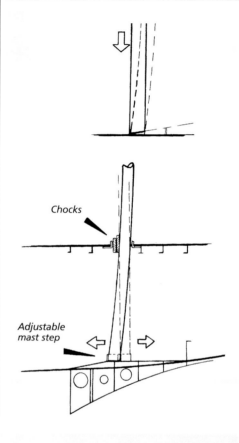

Chocks

Adjustable mast step

Pre-bend.

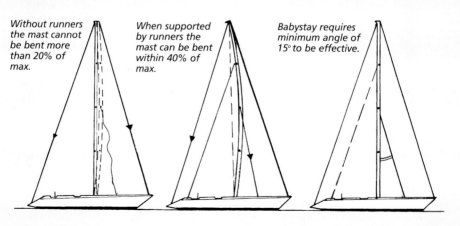

Without runners the mast cannot be bent more than 20% of max.

When supported by runners the mast can be bent within 40% of max.

Babystay requires minimum angle of 15° to be effective.

A classic picture of a crew in perfect control of a fractionally rigged yacht. Wild Thing *is caught surfing at 30+ knots across the Tasman Sea during the 1995 Sydney Hobart Race.*

Adjustable fore-and-aft bend

When the need arises to flatten the mainsail further with mast bend, this is achieved by increasing backstay and babystay tension. Maximum backstay tension can be determined during initial sailing trials by sighting up the forestay as pressure is being applied. Once forestay sag has been taken up in medium wind strengths with the heavy No.1 set, the maximum working load has been reached and further tension merely bends the boat!

Many crews forget that backstays have an ultimate tensile strength factor and should never be tensioned more than half that amount. Calibrate the maximum loading on the dial or use a codline to provide a visual guide to the amount of adjustment being made.

The babystay, an adjustable inner forestay which needs to be angled at least 15° forward of the mast to be effective, is used to promote mast bend in conditions when maximum backstay loading is inappropriate – ie when sailing with a heavy genoa at the bottom of its range, and some luff sag is required. Rigged in conjunction with running backstays, the mast section can be bent to within 40% of the section's maximum but, without runners to check the pumping action on the mast as the boat slams into a head sea, mast bend should be restricted to half this amount. As a general rule, mast manufacturers and sailmakers work to a safe limit of one and a half times the fore-and-aft dimension of the spar.

The fractional rig

There is nothing new about the fractional or non-masthead rig. The concept goes back many decades but, like most fashions, obsolescence led to its rebirth. Current enthusiasm began to re-emerge in the early 1970s when New Zealand designer, Bruce Farr, started a trend towards light displacement boats within the Ton Cup classes, and with them this ever adjustable rig. His wide, flat, very light

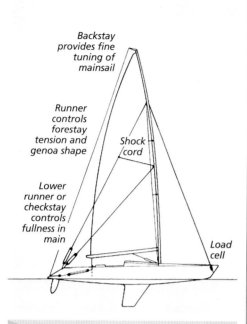

Backstay provides fine tuning of mainsail

Runner controls forestay tension and genoa shape

Shock cord

Lower runner or checkstay controls fullness in main

Load cell

Backstay and runners must provide adequate support to control pumping action of the spar in a seaway. The inclusion of a load cell on the forestay provides an important gauge to correct runner tension. The alternative to runners, is to fit swept-back spreaders.

designs were a marked departure from current thinking which treated Ton Cup yachts and their like as small yachts rather than big dinghies. Those early Farr boats proved to be fast, very fast in fact, and with an ability to surf and plane well above theoretical hull speeds, even in marginal conditions, they dominated the world scene first in Quarter then Half, Three-Quarter and One Ton classes and quickly eclipsed big boat thinking.

Being big dinghies with lightweight dinghy style rigs, the Farr designs required small boat tuning and handling techniques to get the most out of them. Some of their speed advantage was also gained from the measurement rule which penalises yachts with large fore-triangles while offering free rated area to those with large mainsails. It was these international

rules, framed originally to limit a trend towards excessive genoas and ultra-small mainsails on masthead rigs, rather than favour the non-masthead configuration, that really gave the fractional rig its second lease of life. And this in turn encouraged the diehard dinghy men to join the offshore scene, bringing with them a fresh approach to what was then a stagnating situation. The concept has since spread to yachts of all sizes

The masthead rig can be sailed to within 90% of its optimum with comparative ease, requiring only subtle changes to halyard or sheet tension in order to maintain a wide performance groove, but the fractional rig requires far greater understanding before the same or better performance can be achieved. Where this rig does score over the masthead configuration is in heavy weather. The advantage lies within the smaller headsails and spinnakers which, set low, reduce rolling and simplify control, allowing spinnakers to be carried longer with less chance of broaching.

Mast control

In order to have maximum control over the spar it is not only essential to have the correct rigging and deck layout, but the right mast section too, with sufficient taper both fore and aft and athwartships to allow wide variations in bend. Advice on individual specifications is best sought from the yacht designer, spar manu-facturer and sailmaker.

Runners

Double running backstays play an important role in controlling fractional rigs and need to be tacked down as far aft and as close to the centreline as possible to provide the greatest mechanical advantage and least side force on the spar. The upper runner, which requires a

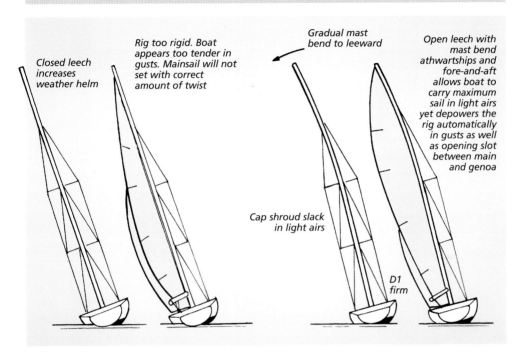

Correct tuning of a fractional rig is essential if mast and sail are to provide enough flexibility to keep the boat upright in a breeze.

Closed leech increases weather helm

Rig too rigid. Boat appears too tender in gusts. Mainsail will not set with correct amount of twist

Gradual mast bend to leeward

Open leech with mast bend athwartships and fore-and-aft allows boat to carry maximum sail in light airs yet depowers the rig automatically in gusts as well as opening slot between main and genoa

Cap shroud slack in light airs

D1 firm

minimal 44:1 purchase, controls headstay tension and genoa shape while the checkstay or lower runner, which runs from the centre panel of the mast to link up with the upper runner or its attachment point, controls mainsail shape as well as limiting the pumping action of the mast generated in a seaway. Adjustment to the checkstay is often made with a simple 5:1 block and tackle arrangement located at the intersection with the running backstay.

A load cell fitted to the forestay is an invaluable aid for fine-tuning these running backstays. It provides a bench-mark to work to for different wind and sea conditions each time the running backstays ground up after tacking. The runner control lines must also be calibrated, not only to show maximum settings but a minimum too, otherwise the spar could invert when sailing off wind.

The permanent or masthead backstay is used to support the spar during a gybe and control fore-and-aft tip bend when sailing upwind.

With smaller tensions involved, a 5:1 purchase is usually sufficient, though the control is best led to either side of the cockpit so that it is within reach of the sail trimmer.

Side bend

Tip bend is critical to performance, helm balance and the sail-carrying capacity on all fractionally rigged yachts. When beating to windward, a boat whose mast has no side bend will appear to be more tender during a gust, but a boat with a well tuned spar with the tip bending off gradually will be stiffer and thus faster, since the tip acts as a shock absorber when the wind increases, allowing the leech of the mainsail to ease and twist open, to de-power the rig automatically. This bending is achieved by tapering the tip of the mast both fore-and-aft and sideways, but to work effectively, it also requires finely tuned rigging. This is achieved by setting the lowers up with greater tension than the D2s and cap shrouds so that they come under load only when the boat is sailing to windward in around 5 knots of apparent wind and above.

Tuning multi-spreader rigs in particular, is often a time consuming task. Once the forestay has been set to produce the required rake (3˚ is a good starting point) and the mast is centred at deck level, the lowers and intermediates are adjusted equally until hand tight. This procedure is followed with the uppers once someone has sighted up the luff track to ensure that the mast remains true. This dockside tuning can only provide an approximation and it will require several hours, days even, sailing in 12-15 knot winds with full main and genoa set, to fine tune the rig. Sail to windward on both tacks to obtain a uniform bend, making small changes (no more than one or two turns at a time) to the leeward turnbuckle before tacking again and checking the results. Never adjust the weather shrouds.

Mainsail control

As the mast bends, so the distance between head and tack shortens, requiring adjustment on the cunningham to maintain correct luff tension. Some sailmakers recommend having an oversized main that can then be adjusted to remain within the black bands using two cunninghams, two flattening reefs and a foot cunningham placed approximately 8in (25cm) along from the foot. Then, when set in its relaxed position with the foot shelf open, the clew is still extended to the outer black band to give

the maximum projected area. Initial flattening is achieved either by increasing mast bend or by applying tension to the foot cunningham which pulls the foot towards the tack, and then to the flattener, thus maintaining a full size sail whether set full or flat.

The most important aspect is for mainsail shape to match mast bend, since this has a critical bearing on leech control. By masthead rig standards, the fractional rig is designed to be quite loose under normal tension, which means that in order to obtain a firm leech, extra load must be exerted either on the mainsheet or boom vang. This extra tension applied usually by the mainsheet, acts like a permanent backstay, twisting off the top of the sail to spill air and reduce the heeling force – and an essential de-powering device when the yacht is hit by a gust. If, on the other hand, the mainsail is cut with a tight leech, mast bend can only be generated by tensioning the permanent backstay, which limits

The fractional rig is particularly sensitive to tune and there is a fine divide between being 'in the groove' and out of it. Correct sail shape is the most important factor in speed and pointing ability. These scale drawings show the relative sail angles for fractional and masthead rigs when beating to windward. Both genoas are trimmed to 9° but note the difference between the main booms.

Fractional rig

Short overlap between genoa and main allows main boom to be set at a wider angle thus increasing lift/drag ratio

Masthead rig

Main is set closer to centreline and is used more to balance the helm than provide a forward driving component

sideways tip bend and the sail's automatic de-powering behaviour.

Genoa control

Compared with a masthead sail inventory, the fractionally rigged genoa differs more than any than any other sail, for it is quite flat by masthead standards and, limited by the shorter J measurement, does not overlap the mainsail by any great degree. Its shape is controlled primarily by the running backstay and success lies in the crew's ability to adjust the runner continually to suit the smallest changes in conditions or trim. When more power is required from a flat headsail to keep the boat moving through a leftover chop in light airs, the running backstay needs to be eased to add luff curve to the sail and pull the draft forward to within 30% of chord length. Once in smooth water and more breeze, the running backstay can be ground up again to produce a flatter shaped entry needed to improve pointing

One advantage of the fractional rig is its short overlap jib, allowing good visibility to leeward.

ability. Tension on the runner to provide 4,000-4,500lb (1814-2268kg) pressure on the headstay of a 35ft (10.7m) yacht or 2,000lb (907kg) on a 26ft (8m) boat will produce the necessary twist required in the top 30% of the genoa – another important aspect with fractional rigs, for the genoa, small though it is, must marry into the mainsail to produce a uniform aerofoil and slot. With masthead rigs, the singular creation of one aerodynamic force within both sails is attained quite easily because both sails intersect at the masthead, and the merging of mainsail and genoa requires only the minimum of twist. But the fractionally rigged genoa intersects the mainsail some 15%-12% down from the head of the main and therefore requires much greater twist to generate the smooth aerofoil shape required.

When trimming the mainsail and genoa for optimum windward performance, the more the mainsheet traveller is offset away from the centreline, the greater the speed potential. While this must be adjusted in harmony with the trim and lead angle of the genoa, the short overlap permits the mainsail to be carried at a wider angle than on a masthead rigged yacht, which increases the forward component within the sail and thus speed. Wider sheeting angles require the genoa to be cut with a flat leech, but the result is to improve pointing ability and speed. This is one reason why a full hoist main and a No. 3, 100% LP genoa provide one of the most forgiving combinations in almost any breeze above the range of the heavy genoa.

Spinnakers

In order to sail to its rating, the fractionally rigged yacht must always make full use of its sail area, especially in light airs when light displacement yachts with their large

The fractionally rigged yacht Sayonara *making maximum use of her sail area on a power reach.*

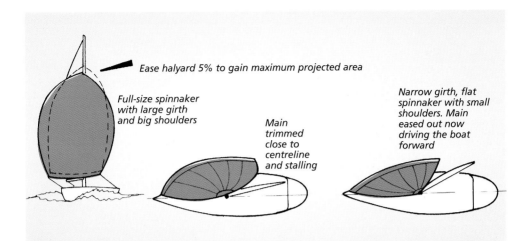

Ease halyard 5% to gain maximum projected area

Full-size spinnaker with large girth and big shoulders

Narrow girth, flat spinnaker with small shoulders. Main eased out now driving the boat forward

Main trimmed close to centreline and stalling

Spinnakers for fractionally rigged yachts are cut with flat middle sections and rounded leeches to encourage the chute to roll out to windward of the mainsail when sailing downwind. The halyard must be eased off 5% to allow the head of the spinnaker to fly out to windward and away from the shadow of the mainsail. For this reason the largest spinnaker is not always the most powerful.

wetted area are often hard to keep moving in a sloppy, leftover sea. So all sails, the spinnaker especially, must be designed and set to provide maximum projected area. This does not mean designing a spinnaker with a maximum head angle, wide shoulders and droopy foot but a chute that will generate sufficient lift to set clear from the blanketing effect of the mainsail. This is achieved by reducing the head angle to approximately 80°, compared to 100° of an all-purpose masthead rig tri-radial, and shaping the sail with a shallow foot that will not pull the shoulders together. In sectional shape these sails are cut with flat middle sections and rounded leeches to encourage the chute to roll out to windward of the mainsail when sailing downwind. But, equally important, the

halyard must be eased off by approximately 5% to allow the head of the spinnaker to fly out to windward and away from the shadow of the main.

The floating star with its small, flat radial head, is an ideal sail for close reaching or running in light airs through a lumpy sea when conditions make flying a larger, fuller spinnaker almost impossible. The golden rule is if the spinnaker needs over trimming to steady it, then replace it with a smaller chute.

When close reaching, the changeover from spinnaker to genoa occurs much earlier, or at a wider sailing angle, than with a masthead rig. This is because the slot created by the intersection between spinnaker and mainsail closes earlier. It is also why the genoa is set with an abundance of twist to create a parallel slot.

Rightly or wrongly, safety margins in inshore and offshore racing circles are often given a low priority by designers and sailors. Minimum weight and windage have long been the important factors, and if a yacht is dismasted, a halyard breaks, or a sail rips as a result, there is always another race tomorrow.

When sailing across oceans, there is no tomorrow. A dismasting, or even continual problems with wear and tear can reduce a year or more of expectation and hard preparation to nothing. A crew may struggle on to finish, they often do, but with all chance of success lost, the voyage invariably degenerates into a morale-sapping struggle.

The wear and tear on each ocean crossing that makes up the various stages of the Global Challenge round the world races, are equivalent to more than two years of hard racing in the Solent, so the lessons learned from what now adds up to 50 circumnavigations are significant. Crews who disregard the wider safety margins required, or fail to make a conscious effort to minimise chafe to sails and cordage are simply courting trouble.

Sailing successfully around the world requires a careful balance between reliability and speed, and good preparation beforehand provides a far greater speed advantage than any paring down on weight and windage aloft.

The initial fleet of 1992 vintage 67ft (20.4 m) Challenge yachts completed two circumnavigations and many more miles besides before being superseded by the 72ft (22m) Rob Humphrey designs which were again built of steel. By and large, the first yachts served their purpose well and continue to be used as training vessels for sailing schools, Britain's Joint Armed Services and by the Challenge Business themselves. The issue of the breaking bottle screws experienced during the first British Steel Challenge led to a serious reappraisal of much of the rigging, deck fittings and safety equipment on these yachts. The wide variations in the metallurgy of the bottle-screw tang castings and the need for much closer tolerances in their manufacturing, led Andrew Roberts and his shore side team of specialists to design and co-ordinate their manufacture. They did the same with the mainsheet traveller, genoa cars, spinnaker pole end fittings and many other items such as lifejackets and personal EPIRBS. Following that first race, The Challenge Business also bought its own mast manufacturer, Atlantic Spars, which now produces purpose-made alloy spars for the fleet and oversee the manufacture of many of the custom-made fittings on the 72ft (22m) yachts.

The design of these second generation yachts, and attention to detail given to their decks and interior arrangements, mirror the wealth of experience gained by the Challenge Team. These are serious all-terrain vehicles designed to scale mountainous head seas in the Southern Ocean, to withstand hurricanes in the Caribbean and collisions with ice, whales – and occasionally each other – while all

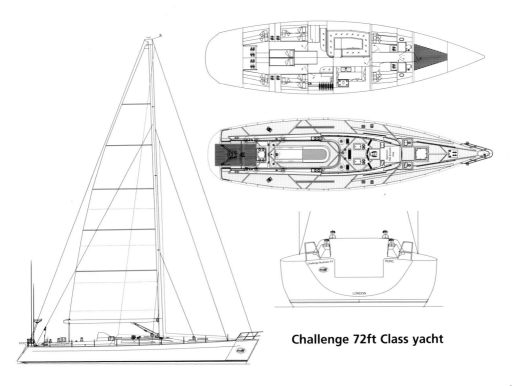

Challenge 72ft Class yacht

the time keeping their 18 strong crews safe from harm.

It is the waves not the wind that does most harm. In the Southern Ocean in particular, they sweep the decks from stem to stern, carrying anything away that is loose, including the crew! Unless you have experienced it first-hand, the bashing and banging that goes on is hard to imagine – until you see the damage sustained to what are in all respect water-born armor plated tanks. After two legs of the Southern Ocean, the bow sections of the 72ft (20.4m) yachts in the first British Steel Challenge were so badly corrugated they looked more like the upturned bonnet of a Citroen 2CV car. Even the second generation yachts, built with thicker plating and better framing, came home with battle scars. One in particular was hit with such force by a freak wave and forcibly flung on her beam ends in New Zealand's Cook Strait that she arrived in Wellington displaying 0.35in (8mm) deep dents along her topsides! Two crewmen

The original safety webbing around the wheel was replaced with heavy netting to stop limbs from getting caught in the spokes.

were swept off their feet so forcibly that the stainless steel carbines on the end of their safety harnesses stripped the plastic sheathing from the jackstays and the bare wire cut deep scores into the hooks. Mercifully, both hook and wire held up to save the crew from falling overboard.

The deck layout on these 72ft (22.4m) yachts is designed to break up these monster waves and protect the crew as much as possible from being swept off their feet. The 'snake pit' just aft of the mast is flanked by winches and control lines laid out so that the crew face side on, rather than have their backs to the waves, so they can see them coming in time to clamp themselves to one of the many handrails around. The glassfibre mini-doghouse protecting the companionway hatch in the middle of this central cockpit acts as a secondary wave breaker and stops green water from flooding below. The design affords considerable protect-ion for those going up or down, there is a jackstay within easy reach to hook onto before emerging, and being close to amidships, the pitching moment is minimal.

The main cockpit has the same high coamings and is divided from the aft cockpit by the mainsheet traveller and a raised companionway hatch leading down to the navigation station. The helmsman is also well protected with a stainless steel, framed, catch fence to stop bodies from being washed into the spinning wheel.

Below decks, the well-lined passage-ways and plethora of handholds make these very safe boats to walk around even in the worst weather. Designed for 18 crew, it is not surprising that the interior is dominated by berths, but these pipe cots are well padded with 2in (5mm) of heavy duty foam, and can be adjusted to lie horizontally whatever the yacht's angle of heel. They are extremely comfortable, and

This aerial picture of a 72ft Challenge yacht in action, shows the split cockpit and protected companionway hatch that allows crew to pass up and down in safety.

for the most part provide a safe haven for exhausted bodies. The galley, sited on the starboard side just forward of amidships, is designed to allow those on 'slave' duty to jam themselves between the sink peninsula and large cooker hob against the hull side. It serves the huge dinette arrangement on the opposite side, which acts as the communal centre of the boat.

The flood-proof engine room beneath the companionway is designed to allow easy access and servicing for the engine, generator and water makers. The navigation station, sited on the opposite side of the aft bulkhead is within hailing distance of the afterguard, via the second hatchway which leads up to the aft cockpit, just forward of the wheel.

The attention to detail given to each area of these 72ft (22.4m) yachts mirrors the vast experience gained from the earlier David Thomas designed war horses used for the first two Global Challenge circumnavigations. This goes down as far as the two sea toilets forward which are hinged to counter the angle of heel and provide a safe haven to er…ruminate in

even the worse weather! Everything, it would seem, has been done to make these yachts as safe as possible in the harshest conditions – without wrapping the crew in cotton wool!

The Mast

The point cannot be emphasised too strongly: minimising weight and windage aloft by paring margins on an ocean racing spar leads to trouble. A mast built for ocean voyages needs to be as specialised in its design and construction as the lightest, cleanest spar on a professional round the buoys racer, but the two design concepts – minimum weight and windage on the one hand; strength, efficiency and ease of maintenance on the other – are simply not compatible.

For yachts embarking on serious ocean crossings, it is often better to start with a clean sheet of paper than rely on a production mast, for sheave boxes and fittings are invariably designed with an eye to rigging shop maintenance – and not a howling gale in mid ocean! One example of this was the Whitbread round the world

The Challenge yacht ocean rig. All rigging connections articulate to minimise fatigue failure. Note the lightweight spreaders.

Close-up of the articulating forestay connection.

race yacht that suffered a broken sheave midway through the first leg from Southampton to Portsmouth. Her crew found that they had to remove the forestay before they could replace the offending part!

Ill-designed sheave boxes are a killer as far as halyards are concerned. If the wires

rub against the mast without guide rollers or through blocks mounted on a crane, then they will wear through on a daily basis. Sheave sizes should be 20 times the diameter of the wire/rope, and are best made from extruded acetyl resin which, unlike other plastics, is self lubricating, hard wearing and does not become over-hardened in the extreme cold experienced in the Southern Ocean. As a secondary precaution, it pays to vary the halyard height to ensure that any wear, even on the sheave, is varied from day to day. Since halyards invariably break in the worst weather conditions, it is also sensible to have smaller secondary sheaves fitted below the main ones, with light messenger lines reeved through ready to take a spare halyard, rather than wait for the weather to abate before sending someone up the mast.

Another essential is to ensure that standing rigging is fully articulating at both the tang connections and spreader tips. There was a time during the early Whitbread races when crews would set off to sail around the world with masts held up by continuous rod standing rigging, and finished up dismasted during the first leg. Invariably, the weak link would be an end or spreader fitting fatigued by constant over rotation.

It was Conny Van Rietschoten and his maxi *Flyer* who introduced the world to discontinuous rigging. His engineering background told him that the common method of rigging masts with continuous stays was flawed, and commissioned the National Aerospace Laboratory in Holland, Rondal Masts, Navtec Rigging and designer, German Frers, to develop a discontinuous system with link plates at the spreader tips that would allow the mast to bend without distorting the rod. At first, other sailors poured scorn on the idea, but when three rival maxis all lost their masts within a couple of months, everyone began to look more closely at *Flyer's* rig. What they found was a system that weighed no more than the continuous system, allowed a full 10° of toggle movement, had a lower centre of gravity and a simplified tuning system that centred on adjusting the lower cap shroud rod. Soon all yachts were rigged this way.

The Challenge yachts are rigged in a similar manner, though with 1x19 wire instead of rod. The forestays which take the greatest loads, are pre-stretched before being fitted to the masts, to avoid adjustment problems later. The standing rigging is set up on each yacht with a tension meter to within 25% of the wire's stated safe working load and these are re-checked in each port to show up any anomalies. Crews are not allowed to adjust the rigging themselves to avoid failures through overload or inexperience. As a precaution on *Flyer*, the crew replaced all the tang fittings at each stop-over and the rod forestay was changed after 20,000 miles, but the pins and 1x19 wire used on the Challenge yachts not only last the entire 32,000 mile global course but for another year in addition. Considering that these 72ft (22.4m) yachts take much more of a battering than their Whitbread or Volvo Race counterparts, this is a considerable advance.

Sails invariably get damaged. The task is to limit 'down time' to a minimum by having a constant eye open for trouble at sea; a comprehensive maintenance programme in port; and a policy of protecting all areas where chafe can occur. This is best achieved by applying self-adhesive patches of cloth to the sails where they rub against stanchions, spreaders and pulpit. The same can be applied to the stanchions and spreader tips too. Some crews go to great lengths to cover these areas in leather, but while this provides a soft finish when new, salt water crystals soon transform the leather into a hard abrasive skin – the exact opposite of what is required. Leather is useful for padding out sharp edges, such as the top of stanchions, but this still needs sheathing in Dacron sticky-back as an outer covering to lessen chafe.

Running rigging

Spectra, with its high UV resistant properties and ability to withstand sharp bending around sheaves, makes this rope a favourite for long distance sailing. The tension on tension factor – its resistance to fatigue from ever changing pressure on the sheet is equally good, which is just as important when for sailing on one tack or gybe for days at a time.

Chafe is another problem to overcome especially where the spinnaker guy passes through the pole-end fitting. Back in the days of those early Whitbread races, a guy would rarely last more than one watch before having to have the outboard end cut of and remade. Conny van Rietschoten's *Flyer* crew extended their life by binding the rope with leather, Dacron tape and passing it through an outer tube of reinforced plastic hose, but this still only prolonged the rope's life by a few hours.

The problem lies, not with the rope, but with the pole-end fitting which cuts into the rope. The Challenge Business have taken *Flyer's* preventative measures a step further by designing their own pole end fittings with the widest possible radius around the claws which extend the life of the rope 10 fold.

Sheets, halyards and control lines will also have their life extended if sheave sizes are no smaller than 20 times the diameter of the rope or wire passing through them. It is also important to 'change the nip' – by easing or taking up on the halyards – once

Spinnaker pole end fitting and guy spindle reduces wear on the rope.

The stopper knot connecting the guy to the tack of the spinnaker.

Knife stowed close to the mast to cut halyards should an emergency arise.

every watch to ensure that the sheaves are not bearing on the same section of rope all the time.

Sail repairs

The 'down time' repairing a sail can be critical in a long distance event. When a spinnaker blows out, invariably a smaller, heavier sail has to be set in its place, and the longer the first sail takes to repair, the greater the distance lost. Some yachts carry a heavy duty sewing machine that is best mounted on the dinette table in open plan arrangements, but this is a luxury Challenge crews have always gone without. The rationale is that these amateur crews would not have the experience to cut and sew new panels into a sail, so they are given needles and palms and expected to form a sewing circle to re-stitch seams using the original holes to reform the sail. In fact, Hood Sails make it easy for them by making the spinnakers, which are the sails that blow out most, with lighter stitching in the centre panels than across radial paneled head and corners. The object is to limit damage to these centre panels which are easier to repair at sea and simpler for the professional sailmaker to replace when the yacht reaches port.

Personal safety

Each crew is provided with a full set of Musto Ocean clothing, a self inflating lifejacket and a personal EPIRB which they carry in a special pocket within their jacket. The lifejackets proved to be a particular problem because they either self inflated whenever the crewman was dowsed by a wave, or the bladder failed through flexing within the folds. During the 1992/3 Race, when crews were issued with an off-the-shelf lifejacket, these suffered a 90% failure rate, so the Challenge Business decided to develop

their own in conjunction with XM Yachting. This addressed the problem of poor bladder wear and auto-inflating when they shouldn't. This design has been under continuous development since, and is now manufactured by Ocean Safety. It is a credit to this research and development that the failure rate for this latest design is down to 10% of what it was in the 2000 race.

The personal EPIRBs also went off far too often, one of them causing a full scale search by Nimrod aircraft after it burst into life following a knock when stored in the foulie locker! The Challenge Business then worked with ARC to develop a far more reliable system which led to far fewer false alarms during the 2004 Global Challenge.

The lifejacket, safety harness, oillies and the personal EPIRB and its fold-out tracking device have all been developed to high levels of reliability during successive Global Challenge races. The initial lifejackets used in the first race suffered a 90% failure rate. The current design now has a 90% success rate. The latest EPIRB design is also far more reliable.

Technology has revolutionised both navigation techniques and sailing efficiency. The old skills of dead reckoning, handling a sextant, and tide charts are now redundant unless the batteries run flat. The emphasis on navigation expertise now rests on an ability to understand and utilise the growing amount of information that modern equipment can provide. Here is an example.

The place is Cowes on the south coast of England. The time is half an hour before the late evening start of the RORC Channel race, a typical medium distance event. The course is east to the Nab Tower, then round the Owers Light, the RORC Offshore Buoy in the central channel and back to Cowes via Poole Bar.

It has been blowing hard all day from the east, but now the wind has eased a little. There is a choppy sea running with wind against tide in the Solent, and the gathering fleet is surging back and forth under an assortment of sail combinations. As in any offshore race, every boat will have a story to tell before the weekend is out. But we have eyes for two boats only.

Both are newly delivered one-designs of the same class. They have consecutive building codes, identical ratings and almost nothing to distinguish one from the other besides their sail numbers – and their instrumentation. Art Abbot, owner of *Adverse* is a fanatical seat-of-the-pants sailor. He has only invested in a basic electronics package with boat speed, wind and depth instrumentation, a handheld GPS, paper charts and a Windex. He heartily disapproves of the latest expensive electronics, and intends to show, by winning his class, that such gadgets are nothing but distractions. *Advance* is owned by Ben Bowline, and he means to win this race, if only to wipe the smugness off Art's face. He is an IT consultant, fascinated by modern technology and as the navigator of his own boat, has equipped her with a complete set of B&G H2000 Hercules integrated instruments. These link GPS, compass, depth, boat speed and wind information – the same system that is fitted to all the Global Challenge yachts. He also has a B&G RaceVision2 computer onboard, a waterproof tablet PC that is wirelessly linked to the instruments and runs the tactical software package Deckman. It is loaded with electronic charts, a tidal database, list of waypoints and a theoretical performance profile of the yacht provided by the designer. He can also link it to his mobile phone using Bluetooth which allows him to pick up the latest weather information from the Internet later on in the race.

Adverse and *Advance* emerge from the marina at the same time and head for the start line. The tide is flooding east, with two hours to go before the turn. The line is set roughly at right angles to the wind, and it will be a windward start. Art takes *Adverse* up to the line and stops head to wind, looking for a bias. His basic instrument system does give him a readout for wind direction but it changes all the time as the boat manoeuvres and tacks, so Art always likes to go head-to-wind to get a better idea of the line bias. He's pretty confident that the starboard end is best, though it is difficult to be absolutely certain because the tide takes him across the line while he's checking his Windex. Although his instruments have the ability to tell Art the

Screen shot from a Deckman computer showing the course by our two mythical yachts Adverse and Advance.

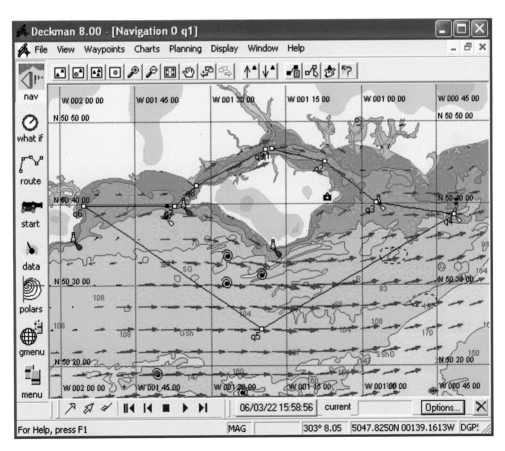

wind speed, they never seem to be consistent upwind or down, so Art relies on his intuition. He gauges that there is too much for the No.1 genoa, so he calls for the No.2, while noting anxiously that a third of the fleet have heavy No.1s set.

Aboard *Advance*, Ben Bowline is confronted with the same problems, but he solves them by different methods. On his way to the start line he has been running a plot of the wind direction and although it has been shifting a little, the mean direction has been consistently around 085°. He also has True Wind Direction showing on one of the 20/20 mast displays which is visible to all the crew. As he swings the wheel to avoid a Class I boat close by, *Advance's* bows swing through 90° but the wind direction display continues to record 085° throughout the manoeuvre, as the instrumentation disentangles the magnetic bearing of the true wind from the apparent wind angle measured at the masthead, and uses advanced correction tables to account for changes in upwash and mast twist on different points of sail. Bowline already has the position of the Squadron flagstaff stored in the RaceVision2, so he now heads for the outer distance mark that has just been laid. As his bow crosses the line at this end, his foredeck drops his arm and Ben clicks on the 'ping' button in the Deckman software to store the position of the line. The display immediately shows the set-up of the start line and that it is set for a wind direction of 090° so there is a small, but nonetheless positive bias to the port end of the line.

The enthusiastic foredeck man on *Advance* is watching the true windspeed on the mast register 20 knots. 'No. 2 genoa' he asks. Ben Bowline checks the wind plot again and notices that although the breeze has touched 20, it has been averaging 13 for the last 15 minutes so he is not sure that the No. 2 is the correct choice. If they start with the No.2 genoa, even given the weather-going tide and the apparent wind speed generated by *Advance's* boat speed, the decreasing wind and lumpy sea will soon force them to change to the No.1. But can she stand the No.1 right now? One way to find out, Ben decides, and confirms the No.2 as he taps away on the RaceVision and starts a Speed Test. As soon as the sail is hoisted and drawing, the helmsman settles *Advance* down for a brief spurt to windward, while Ben monitors the performance of the boat with a plot of VMG percent. It reads 94, informing Ben that his yacht is sailing to windward at 94% of the 'velocity made good' which would be achieved by the designer's theoretical yacht being sailed perfectly. He glances over his shoulder at *Adverse*, and calls for a change to the No.1. Once again the yacht is put through her paces. But this time the VMG percent plot averages out at 98.

'Right, we'll keep the No.1,' he says. Ben then quickly checks the results of the speed test and notes that although the No.1 is the correct sail for the moment, when the wind had peaked briefly at over 17 knots, the No.2 had come into its own with much better VMG. This will be useful information for sail changes on what is a new yacht that they are still getting to know, so he notes it in a spreadsheet he has set up on the RaceVision.

Ben is now watching for the five-minute signal. There it goes, and the computer's timer is started at the same moment. It immediately begins counting down to the start and displays the distance and time to both ends of the line, allowing the crew on *Advance* to time their approach with supreme confidence, despite the strong tide taking them towards the line.

Back on board *Adverse*, the crew are congratulating themselves on stealing a march over their rival who is clearly going to start at the wrong end of the line with the wrong headsail up. The gun goes, the fleet comes crashing and plunging away from the coast, close hauled on starboard tack. *Advance*, however, has bravely started on port. She crosses the majority of the fleet, passes ahead of *Adverse* by three lengths, and then tacks, having scored the first psychological point. Art frets and curses, and eventually demands a change to the No.1, saying the boat isn't going properly. Then he calls for a tack inshore, just as darkness engulfs the fleet.

Concentration is intense aboard *Advance*, but there is also an air of confidence born of knowledge. The yacht is settled on starboard tack, with the tacking performance indicator reading between 97 and 100. It has taken time and one or two adjustments to get her there, but undoubtedly she is going well now. On deck, the helmsman is feeling her along with the help of his computer. At the chart table, Ben Bowline is planning his moves. He has fed the latitude and longitude waypoint of the Nab Tower into the RaceVision. He has also input the latest information about the tide, which has just turned against the fleet. Ben checks the What If? screen in the Deckman software and sees that they are still on the making tack so decides to stand on for a little longer.

Art Abbot is fretting. Navigation lights surround him, and he suspects that one of those white stern lights up to windward may be *Advance*. He shines his torch on the luff telltales, and barks at the helmsman for pinching. Then he peers out to starboard, looking for the Nab Tower. He is not quite sure when to tack again. Meanwhile Ben Bowline has been watching the true wind direction plot and has noted that he has been headed slowly, so that he is on the correct side of the fleet for the shift. This agrees with the forecast that he had

downloaded via his mobile phone just before the start. He had input this into the Deckman to calculate an optimum route and this, coupled with the built-in tidal data, had shown that this was the side of the course to choose. Everything is going according to plan. The true wind speed is now down to 15 knots, but there is still plenty of power to enable the helmsman to point higher – higher in fact than he feels is right. The genoa luff shows the inner tell-tales flicking upwards; but the tacking performance indicator says that this is the way to go; to point high, go a little slower through the water, and make up to the mark at the optimum speed. Now Deckman shows him that the opposite tack has the advantage, and round they go.

By the time *Advance* reaches the Nab Tower, neither Ben Bowline nor Art Abbot knows where the other is. But Bowline is sailing in company with the polars of the perfectly sailed trial horse inside the computer, whereas Art has only his imperfect imagination to keep him on his toes. So perhaps it's just as well he can't see *Advance* 2 miles ahead.

Both skippers turn in at this point to snatch a couple of hours sleep. Both are woken up at 04:00 by the change of watch. The fleet is still hard on the wind, working up to the Owers Light against a foul spring tide. The new helmsmen settle down, and both boats battle on. Art can sense that *Adverse* is going more slowly. 'You're pinching,' he roars, until he feels the increased heel and hears the chuckle of the faster water flow. Then he relaxes.

Ben can tell that *Advance* is going faster, and smiles with satisfaction until he checks with the computer. There is the answer he didn't want to see: they are going faster through the water but not achieving the VMC (velocity made course) towards the Owers Light that Deckman says they should be. In fact, the course for

Optimum VMC is shown as a couple of degrees higher. 'Try sailing a touch closer,' he suggests and gradually the instruments show that *Advance* is edging back towards her optimum performance. Dawn breaks to reveal a distance of 12 miles between the two boats.

Once round the Owers, the front, forecast earlier, goes through. The wind increases and veers to the south, to send the fleet on a fast reach towards the RORC Offshore Buoy in mid-Channel. All around are spinnakers and wild broaches. *Adverse* has a spinnaker which was made for conditions like these, and old Art is grinning fiercely as it powers his yacht along in spectacular fashion. Now he'll catch *Advance*, which hasn't set a kite at all.

Aboard *Advance* there is dissention in the ranks. Spinnaker or blast reacher? It is impossible to draw any conclusions from the other boats, because everybody is going fast. So they begin the leg with staysail and reacher set, while Ben logs the reading of the reaching performance indicator, 98%. Then they break out the flanker, 97%. Now they broach, 54%. Back in business half a minute later, 97% again. Try to improve. Still only 97%. Check apparent wind angle: 85°. Try bearing away a little from the rhumb line course. The computer says that the VMC towards the RORC Buoy has dropped a fraction. Up reacher, down spinnaker. Performance 98%. Sail trimmer adjusts the sheet leads, 99%. *Advance* rounds the RORC Offshore Buoy at 14:30. *Adverse* rounds at 15:25, just as the tide turns against her.

The wind is failing again and *Advance* is setting a course dead downwind for the Poole Bar buoy she only has 5 knots apparent, and 8 knots of true wind speed. Ben reasons that if they tack downwind using the VMG sail, the tide will prevent them from making it to the mark. But if they set the runner and head dead downwind, they will hardly make any way in the light air. Ben tries it both ways, monitoring the results on the RaceVision. He finds that in the puffs it pays to run square, but in the light patches he has to tack downwind, sometimes with an apparent wind coming from forward of the beam. It seems to take forever to bring the mark alongside, but finally they make it as night falls. There is no sign of *Adverse*.

Advance crosses the line at 16:00 on Sunday afternoon. Ben touches the keypad to stop the timer, which began to count automatically from the moment of the starting signal. Now it displays the yacht's elapsed time and calculates the amount of time owed to other boats based on ratings. It has been a long race. But not half as long as it seems for Art Abbot on *Adverse*, who is still out there, sailing by the seat of his pants for all he is worth.

Modern instrumentation systems
How they work and what they can do
Whether Art Abbot likes it or not, technology has revolutionised both navigation techniques and sailing efficiency, and is certainly here to stay. The old skills of DR, handling a sextant, and tide charts are now redundant – unless the batteries run flat. The emphasis on navigation expertise now rests on an ability to understand and utilise the growing amount of information that modern equipment can provide. This may have taken some of the satisfaction out of navigation work, but it has made sailing a more precise, safer sport.

The use of computer chips in marine systems first emerged in the USA in the form of inexpensive electronic position fixing devices. These Decca, Loran, and Omega systems have long since been superseded by the universally common GPS systems, now standard on most yachts and may even be in your car! In the context of yacht instrumentation – monitoring log, wind speed and direction, compass course and boat speed – the B&G Hercules system on board the Global Challenge yachts relays each piece of information to any number of displays around the boat. It also processes this information to compute true windspeed and direction as well as VMG (velocity made good) and VMC (velocity made course).

The opportunity to monitor changes in VMC as opposed to merely watching for fluctuations in boat speed, is one of the greatest benefits this technology offers to navigators. Merely enter a waypoint (or the position of the next mark) and the VMC reading, computed from the vector sums of true wind speed and direction with boat speed, tells when to tack or gybe. Providing there are only small fluctuations

in the wind, the log reading will remain constant but the VMC will drop as the yacht starts to overstand the next mark. With the Hercules and other systems, it is also possible to monitor performance from an absolute standpoint. Stored within the computer memory is a set of polars that give an optimum performance value for all angles to the wind, which is enhanced using empirical data gained during early sail trials.

This facility is particularly useful to owners of one-designs. The performance characteristics gained from other yachts of that type can be fed into the computer to provide a standard to aspire to when determining the best trim, sail settings and reefing patterns during early sailing trials. The readings can also save a great deal of embarrassment. No one likes being told he is a second-rate helmsman but the little

A typical computerised sailing instrument system aboard a performance yacht.

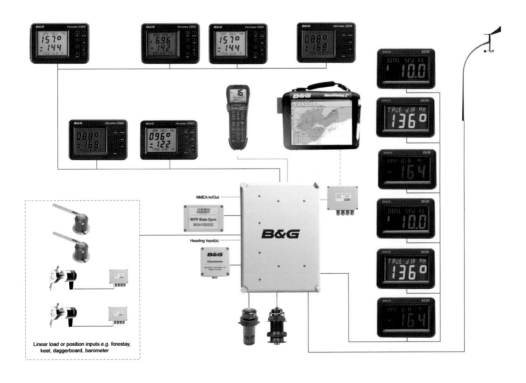

black box acts as judge and jury. The percentage figure lit up on the display reflects its verdict for all to see. If the percentage figure does not rise to within a point or two of optimum there is something basically wrong either with sail trim or the helmsman's technique – and it doesn't take long to find out which!

One point of sailing where the constant VMG value is particularly useful, is sailing downwind in light airs when the winds can fluctuate considerably, taxing the most agile mind. The computer removes all the guess work from determining the best course, taking account of the increased apparent wind and boat speed when the yacht heads higher than the required course. Which is better – to sail dead downwind for the mark at 12 knots or reach twice as far at 14 knots? The VMG reading tells you immediately.

Position fixing

Introduced in the 1990s, the Global Position System or GPS for short, based on up to 24 satellites, has given all sailors an affordable and reliable means of position fixing with an accuracy within 33ft (10m). Standard antennas update this position once a second and more expensive antennas can update it at up to ten times per second. Sub 33ft (10m) accuracy is becoming increasingly common with dGPS which uses differential corrections to position errors provided by land based radio transmitters when in range. More recently these position corrections can also be obtained via the satellites themselves with the WAAS system (Wide Area Augmentation Service) already launched in the USA and EGNOS (European Geostationary Navigation Overlay Service), soon to be started in Europe.

Screen shot of a wind plot displayed on a Deckman computer linked to a yacht's electronic sailing instruments.

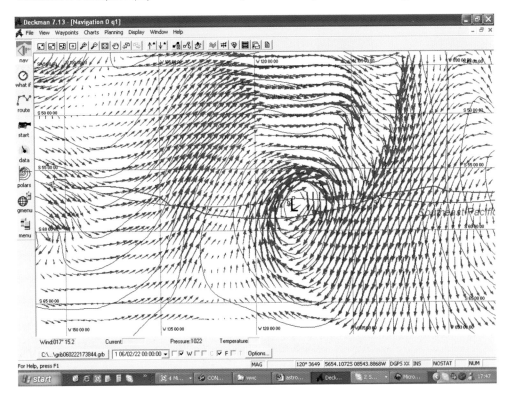

Communications

Recent advances in global tele-communications are simply staggering. In our example race, Ben Bowline uses his pocket mobile phone to connect to the Internet and download the latest weather forecast on the way out to the start line. Ocean racing boats use satellite based telephony such as Fleet 77 to provide voice and data communications anywhere on the planet. This even allows them to send video clips back to the media ashore. With access to the Internet available any time and anywhere it is always possible to get hold of the latest weather data from a wide array of sources. This has led to some boats having huge communications budgets as they rack up expensive international satellite phone bills. In the recent Global Challenge race and Volvo Ocean Race, organisers chose to limit this expense by only allowing teams to access weather data provided by the race office as part of a communications package sent regularly to every team.

Instrument layout

The only problem with computerised information is that the wealth of data can lead to confusion. The instrumentation is designed to dissect all the information then channel it to the crew member who requires it. The helmsman, for example, needs to see the compass, wind direction, and boat speed indicators to keep the boat on course and going as fast as possible. But if he can see all the other information as well, he may start thinking about problems that are not necessarily his to worry about. This is particularly so with VMG, which can easily lead the helmsman astray if it is within his field of view. This is because the VMG reading is designed to provide a long term measurement of overall per-formance, and not a moment-by-moment indication, since it takes 45 seconds or so for a yacht to stabilise its speed after each change of course. The computer cannot

A clear display at the steering console allows the helmsman to focus on the information that relates to his task, and not be distracted by extraneous information.

take account of this, so VMG climbs initially when the helmsman starts to pinch and decreases when he bears away. Thus, the man at the wheel is tempted to head up a little until the VMG reading begins to drop, but when he then tries to bear away, the reading drops even further so he instinctively heads up again – a move encouraged by the steadily climbing VMG reading until the headsail is completely back winded and the boat stops dead in the water!

Similarly the crew are concerned not so much with the compass but numbers that relate directly to sail trim, showing changes in speed and other performance factors. Other instruments clearly belong to the navigator or tactician and need to be placed accordingly.

It is now possible to portray almost any function either digitally or in the more conventional analogue form. These days, racing crews tend to use only digital displays. When sailing at night hard on the wind, it is easier to sail to a figure (say 28°) than measure a needle that is constantly moving around. Crews can then play boat speed against wind angle and discover the angles at which the boat performs best in set wind strengths. For example, a Transpac 52 might have an optimum windward sailing angle of 40° true wind angle with a target speed of 8.02 knots. Having a target boat speed figure like that prevents the speed from dropping too much when a new helmsman takes over, for there is always a guide line to refer to while they spend the first two or three minutes getting a feel for the boat and conditions.

The most popular position for digital displays is on the mast where large 20/20 type readouts can display the most important information for all the crew to see. These mast displays are in the direct line of sight of the helmsman and trimmer

Jumbo instrumentation panel on the mast gives the crew a clear view of the readings.

as they look forward to the bow and sails. Additional digital displays are often placed in convenient positions for the main sheet trimmer, navigator and headsail trimmer to display secondary information such as heel angle, forestay load or rudder angle.

Just as display technology on deck has advanced and changed the way crews look at the numbers available, it has also transformed the look of the chart table. The Volvo Ocean Race yachts have two computers side by side for redundancy and then a small, dedicated radar screen that is used to monitor competitors and identify icebergs in the Southern Ocean. In some cases even the radar screen functionality is provided by the computer screens. The computers themselves are then used by the navigator to access and manage all the data available. This information can then also be accessed by the navigator on deck using a dedicated

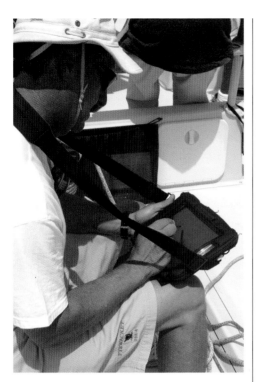

The Deckman allows the navigator to come up on deck and see where he is going!

waypoints. This may seem to have taken all the skill out of the navigator's role, but in fact it has increased the demands on the navigator. He is now expected to make use of all the extra information available and feed this back to the crew with more accurate information on boat performance and routing strategy. A navigator in the Volvo Ocean Race can now expect to spend around 16 hours a day staring at a computer screen!

In the America's Cup, investment in technology far exceeds any other area of yacht racing. The best equipped campaigns have two boats sailing that are bristling with sensors and displays which are wirelessly networked together so that the crew of one boat can tell what is happening on the other. This information is also shared with the tenders out on the water and the design office back at base – and can be analysed before the boats return to the dock. This level of information requires vast databases to compile all of the sailing data and link with video images of the sails and sometimes even audio commentary from the teams. The tenders are also fully equipped with instrument systems that are then networked together and used by the meteorology teams to use in the information they pass to the crew moments before racing begins. The instrument systems now used on these boats measure sensor data 100 times a second and even correct wind measurements for the effects of yacht motion. Meanwhile the navigator tracks the opposition boat using a laser range finder and informs the tactician about gains or losses.

wireless display or computer such as the RaceVision2, meaning that there is no longer any excuse for navigators to go below and avoid the wet and cold!

The Deckman tactical software installed on the onboard computers is used to combine the sailing information from the instrument system with positional information from the GPS. This shows the position of the yacht, its track and laylines overlaid onto the electronic chart. It is also used to plot graphs of instrument data to track performance and wind shifts over time. Weather data downloaded via the Internet using mobile phone or satellite communications is then used to calculate optimum routes to

Too few people place enough emphasis on the need for compatibility at sea. Yet in the damp, cramped and often limited comfort of even the most well endowed yacht, clashes of personality or discontent can destroy morale and enjoyment.

Crew choice and training

There are sprinters and marathon runners in every sport, and it rarely pays to match them. Hard-living, fast-talking hotshots with outsize egos undoubtedly have their place in the sport, but marathon material for trans-ocean events they are not.

The Global Challenge races attract ten applicants for every berth and all undergo a rigorous assessment before 'winning' their place on board. Burning ambition tops the list of requirements. The ability to pay straight up, and previous sailing experience are at the bottom. Staying power is tested during the training.

'We look for people who are prepared to move mountains in order to take part in the Challenge,' says Sir Chay, adding, 'Those with a burning ambition will always find ways of raising the money. We prefer those who have little or no previous sailing experience because they don't come with any preconceptions or bad habits. Each person undergoes a rigorous training programme covering up to 5,000 miles before the race. By the start time, they have more experience than most 'weekend' sailors who have been doing it for a lifetime. And for those who have the money and time to spare, we set a challenge to prove their commitment – to raise £2,000 for Save The Children.'

Events like the Global Challenge races attract men and women from almost every walk of life. There have been lorry drivers, vets, undertakers and salesmen sharing the experience, if not the same night watches, with doctors, market gardeners, city types, policemen and prison officers. There was even an ex-convict, though not on the same watch!

By the end of their training, which includes working up to doing a 3-mile run, each successful applicant will know exactly what to expect in racing the wrong way around the world, having endured winter training trips out into the Atlantic, sleep deprivation during non-stop weekend courses and testing delivery trips around Britain and Europe. Some have taken their training so seriously that they have devoted extra time and energy to earning their Ocean Yachtmaster™ tickets.

Pete Goss, the former Royal Marine responsible with Sir Chay for setting up the training programme that turned what was a disparate bunch into true blue water sailors for the first Global Challenge race in 1992, recalls: 'When they first joined for training, most were starry-eyed enough just to want to sail around the world. But the training programme that Chay and I put together soon knocked that out of them. After enduring months of cold night watches, wet clothes, fitness runs and 6:00am swims through the winter, their one wish was to win!'

Many, going to sea for the first time,

clamber aboard in trepidation. Some even have to be shown how to climb over the lifelines. A year later, they are happy working up a wildly gyrating mast or swinging out on the end of a spinnaker pole. The Challenge itself becomes the motivating factor, and for some the learning curve will have been extremely steep, but through sheer tenacity, deep questioning and some tears, each person becomes a responsible seaman in their own right.

For many, just raising the considerable sum to compete in these races is challenging enough. Some sell every asset from business to home, parts of their car, to the vehicle itself. Valerie Elliot, a strong-willed teacher and grandmother, gave up her marriage and much else, and used the Challenge as a stepping-stone to start a

Team buiding. The 18 crewmembers aboard each Challenge yacht probably have 18 different reasons for choosing to sail around the world. It is the task of each skipper to meld these disparates into one cohesive force.

new life. By the time of the race, the grip-bag she flung aboard her yacht represented everything she owned.

On the way, she also had to conquer a fear of heights. 'Going up the mast was her personal Everest' recalls Ian MacGillivray, another of Chay Blyth's first training skippers. 'She tried several times and failed. Then one day we had a problem at the masthead and I said, 'Quick, Valerie, grab the harness.' She was half way up the mast before she knew what was happening. I went up with her, but she got to the top and did the job on her own. By the time she was back on deck, she was standing 10ft tall. It was a real turning point in her life, giving her confidence a tremendous boost. She could tackle any job after that!'

Another crew with an iron will was Lisa Marie Wood, a former Wren who had been invalided out of the Royal Navy after sustaining horrific burns. At the time of signing up, she was earning £6,000 a year as a nurse in an old people's home and had nothing in the way of assets or savings. Yet, so determined was she to take part, that her fundraising exploits made her something of a legend. She sold the fog lights off her car to pay for the petrol to get herself down to Plymouth for a week of training, and then flogged the car radio to get home again. She got the rest of the money by selling the car bit by bit and writing persuasive begging letters to more than 200 companies. After the race, she threw herself enthusiastically into anything to do with sailing, acting as assistant shore manager for fellow crew Samantha Brewster during her solo non-stop round the world record bid, subsequent entries in other Challenge

After a series of dawn runs, 6am swims, and winter sail training out in the Atlantic, none of the Challenge crew are under any starry-eyed illusions when they set out to sail around the world.

Events like the Global Challenge races are as much about team building are they are about providing individuals with the adventure of a lifetime.

races, and most recently, the Volvo Ocean Race.

Some of these crews have never been on a yacht since. Others have gone back into industry and made a second success of their careers. A few, like Andy Hindley and Dougie Gillespie, have gone on to skipper Global Challenge yachts in their own right, and some skippers, like Mike Golding and Pete Goss, have gone on to make a considerable mark in other areas of the sport.

It doesn't matter if you are planning to sail around the world or around the Solent; there are skill-sets and levels of teamwork required to avoid damage or drama. This chapter lists the basic job descriptions for each crew member and the roles each must play during each manoeuvre and sail change.

Cornelis van Rietschoten, whose *Flyer* yachts won two Whitbread Round the World races, took man-management and preparation to new levels in the sport. Having employed some 2,000 people in his electrical company in Holland, he knew a thing or two about leadership, teamwork and training people. He was also a good judge of whom to have around him. He wrote in the original book *Blue Water Racing*:

'My own preference is for quiet, easy going characters with a ready smile and sense of commitment that produces 100% effort without being asked. Those that spend their time on deck looking for tasks to perform are immensely valuable. Those that stand around with their hands in their pockets are not.

Shouters are also discouraged. Efficient teamwork comes through practice, set routines and a positive chain of command running from stem to stern. Shouted commands are lost on the wind or worse,

Conny van Rietschoten at the helm of Flyer *deep in the Southern Ocean, en-route to winning his second Whitbread Round the World race.*

misunderstood. Raised voices only aggravate what are invariably tense situations already. The best way to reduce foul-ups or 'down time' is to practice beforehand and to rely on a system of hand signals which can always be seen and understood, whatever the weather.

Nor is there room on board for a committee. Decisions have to be made at the top and it is the quality of this leadership in making consistent, firm but fair decisions that dictates whether the crew are efficient or not. Any sloppiness or inconsistency at the top is quickly reflected throughout the crew, adversely affecting morale and boat speed.

Both *Flyer* campaigns were run as a business, using normal management practices. The skipper took ultimate responsibility, the watch leaders acted as middle managers and individual jobs on board were delegated according to experience and qualifications. The general rules that I drew up will come as second nature to an experienced hand, but from my experience of running a large company, youngsters drawn from all walks of life need a common code to live by if team spirit is to work effectively for extended periods at sea. The two subjects most likely to create friction are politics and food. By banning these as topics of conversation, we cut out most opportunities to argue.

I drew up specific job descriptions for key crew members, which directed them and cut out further disputes over job allocations. Any griping was then quickly quelled by telling recalcitrant crew to get out their list of duties!'

General Rules On Board

1 No smoking!
2 Keep politics out of the conversation.
3 This is a hospitable ship, and almost anyone is welcome aboard. Introduction to the skipper is appreciated.
4 No throwing of food.
5 Daily freshwater allowance (except for rainwater) is restricted to the contents of the day-tank – 8 cups a day per person.
6 The cook can ration certain foods, beverages, water and other articles only on orders from the skipper.
7 Turn the gas supply off after using the stove.
8 Light is scarce. Switch off after use.
9 Switch off music system after use and replace CD in its box.
10 Specific jobs on board described in the job descriptions are the responsibility of that particular crewman. Comments or ideas to improve jobs are welcome but should be channelled via the responsible crew member.
11 No personal gear to be left around the deck or cockpit except when drying out.
12 Mugs to be returned to the galley after use.
13 'Dodger dwelling' is restricted to the off-watch only.
14 At night, the 'off-watch' is called 15 minutes before their watch starts. Hot drinks are prepared by one of the 'on-watch' in time for them to be consumed below decks before the watch changes.
15 No fresh 'on-watch' to come on deck with a cup in their hands.
16 Day watches are called 40 minutes before their watch and meals should be ready 30 minutes before the watch change.
17 Cleaning below deck is done by the morning watch. Cleaning of dishes is done on a rota basis.
18 Sail packing is done by the watch that effected the sail change.
19 The 'on-watch' should always remember that the 'off-watch' crew is trying to sleep.
20 The 'off-watch' crew can be called on deck only on the orders of the skipper.
21 Crew to station themselves on the weather rail whenever conditions demand.
22 No crewman other than the helmsman, watch leaders and navigator should remain in, or around, the aft cockpit.
23 Conversation with helmsman is restricted to essential items only, to ensure maximum concentration.
24 Only when off watch can a crew member:
   ■ Take a shower
   ■ Take photographs
   ■ Read books and magazines
   ■ Listen to music on pocket stereos
25 Drying of towels should be done below.
26 Drying of clothing and boots should always be carried out in the drying locker.

1 Lifelines must be carried in lifejackets ready for use at any time.
2 Each crew member must carry at all times:
   ■ Personal transponder or mini-flares
   ■ Whistle
   ■ Knife
   ■ Torch – during night watches
3 The wearing of a lifejacket is advised but optional.

Job Descriptions

Watch leaders
The skipper delegates the following responsibilities to each watch leader

1 Maintain a cohesive functioning team.
2 Coordinate sail handling and trimming.
3 Maintain course control and standard of steering.
4 Crew punctuality at each watch change.
5 Daily check on standing rigging, halyards, sheets, blocks, shackles. Repair and renew where necessary.
6 Oversee packing and stowing of sails in their assigned bags and bins.
7 Maintain peace and quiet on deck – NO SHOUTING.
8 Station crew on weather rail when conditions demand.
9 Ensure that crew members keep clear of aft cockpit.
10 As little as possible to be said to helmsman to maintain concentration.
11 Keep deck and topsides clean.
12 General tactics and strategy are based on factual information and experience on the part of skipper, watch leaders and navigator. The skipper has the final authority at all times and must be consulted and informed accordingly. When resting, the skipper should be called by the watch leader when:
   ■ A change in weather calls for a sail change or reef
   ■ For gybing
   ■ In case of emergency

Navigator
Is responsible for:

1 Charts, pilots and tidal information.
2 GPS positioning and dead reckoning.
3 Updating weather information.
4 Maintaining the ship's log.
5 Maintaining and monitoring navigation equipment (together with Electrician):
   ■ Sailing instrumentation
   ■ Computers and programmes
   ■ Emails
   ■ Satellite phone

- ■ Radio equipment
- ■ Water temperature sensor
6. Non-electrical systems:
   - ■ Ship's clocks and chronometer
   - ■ Barometer
   - ■ Compasses
   - ■ Code flags

Doctor/ship's medic
The doctor's tasks are:

1. Keep crew in good physical condition.
2. Administer first aid.
3. Monitor individual medication.
4. Restock medical kit at each port of call.
5. Investigate what medical restrictions are in force at ports of call.
6. Ensure that everyone has the correct inoculations.
7. Offer medical advice to other crews in event of emergencies.
8. Responsibility for balanced diets and quality of food (together with Cook).

Electrician
Is responsible for:

1. Electrical installations:
   - ■ Alternators (together with Engineer)
   - ■ Starting and lighting batteries
   - ■ Switchboard
   - ■ Shore power system
   - ■ Lights and outlets
   - ■ Inverter
2. Electronic equipment (together with Navigator):
   - ■ Sailing instrumentation
   - ■ VHF and SSB radio
   - ■ GPS equipment
   - ■ Water temperature sensor
   - ■ Computers
   - ■ Music system
3. Ship's wiring diagram and equipment instruction books.

Shipwright/engineer
Is responsible for the maintenance and repair of:

1. Hull and deck structure.
2. Winches.
3. Steering mechanism (including emergency tiller).
4. Ventilation.
5. Leaks.
6. Water and fuel tanks.
7. Valves, piping and plumbing.

8   Sea cocks.
9   Toilets.
10 Washbasins.
11 Engine (weekly oil check and maintenance).
12 Generator (weekly oil check and maintenance).
13 Desalinator.
14 Woodwork.
15 Scuppers.
16 Running rigging (together with Rigger and Sailmaker).
17 Non-slip deck covering.
18 Locks and padlocks.
19 Ship's toolbox.
20 Zinc anodes.
21 Spare equipment and repair materials.
22 Instruction manuals.
23 Know exact positions for strops and shores when yacht or equipment
    is to be hoisted or slipped.

Rigger
Is responsible for the care, maintenance and repair of:

1   Mast and spars:
    ■ Mast and track
    ■ Boom
    ■ Spinnaker poles
    ■ Reaching strut
    ■ Shroud rollers
    ■ Spreaders
    ■ Mast collar
    ■ Masthead aerials and wind instruments
    ■ Sheaves
2   Standing Rigging:
    ■ Blocks, rigging fittings, cleats, turnbuckles
    ■ Anchors
    ■ Cables and dock lines
    ■ Fenders
    ■ Flag halyards and flag staff
    ■ Lead line
3   Running rigging (together with Sailmaker and Shipwright/Engineer)
4   Safety equipment:
    ■ Stanchions, pulpit, lifelines and pushpit
    ■ Jackstays
    ■ Lifejackets
    ■ Liferafts and emergency equipment
    ■ Life rings and man-overboard equipment
    ■ Radar reflector

Sailmaker

Is responsible for:

1 Care and maintenance of sails and equipment (battens etc).
2 Care and maintenance of repair tools and materials.
3 Running rigging (together with Rigger and Shipwright/Engineer).
4 Restocking of repair materials at each port of call.

Cook

Is responsible for:

1 Cooking and galley organisation.
2 Water distribution.
3 Stowage of food and recording daily usage.
4 Distribution of linen, towels and toilet paper etc.
5 Stove maintenance and gas supply.
6 Cleaning materials and keeping below decks clean and tidy.
7 Restocking of food and water at ports of call.
8 Responsibility for balanced diets and quality of food (together with Medic).

A good galley design allows the cook to wedge themselves in. Oilskin bottoms guard against any danger of scalding.

The raw recruit

With the benefit of four Global Challenge races, Sir Chay Blyth and his team have developed an excellent Training Manual which is issued to all new recruits. They are expected to read and digest it before their first sail, then use it to test themselves on procedures, equipment maintenance and stowage. By the time the race starts, the learning and training programmes will have made the whole business of working and living on a yacht for 5-6 weeks at a time second nature.

For those taking their first training sail, these are Sir Chay Blyth's 11 Golden Rules: 'Good seamanship is directly attributable to anticipation. You need to be like a coiled spring, leaping to action whenever something needs doing.'

1 Keep one hand for the boat – and one for yourself!
2 Be aware.
3 *Always* work on the windward side:
   ■ Clip your safety harness on windward side
   ■ *Never* stand downwind of sails being dropped
   ■ *Never* stand on the boom
4 If you think something needs doing, it's time to do it!
5 When 'on watch' check all around:
   ■ Will the sheets run in an emergency?
   ■ Check the mast. Are there any sails chafing on the rigging?
   ■ Before departure – is everything in place?
   ■ Before returning – is everything ready?
   ■ Make sure that there are no ropes hanging over the side
6 Never open hatches more than 60° – apart from the forehatch.
7 If doors or hatches won't shut – don't force them. Find out what the problem is and rectify it.
8 Below decks – make sure everything is secure.
9 Don't bang latch or locker doors.
10 Don't chip the paintwork – especially easy with winch handles.
11 The longer bad weather lasts, the less time there is to go!

Reefing the mainsail is one of those times when sail ties have to be at the ready.

Sail ties

Next to your lifejacket, sail ties are your best friend. A good crew will always have one on them, in their pocket, when on watch. Never wear them around your neck. When you go off watch, leave the tie looped through itself on a grab rail in the companionway, ready for someone else to use. Don't leave it lying around on deck.

When using the tie to secure a sail on the foredeck, wrap the sail tie around the sail only and secure with a slip knot. Do not secure it to any part of the deck, fittings or trap ropes or lines in it. Waves can have the force of 1.5G and will not only damage a tethered sail, but rip out the fittings it is tied to! The one exception to this is when bricking a headsail in preparation to fly a spinnaker.

Sheets and halyards

Whenever you pull on a piece of string, remember that something happens at the other end too! Too many people have wound in a halyard on a powerful winch without checking, and the first they knew something was wrong was when the pulpit was catapulted up into the rigging!

Be aware. If a halyard or sheet starts to run – let it go. There is no excuse for, and nothing more painful than a sheet burn on the hands.

Every activity can be broken down into three phases:

1 Preparation
2 Action
3 Tidy

When preparing to pull on a rope, check it is the right one, check it is not twisted and always put three turns around the winch.

Never sweat down a line that is fed directly to a winch. It will simply cause a riding turn.

Tidy up and recoil ropes only after the action is complete.

Winches are powerful and dangerous. Sail loads can amount to 3.5tons on a large yacht so keep hands well clear of the drum when paying out the rope. Too many fingers have been crushed this way!

When pulling in on a line, have three turns on the winch. Any less and you will

Sheets and halyards should be coiled and stowed ready for immediate use.

be unable to hold it when the load comes on. Any more turns and a wrap or riding turn may occur. If you see a wrap occurring, stop winching and remedy it. If it is caught early enough, you may be able to deal with it by easing the line out slowly.

Riding turns come in two forms. One can be dealt with by taking the line out of the self-tailer and pulling on the rope while someone else continues winding. The second type requires the line to be taken out of the self-tailer, fed around another winch and tension applied until the wrap has been winched out. If other winches are in use, then tie a short length of line with a clove hitch to the sheet and secure this to something substantial, then unwrap the winch and reload the sheet.

Beware of riding turns on winches and underestimating the sheet loadings. These can be as much as 3.5 tons on a 72ft (22m) yacht, so keep fingers clear of winch drums when paying out sheets.

Ropework
*These are the basic knots that every crewman needs to be able to do blindfold because there
will be times at sea when ropes have to be tied at night or half hidden behind a sail.*

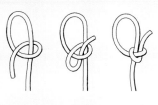

Slip hitch
A quick knot to tie that is
easy to release and used
for securing sails.

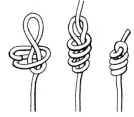

Admiralty stopper knot
Used as a stopper knot in the end of
sheets, and halyard to stop the rope
from running through the sheave.
(This is preferred to the simpler figure
of eight knot, which is easily washed
out by the force of water.) Lines used
for flying spinnaker (sheets, guys and
halyard) must NEVER have stopper
knots in them, to ensure that in the
event of an emergency, the ropes
will run free.

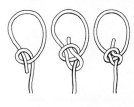

Bowline
Ties a non-slip loop in the
end of a rope and is used to
secure a sheet to sail clew
and mooring lines.

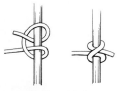

Clove hitch
Also used to attach a
line to an object such as
fenders to the stanchions.

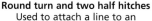

Reef knot
Used to attach two lines of
equal thickness together
such as sail ties when
something more secure
than a slip knot is required.

Rolling hitch
Used to tie a line to an object when
the load is parallel such as a sheet
when taking a riding turn out of a
winch or when transferring the
sheet load to allow fairlead cars to
be moved up or down the track.

Round turn and two half hitches
Used to attach a line to an
object such as a tender to the
yacht or pontoon. Easy to
untie under load.

Coiling rope
Loose rope ends should be
coiled and secured with the
tail so that they are ready to
be shaken out at a moment's
notice.

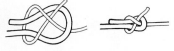

Single sheet bend
Used to attach two lines of
unequal thickness together
such as sail ties.

Double sheet bend
More secure version of single
sheet bend and preferred method
for tying mooring lines together.

Preparation for sea

When preparing the yacht for sea, the following things need to be done before departing from the dock:

- Sailing instruments turned on and covers taken off
- Winch handles out
- Halyards moved to at-sea positions
- Mainsail cover off and halyard on
- All working lines run around the yacht
- Headsails hanked on and sheets attached
- Hatches shut and dogged down
- Engine check
- Bilge inspection
- Stowage check
- Personal preparation
- All sausage fenders singled up
- Two large fenders held ready to rove
- Shore lines removed and slips rigged
- Final walk round check of the yacht

Preparation goes a long way with any manoeuvre, so the skipper or watch leaders must ensure that everyone knows what is expected of them. Crews need to check to see what working lines, headsails and slip lines are required and have them ready before leaving the dock. The skipper may want to keep his options open on which headsails to raise up until the yacht is out in open waters, so be prepared to have a second sail ready to hand. When running the working lines around the boat, start from the bottom and work upwards. ie start with the spinnaker pole foreguy, then the headsail sheets, then spinnaker guys, and finally with the spinnaker sheets. These must be run outside of all rigging and lifelines.

Anyone without a specific task needs to keep a lookout, but well out of the way; either on the centreline of the yacht forward of the mast; in the cockpit; or on the side decking opposite the dock.

Everyone should keep a low profile to ensure that the skipper has a clear line of sight to the bow and is able to communicate quietly and efficiently with hand signals whenever possible. A 'thumbs up' will signal that the slip lines are clear. Fingers are used to signify the distance between the bows and other objects. If voice communication has to be employed, then it must be clear and simple. A call such as 'Bow clear' signifies that the bow slip line is free.

When preparing to leave the dock, it is best to use the shore lines as slips to ensure that the yacht is always attached with a bow and stern line. The skipper may want to use one of the slips as a spring to set the boat up at an angle to take advantage of the tide to get out of a tight spot. Be alert to the effects wind and tide might have on the yacht and expect the unexpected. Keep fenders to hand and two lines ready to throw back to the dock in the event of engine failure or mishap.

Returning to the dock

1 Run warps
2 Attach fenders

When arriving at a dock, the warps require a bowline tied with a waist-high loop at their outboard end, have their inboard end ready roved through the fairlead and be coiled ready to throw ashore. Ensure that warps do not trail in the water, as the engine will invariably be on and they could foul the propeller.

Fenders should be tied with a clove hitch at the correct height around the stanchion posts, and put overboard when instructed. Two crew should each keep a fender free ready to deploy it at either end of the boat to cushion against collision with other yachts or objects.

As soon as bow and stern lines are secure, the springs are set up and fenders are checked for height and doubled up.

When returning to dock, check:

1 Shore lines (electricity, phone etc) are plugged in.
2 Navigation lights switched off.
3 Engine turned off (check with skipper first).
4 Ensign dropped.
5 Time logged in ship's log.
6 Sails checked for damage, folded and packed.
7 Working lines coiled and stowed.
8 Halyards stowed.
9 Boom set and mainsail cover fitted.
10 Winch handles stowed.
11 Instrument covers fitted.
12 Deck cleaned.
13 Below decks made presentable.
14 Ashore for a beer!

At sea

Watch and learn. Those that take an active interest in what is happening around them are most likely to be invited back! Be aware of the big picture. Swot up on sailing basics beforehand so that you are able to answer the following questions:

■ What point are we sailing on?
■ Which tack are we on?
■ Is that vessel on a collision course?
■ What is that light or land over there?
■ What needs to happen if there is a man overboard situation now?

Finally, be prepared personally. Remember that it is often colder at sea than on land and it may well be windier and wetter than it looks. Once your clothes are wet, they remain wet, so wear oilskins and boots as a matter of course. Taking layers of clothing off is far easier than putting them on later. Also, make sure that any items you may need during the next few hours are readily accessible, including sun cream and a water bottle!

Safety

Risk and Safety – the overriding aim is to eliminate the first to preserve the second! Accidents are inevitable, but the ability to minimise them comes only with a conscious decision to be aware of potential dangers and to minimise risks.

Night watches are a danger time. Always wear a lifejacket and have your harness clipped on to a jackstay. Carry a torch and have a knife and sail tie to hand.

Overall safety of yacht and crew is the responsibility of the skipper, but personal safety is also down to individuals looking after each other. When getting dressed for a watch during a dirty night at sea for instance, the crew should check that each other's lifejackets are worn correctly, and maintain a buddy approach when working on deck. The golden rules are:

1 Never run around on deck.
2 Never go barefoot.
3 Never pass to leeward of a sail being carried, dropped or hoisted.
4 Never hold on to ropes or running rigging.
5 At night or in windy conditions:
- Always wear a lifejacket
- Clip on to the jackstays
- Always stay on the weather side unless required to go to the lee side
- Have a knife and sail tie at the ready
- Carry a torch, emergency light and whistle
- Look out for others around you
- Use the safety strops below. Do not rely on doors to take your weight

Lifejackets and harnesses

Your lifejacket could save your life – look after it with your life!

Know which jacket is yours; know how to put it on; know that it fits; know that it is in good working order – and know how to use it!

Lifejackets should be worn:

- Whenever you want to
- At night
- In restricted visibility
- Whenever your skipper asks you to

When fitting your lifejacket, allow a fist-sized gap so that in the event of inflation you can still breathe, but not so loose that you could fall out of it! Make sure, too, that the crotch strap is done up. Before each sail, check for signs of wear and tear, especially around the webbing, reflective tape and safety line. Unscrew the CO_2 cylinder and ensure that the seal has not been pierced. If in doubt, REPLACE IT, applying a small amount of petroleum jelly around the thread to prevent corrosion. Check that the light works and the battery is within its expiry date. Finally, orally inflate the jacket and leave it for an hour to check that it holds air, then carefully deflate and repack.

Keep your lifejacket either around your neck or stored with your foul weather gear in the oily locker. Never leave it lying around, and never loose on deck. If it is stepped on, it might not save your life!

Most lifejackets now incorporate a safety harness, so there is no excuse for not clipping on. Clip on at night (unless it is very calm) and whenever you feel the need or when working on the foredeck. The object is to stop you falling overboard, so clip on to an object uphill, not to leeward. When steering, clip on with a short strop, but never to the wheel. If you fall, then you are likely to pull the wheel, which could result in a violent and dangerous alteration in course.

Do not clip on to:

- The steering wheel or pedestal
- The pulpit
- Sheets or running rigging
- Guard lines or stanchions

Do clip on to:

- Jackstays
- Fixed eyes provided for the purpose

Practice clipping on in calm conditions and work your way from bow to stern. You should be able to go from the cockpit to the bow without unclipping, simply by passing lazy sheets and other lines over your head. If you do need to unclip and refasten to another jackstay, then sit or kneel on deck and hold on with one hand while moving the clip with the other. If conditions are bad, then hold on with both hands and ask a buddy to move the clip for you.

Whenever unclipping, follow your safety line down to the jackstay to avoid undoing someone else's clip! When moving around deck, walk your safety line like a dog on a short leash. When a number are going up to the foredeck, clip on in order and go together. When conditions are rough or it is dark, never leave one person on the foredeck alone. There must always be a buddy nearby.

The Bowman

The bowman has to be agile, strong, have a good reach – and a head for heights. He or she leads the foredeck team and is responsible for everything that happens forward of the mast. When reefing the mainsail, the bowman can also provide an extra pair of hands, to help control the luff of the mainsail.

When conditions are rough, the cockpit crew need to be ready in position before the bowman leads his team out on the foredeck in the order that they work, to avoid tangling safety lines. The other foredeck crew need to be able to step into the bowman's shoes in the event of injury or call for the mother watch.

The bowman's essential kit includes a harness, spike, knife and pliers, which are stowed in a pouch on his belt. It also makes sense to have a crash helmet. These tools should all be attached with chord or bungee so they can't be dropped on the crew below.

When going out to the end of the spinnaker pole, the bowman first clips on to the foreguy, then hauls himself out to the end and clips a second short safety line on to the pole to take his weight. He can then dangle in relative comfort while awaiting the call to 'spike' the spinnaker guy to release the tack. When performing this job, keep below the pole and out of any trap points, since the pole has a nasty habit of springing back in strong conditions, whenever the loaded guy is released.

The Mastman

The mastman and his team have to haul halyards up quickly by jump hoisting in unison. They also double as the last member(s) of the foredeck team. The mastman also requires a strong head for heights and should practice going up the mast when in harbour. The mastman's essential kit includes a harness; two short safety strops to clip on when at the masthead; a spike, knife, and pliers (stowed in a pouch and tied to his belt); together with a crash helmet.

When going up the mast at sea, have the halyard secured tight against the mast to prevent swinging uncontrollably. Have a downhaul attached to your harness so that the crew can control your descent back on

deck (not so easy when the yacht is heeled at 25°!) In strong conditions a back-up crewman should be readily on-hand and harnessed up to assist if needed.

Each time you go up and down the mast, check the halyards for chafe, and shrouds and fittings for signs of fatigue.

Cockpit crew

The central cockpit crew control all sail manoeuvres from hoisting and lowering headsails and spinnakers to dealing with reefs and setting the boom vang. On medium-sized yachts and larger, they also take control of the spinnaker foreguys and some hydraulics. This is the control area of the yacht, and while some roles may appear minimal, do something at the wrong time, and it will ruin a routine, and may cause considerable delay/damage. Every cockpit crew must know what each halyard or control line does and be able to lay their hands on them instinctively, day or night. They must also learn every routine and take on any role.

On larger yachts with a forward cockpit, this area is often known as the Snakepit, not because of the type of characters that dwell there, but the mass of ropes that quickly become entwined around them. A good cockpit crew is always one step ahead of the game, having each line ready the moment it is needed. When extra horsepower is required, the mastman can be brought in to man a winch, but they will require clear directions on what to winch, when, and for how long! Communication has to be clear and precise, not just within the snakepit, but also between mast, bow and helms-man/tactician. When manoeuvres are run right, a good cockpit crew will make everyone else look good too!

Afterguard
The aft cockpit is where the brains trust resides. Between them, they call all the shots. Communication has to be clear and precise. Hand signals are invariably better than bad-tempered shouts. When the routines on board are well oiled, the rest of the crew need hear only the call to tack, peel spinnaker or reef etc and the rest will be between the cockpit, mastman, bowman and trimmers.

Tactician and Navigator

These are the boffins in the boat; the guys that must have a smell for the wind, can read the weather around them just as well as the isobars on the charts, and know how to take most advantage from the prevailing conditions. They must also know precisely where they are in the world, have a clear idea of any coastal dangers, and the waypoints ahead. On smaller yachts, the tactician and navigator will be one and the same. On larger trans-ocean yachts, the tactician's role is often played out as a brains trust between skipper, watch leaders and navigator.

The navigator is also responsible for communications on board, monitoring the radio, emails and phone, and maintaining 'chat-show' schedules with other yachts. He will also be taking down the weather forecasts and monitoring the weather websites. These are the guidelines for Global Challenge navigators to follow:

- Use the largest scale chart on board
- Use *soft* pencil only on charts
- The chart should show the past, present and intended future positions of the yacht, as well as the mean track when tacking to windward
- Intended track should be marked hourly, with allowance made for tidal flow

- Fixes should be taken hourly when sailing offshore and at least half-hourly when in coastal waters
- Each fix should be marked with the time, log reading and a letter to indicate the source ie V (Visual), R (Radar), GPS (Global Positioning System)
- Electronic fixes should be checked visually or with other methods
- The echo sounder should be monitored continuously in shallow water and thick fog when sailing in coastal waters

Yacht's log

It is a legal requirement to maintain a ship's log. It should contain enough information to maintain the yacht's dead reckoned position, should the electronic navigation system fail. The following is the minimum information that should be entered in the log:

Hourly
- Log reading – distance run in past hour
- Course ordered
- True wind direction and speed in knots
- Bilges pumped (and number of strokes)
- Barometer reading
- Weather/visibility
- Position
- Day tank levels

As it happens
- Major course alterations, time, fix, log readings
- Sail changes
- Wind shifts and weather changes
- Weather forecast in area
- Engine start/stop
- Battery charging start/stop
- Boat heater on/off
- Any unusual occurrence

The Helmsman

The helmsman has to have a natural feel for the yacht; how to get the most out of her, and above all, maintain a steady course. This all comes with practice, a clear understanding of the theory, and strong concentration. A wandering mind leads to a wandering wake!

The rudder acts like a break causing increasing drag the more it is pulled out of line. If the helm is heavy and the boat is constantly wanting to head up towards the wind, then the rig is out of balance and invariably requires a reef taken in on the mainsail. If the weight in the helm is unduly light for the conditions and the boat requires lee helm to correct the bow from falling away from the wind, then either the genoa needs to be changed down to a smaller sail, or a mainsail reef needs to be shaken out. If the boat is heeling more than 25°, then invariably there is a need to shorten sail.

Steer a steady course. A yacht that is 1° off course over 60 miles will finish 1 mile off its target. Over 6,000 miles across the Pacific and that could mean finishing up mid-way between San Francisco and Los Angeles. It is almost impossible to hold a an exact course. One to five degrees is a more reasonable, but the 500 mile difference this makes will add an additional two day's sailing to the voyage!

The key is to spend as much time as possible looking up at the horizon rather than staring down at the compass. Start with aiming at easy targets like a buoy, the crest of a hill, church spire or clump of trees and then move on to harder targets such as stars or clouds (though remember that these move too!). Passing ships and the direction of the waves give an indication of course swinging. The yacht will feel different at various angles to the wind and as you get to know these variances, so course accuracy will improve.

Never alter course while looking at the compass, or look at the rose for more than a few seconds at a time. The compass gives no idea as to the rate of turn and the instruments also have a degree of dampening built in, so a steady course needs to be held for half a minute or so before referring back to them. When steering to an apparent wind angle, the digital display is far more accurate than the analogue one.

Steering upwind

Bearing away in strong winds can be impossible unless the mainsheet is eased first. Helmsman and tactician/mainsheet trimmer need to work in unison, especially when passing just astern of another vessel! When sailing upwind, it is critical to get the balance right between pointing and speed. The higher you head into the wind, the slower the boat goes. Speed increases the lower you head away from the wind, but there comes a point when velocity made good to windward (VMG), the equation computing speed and pointing angle, starts to lower. The key is to keep the yacht powered up and to find the sweet spot between pointing too high and when the helm starts to feel sluggish.

When gusts come through, head higher into the wind to maintain the same heel angle, and both speed and VMG will increase. When there is a lull, you may have to bear away a degree or two to maintain the best momentum. The key is to keep a close eye on boat speed, apparent wind angle, wind speed and angle of heel.

Steering off the wind

With a steady wind angle between 50°–100° apparent, it should be possible to maintain a steady compass course and for the trimmers to maintain the sails at the best angle to the wind. Waves will be running across your course, but by anticipating their effect, it should be possible to keep a steady course. When the waves are high, learn to bear away a little down their backs to increase speed and resultant narrowing of the apparent wind angle, and steer higher into wind when climbing the wave when the slowing speed will widen the apparent wind angle. The key is to keep a close eye on the compass heading, boat speed and apparent wind angle.

Steering downwind

VMG is key to sailing the best course downwind. It never pays to sail directly downwind. Not only do you run the risk of going into an accidental crash gybe, but also it is slower than sailing 15° or so off, on one gybe or the other. Each yacht will have an optimum downwind course angle, which will vary with the strength of the wind. In light airs, it will require a higher angle to generate a steady wind flow across the sails than in stronger conditions. Once boat speed has built up, a good helmsman is able to 'drag' that wind flow down to a lower angle, which will improve VMG considerably. In moderate conditions steer a straight course, and in stronger winds take advantage of the waves, sailing a higher angle in the troughs, then bearing away as boat speed increases down the back of each wave.

Watch out for gybing. If there is a risk, then warn the crew and try to turn the yacht towards the wind. The key is to keep a close eye on the apparent wind angle, true wind and boat speed.

Changing the helm

Before handing over, the helmsman being relieved must tell his relief:

- Ordered course and course made good
- Degree of helm carried and any steering problems experienced
- Normal instrument readings – log speed, apparent wind angle and wind speed
- Movement of any shipping in sight or on radar
- Any instruction ie: watch the echo sounder for depth changes
- Weather: wind, cloud and waves – changes during the last watch

The new relief must stand beside the helmsman for five minutes before taking over control, to get used to watching waves, sails and wind. On taking over, the new helmsman must call out to his watch leader and navigator his name and course, ie 'Andy at the wheel – course 135°'. This is particularly important at night.

The helmsman being relieved must then stand beside the new helmsman for a further five minutes to make sure that he has settled.

Watch systems

Watch systems vary from one yacht to another. For short overnight or weekend voyages, it is often simplest to split the crew into two watches and have the skipper, navigator and cook floating. Certainly, the friendly rivalry between port and starboard watches to out-sail each other or score the best day's run helps to keep spirits and interest levels up, but on transoceanic voyages, this can divide the crew too much and a rotational system, allowing a greater mix, can prove a better arrangement. This way, the crew rotate automatically to give one crew member 24 hours out of the watch system every day, before joining the other watch for 10 days. During their 'day off' the crewmember acts as the standby and remains on call to help with sail changes and is responsible for cleaning up below decks and washing the dishes. Sailing in the trade wind latitudes, the constant winds often allow a second person to go on standby too, which increases the number of breaks and lessens monotony.

Another system practiced by crews competing in the Global Challenge races is to divide the crew into three watches: one on watch, a 'mother' watch acting on standby, and an off watch. The on watch is responsible for running the yacht; the 'mother' watch cooks, cleans and remains on standby for sail changes etc and the off watch carry a 'Do Not Disturb' sign.

Some watch systems are run so that the morning watch also cleans the deck and the afternoon watch takes care of general maintenance. This is a good routine to have when there are no specialists to assign specific tasks to.

Watch times can also vary. Some divide the day up into four 6-hour periods while others prefer to reduce the night watches to 4-hour stints. This has the advantage of moving the watch groups up one time schedule each day and thus rotate the worst 'night-watchman' hours and relieve the monotony.

Thus, a normal day would run:
- 08:00 – 14:00 – Port watch
- 14:00 – 20:00 – Starboard watch
- 20:00 – 00:00 – Port watch
- 00:00 – 04:00 – Starboard watch
- 04:00 – 08:00 – Port watch
- 08:00 – 14:00 – Starboard watch etc

Night watches should be woken with a hot drink 15-20 minutes before they are due on deck, and day watches are given 40 minutes to allow them time to have a meal. The on going watch should put on their oilskins and lifejackets *before* going on deck (unless briefed otherwise) and harnesses must be clipped on before leaving the doghouse. At night, hands must call out their names as they come on deck and before going down below. The on going watch need to be settled on deck *five minutes* before the watch change to give themselves time to settle in and be briefed.

The watch leader (or anyone navigating on their behalf) must study the chart carefully with the navigator or person he is relieving *before* going on deck, then be briefed by his opposite number before taking over on deck. The following points should always be covered:

1 Course ordered and any navigational hazards expected during the next 4-6 hours.
2 Sails set and present weather conditions.
3 Wind/weather trends during previous watch.
4 Tactical situation and skipper's policy, ie tack if wind backs.
5 Movement of any shipping in sight or on radar.
6 Any other instructions from the skipper.
7 State on deck.

'State on deck' refers to anything unusual such as barberhaulers or preventers set, poled out headsails and changes to normal routines such as: 'The starboard genoa halyard is on the middle winch because the stopper on the port winch keeps slipping.' Or 'the vang is on the starboard winch so that it can be eased whenever the boom goes into the water.'

Calling the standby or mother watch

The standby crew needs to be dressed and ready to be called up by the deck watch leader at a moment's notice to provide extra hands when necessary for sail changes and emergencies. Mother watch duties include:

- Assist the on watch as required
- Prepare meals and wash up
- Re-pack sails
- Keep below decks clean and tidy
- Clean heads, galley and grab rails at least twice a day
- Provide a stand-in for any injured or sick crew

Calling the skipper

The skipper is on call 24 hours a day for any form of emergency or if the watch leader has any doubts concerning:

- Rules of the Road
- Close approach of another vessel
- Change in wind strength and direction
- Navigational position or dangers
- A sail change

Good husbandry

The yacht is your home for the duration of the voyage, so good habits of seamanship and yacht husbandry should become second nature. Always tidy up after a job. Everything has a home, and putting it away every time means that it will be there the next time it is needed – perhaps in an emergency.

Remember the old saying – A stitch in time saves nine…

On deck

Halyards, sheets and control lines must be stowed and coiled away for instant use, and re-coiled and stowed whenever they are disturbed. Other pointers include:

1 Don't lash sails to the guardrails.
2 Keep a constant check for chafe on sails and ropes. Use binoculars to inspect the rig.
3 Keep leech lines to the correct tension to avoid them flogging.
4 Don't drop hatches.
5 Keep ropes taut. Halyards not in use should be secured clear of the mast.
6 Stow winch handles in their correct places.

Sheets and halyards should be adjusted regularly so that the section in the sheave gets varied. Sail chafe on spreaders, running backstays, shrouds and guardrails can be reduced by stitching leather patches over the chafe points. Keep a weather eye open for any sail cringles that work loose, always fold the sails carefully and never walk on them!

- If you see a job – do it
- If you do a job – do it properly
- Time spent on preparation and maintenance is never wasted

Below decks

After 2-3 weeks at sea, many yachts would be classed as 'unliveable' by Third World agencies and Prisoners' Rights groups. Germs love the damp putridness of a long distance yacht, and the galley and heads are particularly vulnerable. Prevention is better than cure, as the crew on *Heath Insured* will attest to. During the 1992/3 Global Challenge Race, when one crewman caught a bad dose of 'gunwale bum', it quickly spread throughout the crew simply because hygiene standards on board were not up to scratch, and the infection remained until the end of that leg.

The heads are easily fouled in bad weather. Clean them after use, leaving the area as you would wish to find it. They also need to be cleaned once a day with disinfectant, along with all handrails below deck. The same applies to the galley, with particular attention paid to work surfaces, which need to be cleaned down in a similar manner twice a day.

Personal hygiene is vital. It is so easy when coming off watch in a fatigued state to crash out in a bunk, and then rush up just in time for the next change of watch without washing. But it is also a sure way to pick up fungal infections, which then quickly spread throughout the crew.

Always wash hands after visiting the heads AND before preparing or eating food. Never dry your hands on the tea towels. Preferably use disposable paper towelling.

Water

Fresh water is a precious commodity at sea. Yachts may well be fitted with desalinators, but these, or the generators that power them, can and do break down. Water supplies require careful husbandry.

- Use salt water for the washing of dishes and personal washing with salt water soap
- Clothes can also be washed in salt water, saving fresh water to rinse them through
- Limit personal intake to 2-4 litres a day
- Use a small cup of water when brushing teeth

Garbage

Never throw rubbish overboard. Even biodegradables take a long time to rot down. Plastics never do and become traps that entangle fish, seabirds, seals and turtles, and slowly choke them to death. It is now illegal to dump any ship's waste within 12 miles of land, and any vessels that do so run the chance of a hefty fine. Keep garbage in sealed plastic bags and dispose of everything in the proper manner once you reach port.

These are the primary positions on deck. On smaller yachts some positions, such as tactician and navigator, may double as watch leaders, and grinder and trimmer may well be combined. On larger yachts, there will be two or more working in the forward cockpit or 'snakepit', multiple grinders and several foredeck hands. Here we list the principle responsibilities for each area which, on large yachts, will be divided up among a number of crew. Crew routines need careful choreographing. Practice not only makes perfect – it will save enormously on wear and tear!

H: **HELMSMAN:** Concentrates solely on steering the yacht. Discusses tactics with the navigator/tactician and gives commands when changing course and reefing. Speed and compass course are king!

T: **TACTICIAN:** Watches other yachts. Looks for favourable wind shifts and areas of stronger pressure. Calls tactics and sail changes. Takes care of the running backstays.

N: **NAVIGATOR:** Responsible for navigation, communications and weather information (and sometimes cooking). May also double as **T**. When on deck, trims mainsheet, main traveller and hydraulics/backstay.

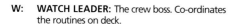

W: **WATCH LEADER:** The crew boss. Co-ordinates the routines on deck.

G: **GRINDER:** Powers the main genoa/spinnaker winches.

P: **PORT TRIMMER:** Responsible for trimming genoa/spinnaker sheets.

S: **STARBOARD TRIMMER:** Adjusts sheeting tracks, calling halyard tension and communicating with helmsman.

M: **MAST HAND:** Responsible for jump-hoisting halyards, sets up inboard end of spinnaker pole; trips pole when dip-pole gybing; sets up guy jockey pole; helps bowman with headsails and spinnakers.

C: **COCKPIT:** Tails halyards; handles foreguy and spinnaker pole topping lift; reefing lines; boom vang control; any hydraulics controlled from the forward cockpit.

B: **BOWMAN:** Acts as forward lookout. Responsible for executing headsail/spinnaker sets and changes; trips spinnaker when gybing or during takedown. May also take responsibility for the luff of the mainsail when reefing. Must have a head for heights!

SAILING TO WINDWARD – PORT TACK

H: Positioned to windward in heavy air, and to leeward in light winds to get a better view of sail tell-tails and other yachts.

T: Sits to weather to get a good view and watches for changing wind patterns. Also plays the weather running backstay (if fitted) to flatten or broaden mainsail shape to suit changes in wind or sea patterns.

N: Alternates between nav station and weather rail, trimming mainsail as appropriate.

W: Co-ordinates instructions from **H** and **T** and acts as troubleshooter during routines.

G: Powers the primary sheet winches when called by the trimmer.

S: Adjusts the headsail sheets continually to suit changes in wind and sea patterns. Keeps weather eye open to leeward for converging vessels.

P, C, M, and **B:** Sit on the weather rail in heavy airs and to leeward in light conditions.

B: Also keeps a weather eye open for cross-tacking yachts, calling their position regularly to the helmsman

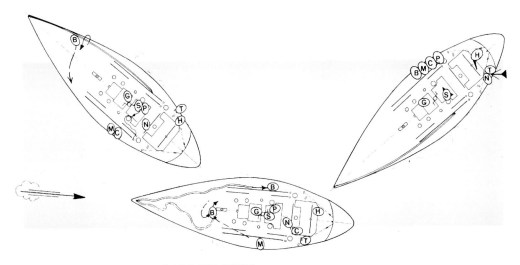

TACKING FROM STARBOARD TO PORT

T/N: Make decision to tack.
T: Calls warning 'Ready to tack'.
P: Flakes down port genoa sheet.
H: Calls 'Ready about' and bears off slightly to accelerate yacht into tack.
P: Releases port genoa sheet from self-tailer on winch and takes strain.
H: Calls 'Lee-ho' to warn crew and puts the helm over to commence tack.
P: Casts off port genoa sheet from winch.
N: Slackens mainsheet and/or mainsheet traveller.
T: Casts off starboard (weather) running backstay.
B: Runs genoa clew round mast.
S: Tails starboard genoa sheet around winch.
G/P: Grind winch.
B: Runs sheet aft.

T: Tensions port (new weather) running back stay.
G/P: Continue grinding winch until told by **S** to stop.
B: Skirts genoa foot inside lifelines.
C: Calls out changes in boat speed.
S: Trims in last few inches of sheet once yacht has built up speed.
H: Steers optimum course.
N: Trims mainsheet and main traveller.
P: Sets up genoa sheet around port winch ready for next tack.
Crew: Tidy up and move back to standard positions.

REEFING MAINSAIL

The mainsail is reefed whenever the yacht becomes overpowered ie heel angle exceeds 25°, and/or **H** is experiencing increasing weather helm.

T/H: Makes decision to reef mainsail.
W: Calls 'De-power'.
M/C: Flake down main halyard.
C: Load main reefing pennant with three turns on winch.
N: Releases mainsheet.
W: Calls 'Ease halyard – winch pennant.'
M/C: Ease main halyard to pre-set mark.
C: Winds in reefing pennant and set jammer.
C: Calls 'Pennant made up – power up.'
M: Attaches and tensions Cunningham, then calls 'Cunningham made.'
C: Releases boom vang.
M/C: Re-tension main halyard, then call 'Halyard made.'
N: Re-sets mainsheet.
C: Re-tensions boom vang.
Crew: Tidy up and move back to standard positions.

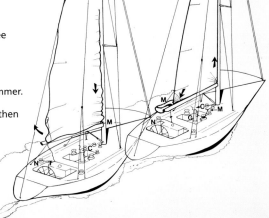

SHAKING OUT A MAINSAIL REEF

This is the reverse manoeuvre to reefing the mainsail on the previous page.

T/H: Make decision to increase mainsail area.
W: Calls 'De-power.'
M/C: Flake down main halyard.
C: Flakes down reefing pennant in use, loads winch and opens jammer.
C: Flakes out (or prepares to release hydraulic pressure) boom vang.
M: Attaches second cunningham to selected reefing cringle (if moving up one slab).
N: Releases mainsheet.
W: Calls 'Ease halyard – winch pennant.'
C: Releases reefing pennant in use, and removes from winch.
M: Spikes cunningham in use.
C: Releases boom vang.
M/C: Ease main halyard.
N: Releases mainsheet.
C: Tensions new reefing line (if moving up one 'slab').
C: Calls 'Pennant made up – power up.'

M/C: Re-tension main halyard then call 'Halyard made.'
N: Re-tensions mainsheet.
C: Re-tensions boom vang.
C: Re-tensions cunningham.
Crew: Tidy up and move back to standard positions.

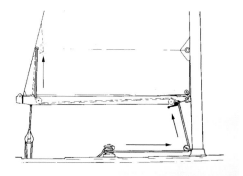

LEEWARD GENOA CHANGE – PORT TACK

For yachts with twin slot headfoil.

T/C: Make decision to change headsail.
W: Calls warning 'Leeward genoa change.'
M/B: Bring up new genoa and attach tack.
S: Sets up temporary sheeting system on set genoa.
S: Releases old sheet and connects to clew of new genoa and changes track car to correct position.
C: Flakes down existing genoa halyard ready to run.
B: Leads second halyard to leeward of headsail and clips on to head of new genoa.
M: Fastens new sheet to clew.
W: Gives order to hoist.
B: Feeds luff into headsail foil.
M: Jump hoists halyard at mast.
C: Tails halyard around deck winch.
S: Tails new genoa sheet.
G: Grinds winch.
C: Casts off old halyard.
M/B: Gather old sail and fold.
T: Monitors speedo to check for improvement.
P: Leads lazy (port) genoa sheet through correct lead.
Crew: Tidy up and move back to standard positions.

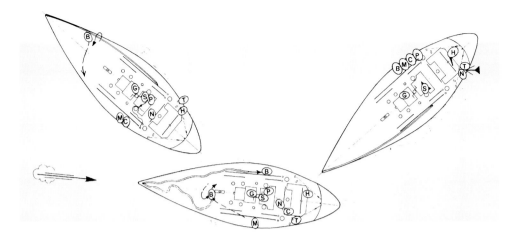

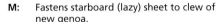

TACK GENOA CHANGE FROM STARBOARD TO PORT

For yachts with twin slot headfoil.

T/C: Make decision to change headsail.
W: Calls warning 'Tack genoa change.'
M/B: Bring up new genoa and attach tack.
S: Leads new sheet through correct lead on starboard (leeward) side.
C: Flakes down existing genoa halyard ready to run.
B: Connects second halyard to head of new genoa.

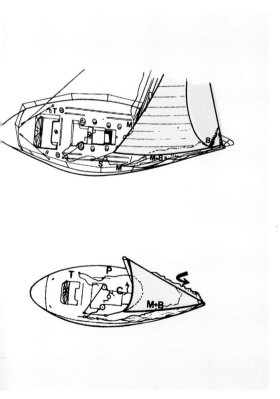

M: Fastens starboard (lazy) sheet to clew of new genoa.
W: Gives order 'Ready to tack.'
H: Calls 'Ready about.'
P: Releases port genoa sheet from self-tailer on winch and takes strain.
H: Calls 'Lee-ho' to warn crew and puts the helm over to commence tack.
P: Casts off port genoa sheet from winch.
W: Calls order to 'Hoist.'
N: Slackens mainsheet and/or mainsheet traveller.
B: Feeds luff into headsail foil.
M: Jump hoists halyard at mast.
H: Steers slowly into tack and momentarily holds bows head to wind.
T: Releases starboard (weather) running back stay.
C: Tails halyard with three turns around winch.
W: Calls 'Halyard made – release halyard.'
S: Tails new genoa sheet.
G/P: Grind on winch.
B: Skirts genoa foot inside lifelines.
C: Casts off old halyard
M/B: Pull down old genoa, fold on deck and pass down hatch.
T: Tensions port (new weather) running backstay.
G/P: Continue grinding winch until **S** calls 'Stop.'
T: Calls out changes in boat speed.
S: Trims in last few inches of sheet once yacht has built up speed.
H: Steers optimum course.
N: Trims mainsheet and main traveller.
T: Monitors speedo to check for improvement.
P: Leads lazy (port) genoa sheet through correct lead and around winch ready for next tack.
M/B: Gather old sail and fold.
Crew: Tidy up and return to standard positions.

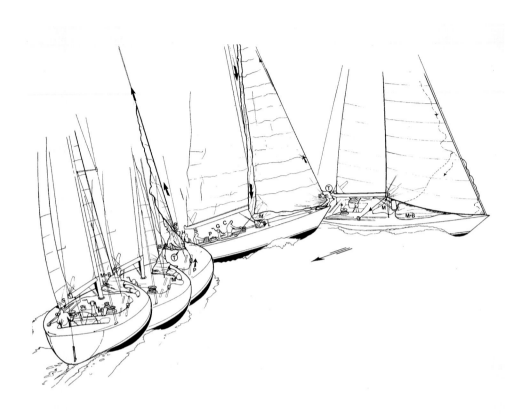

BALD HEADED GENOA CHANGE – PORT TACK

For yachts without a twin headstay foil.

T/H: Make decision to change headsail.
W: Calls warning ' Genoa change.'
M/B: Bring up new genoa and attach tack and secure with sail tie.
C/M: Flake down existing genoa halyard ready to run.
B: Leads second halyard to pulpit ready to attach to head of new genoa.
W: Gives order to 'Drop.'
C: Releases genoa halyard.
P: Releases sheet from winch.
M/B: Take down genoa and secure with sail tie, with hanks still connected to headstay.
B: Hanks new genoa to headstay above hanks
of earlier headsail and connects halyard to head and calls 'Halyard made.'
M: Attaches sheets to clew.
P: Repositions sheet car to correct position for new sail
W: Calls 'Hoist.'
M: Jump hoists halyard at mast.
C: Tails halyard around deck winch. When fully hoisted, calls 'Halyard made.'
P: Tails new genoa sheet.
G/S: Grind winch until P calls 'Stop.'

M/B: Disconnect old halyard, unhank old genoa and fold.
T: Monitors speedo to check for improvement.
S: Leads lazy (starboard) genoa sheet car to correct position for new sail and tails round starboard winch ready to tack.
Crew: Tidy up and move back to standard positions.

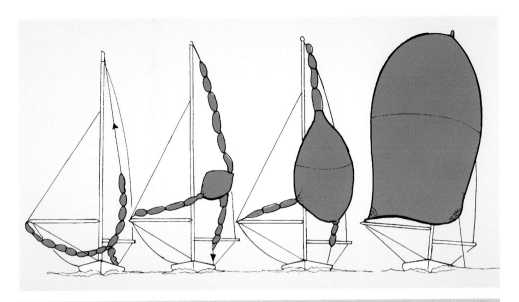

Rubber bands or light wool stops attached around the spinnaker when it is packed, will stop the sail from filling prematurely when hoisting.

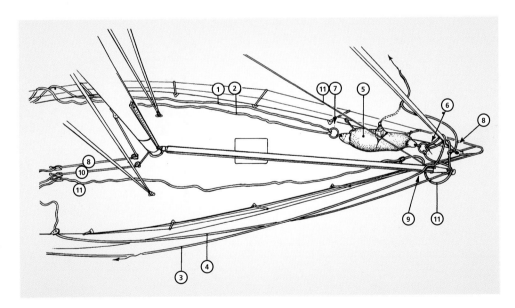

SPINNAKER SETTING PREPARATION

Layout of gear with pole set and spinnaker ready to hoist.

1: Sheet.
2: Lazy guy.
3: Lazy sheet.
4: Guy (sometimes called afterguy to distinguish from foreguy (12))
5: Spinnaker.
6: Guy and lazy sheet attached to spinnaker tack.

7: Sheet and lazy guy attached to spinnaker clew.
8: Halyard clipped temporarily to guy running through jaws of pole.
9: Lazy sheet led over pole.
10: Pole lift or pole topping lift.
11: Foreguy or pole downhaul.

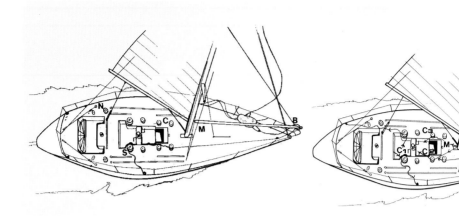

SPINNAKER SET – STARBOARD GYBE

T/H: Make decision to set spinnaker.
W: Calls warning 'Up spinnaker.'
M/B: Bring up new spinnaker and connect halyard, sheets and guys.
C: Flakes down genoa halyard ready to run.
M/B: Set up spinnaker pole.
C/S: Set guy and afterguy to match pole to wind angle.

W: Calls 'Hoist spinnaker.'
M: Jump hoists spinnaker halyard.
C: Tails halyard around deck winch and v fully hoisted, calls 'Halyard made.'
P: Sheets in spinnaker with **G** grinding w
C: Flakes down genoa halyard ready to r
W: Calls 'Drop genoa.'
C: Casts off genoa halyard.

SETTING STAYSAIL

T/H: Make decision to set staysail.
W: Calls warning 'Set staysail.'
M/B: Bring up staysail and attach tack in appropriate position ie on centreline when running/broad reaching with spinnaker or to weather when close reaching with spinnaker.

M/B: Attach halyard and sheets.
C: Prepares halyard on winch.
W: Calls 'Hoist.'
B: Jump hoists halyard at mast.
C: Tails halyard around deck winch and when fully hoisted, calls 'Halyard made.'
M: Trims staysail sheet. (**S** & **P** are busy trimming spinnaker.)

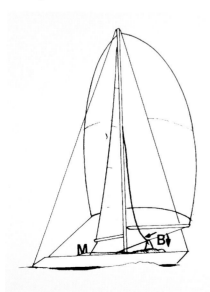

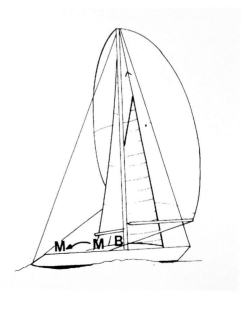

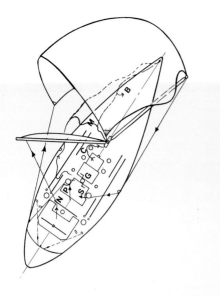

SPINNAKER LEEWARD TAKE DOWN – STARBOARD GYBE

T/H: Make decision to take spinnaker down and replace with headsail.

W: Calls warning 'Spinnaker leeward takedown – up genoa.'

M/B: Bring up new genoa and attach tack, halyard and sheets to clew.

P/S: Run sheets through track cars and back to winches.

C: Flakes down spinnaker halyard ready to run.

W: Calls 'Hoist.'

M: Jump hoists halyard at mast.

C: Tails halyard around deck winch and when fully hoisted, calls 'Halyard made.'

P: Tails new genoa sheet.

G/S: Grind winch until **P** calls 'Stop.'

W: Calls order to 'Drop' spinnaker.

B: Takes up position on outboard end of pole ready to spike the tack.

P: Takes up on lazy (leeward) spinnaker guy.

W: Calls **B** to 'Spike' spinnaker tack.

C: Casts off spinnaker halyard.

H: Rounds yacht up towards the wind.

P: Pulls spinnaker on the lazy guy under the boom into the cockpit.

S: Eases the spinnaker after guy.

S: Eases the spinnaker sheet.

S/M: Gather spinnaker in under boom and pass down hatch for packing.

P/G: Trim genoa.

N: Tensions backstay for beating to windward.

B/M: Stow spinnaker pole and prepare to tack.

Crew: Tidy up and return to standard positions.

S: Releases port genoa sheet.

M/B: Gather in genoa and fold.

N: Slackens backstay for running/reaching.

Crew: Tidy up and return to standard positions.

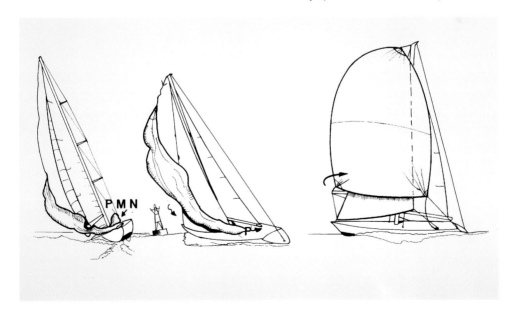

The choice of inside or outside peel is dictated by the line of spinnaker halyards. Beware of forming a twist at masthead.

SPINNAKER – FOREDECK STARBOARD TAKE DOWN

T/H: Make decision to take spinnaker down and replace with headsail.

W: Calls warning 'Drop spinnaker – forward takedown – up genoa.'

M/B: Bring up new genoa and attach tack, halyard and sheets to clew.

P/S: Run sheets through track cars and back to winches.

C: Flakes down spinnaker halyard ready to run.

W: Gives order to 'Hoist genoa.'

M: Jump hoists halyard at mast.

C: Tails halyard around deck winch and when fully hoisted, calls 'Halyard made.'

P: Tails new genoa sheet.

G/S: Grind winch until **P** calls 'Stop.'

W: Calls order to 'Drop' spinnaker.

B: Takes up position on outboard end of pole ready to spike the tack.

P: Takes up on lazy (leeward) spinnaker guy.

W: Calls **B** to 'Spike' spinnaker tack.

C: Casts off spinnaker halyard.

H: Rounds yacht up towards the wind.

M/B: Pull in lazy spinnaker sheet under genoa.

S: Releases spinnaker after guy.

P: Releases spinnaker sheet.

P: Pulls spinnaker on the lazy guy under the boom into the cockpit.

S/M: Gather spinnaker in under genoa and pass down hatch for packing.

P: Tails genoa sheet as **H** rounds yacht up towards the wind.

G/S: Grind winch until **P** calls 'Stop.'

N: Tensions backstay ready for beating to windward.

B/M: Stow spinnaker pole and prepare to tack.

Crew: Move back to standard positions.

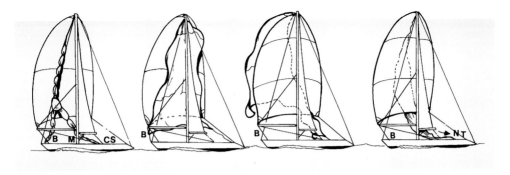

SPINNAKER CHANGE – INSIDE PEEL – PORT GYBE

T/H: Make decision to change spinnaker.
W: Calls warning 'Spinnaker change – inside peel – up spinnaker.'
M/B: Bring up new spinnaker.
C: Flakes down spinnaker halyard ready to run.
B: Prepares new spinnaker ready for hoisting inside existing sail. Takes lazy guy off set spinnaker and clips it on to clew of new sail as temporary sheet. Clips foredeck stripper to tack of old sail and ties temporarily to deck, then transfers guy to new sail.
W: Calls 'Hoist spinnaker.'
M: Jump hoists second spinnaker halyard.

C: Tails halyard around deck winch and when fully hoisted, calls 'Halyard made.'
C/S: Ease guy and after guy to allow pole to swing forward.
W: Calls **B** to 'Spike' spinnaker tack.
B: Spikes guy to release old spinnaker, then re-attaches guy to tack on new sail.
C: Takes up on spinnaker guy.
B: Releases stripper.
C/P/S: Adjust spinnaker set.
W: Calls 'Drop' spinnaker.
C: Releases spinnaker halyard.
M/N: Gather spinnaker in under boom and pass down hatch for packing.
Crew: Tidy up and return to standard positions.

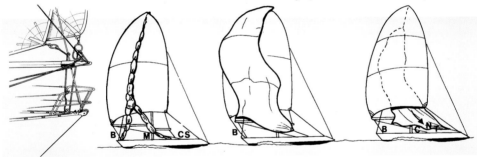

SPINNAKER CHANGE – OUTSIDE PEEL STARBOARD GYBE

T/H: Make decision to change spinnaker.
W: Calls warning 'Spinnaker change – outside peel – up spinnaker.'
M/B: Bring up new spinnaker.
C: Flakes down spinnaker halyard ready to run.
B: Prepares new spinnaker ready for hoisting outside existing sail. Takes lazy guy off set spinnaker and clips it on to clew of new sail as a temporary sheet. Clips foredeck stripper to tack of old sail and ties temporarily to deck, then transfers guy to new sail.
W: Calls 'Hoist' spinnaker.
M: Jump hoists second spinnaker halyard.
C: Tails halyard around deck winch and when fully hoisted, calls 'Halyard made.'

C/P: Ease guy and afterguy to allow pole to swing forward.
W: Calls **B** to 'Spike' spinnaker tack.
B: Spikes guy to release old spinnaker, then re- attaches guy to tack on new sail.
C: Takes up on spinnaker guy.
B: Releases stripper.
C/P/S: Adjust spinnaker set.
W: Calls 'Drop' spinnaker.
C: Releases spinnaker halyard.
M/N: Gather spinnaker in under boom and pass down hatch for packing.
Crew: Tidy up and return to standard positions.

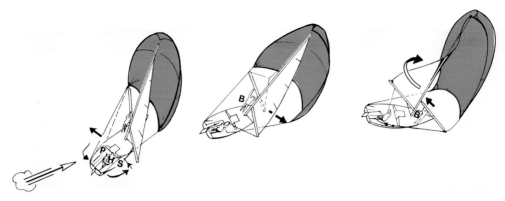

END-FOR-END POLE GYBE – PORT TO STARBOARD

Standard gybing technique aboard small yachts with pole uphaul and downhaul lines connected centrally to universal pole.

T/H:	Make decision to gybe.
W:	Calls warning 'Prepare spinnaker gybe.'
P/S:	Square spinnaker aft as **H** bears off straight downwind.
M:	Releases mainsail boom preventer.
T:	Pulls mainsail in to centreline.
B:	Trips spinnaker pole from mast and connects this end to new clew.
P/S:	Keep spinnaker flying.
W:	Calls 'Gybe-ho' and **H** turns bow 15° on starboard gybe.
N:	Releases starboard running backstay (if fitted).

T:	Lets mainsail out and adjusts traveller.
N:	Winches in port running backstay (if fitted).
B:	Trips old spinnaker clew and connects this end to mast track.
P:	Eases spinnaker guy for new course.
C:	Adjusts spinnaker pole topping lift.
S:	Trims spinnaker sheet.
M:	Resets mainsail boom preventer.
Crew:	Tidy up and move back to standard positions.

DIP POLE GYBE – PORT TO STARBOARD

Standard gybing technique aboard medium and large yachts when sailing in light/moderate conditions.

T/H:	Decide to gybe.
W:	Calls warning 'Prepare spinnaker gybe.'
B:	Removes inner forestay/babystay.
N:	Pulls mainsail in to centreline and cleats off main traveller.
P/S:	Square spinnaker aft as **H** bears off straight downwind.
M:	Trips spinnaker pole from inner end.
P/S:	Keep spinnaker flying.
C:	Lowers spinnaker pole topping lift and takes slack out of foreguy.

M:	Swings spinnaker pole forward.
B:	Snaps lazy guy into pole end fitting and push pole out to new weather side.
M:	Releases mainsail boom preventer.
W:	Calls 'Gybe-ho' and **H** turns bow 15° on starboard gybe.
T:	Releases port running backstay.
N:	Gybes mainsail and adjusts traveller.
T:	Winches in starboard running backstay.
P:	Eases foreguy for new course.
C:	Adjusts spinnaker pole topping lift.
P:	Takes up on afterguy.
S:	Trims spinnaker sheet.
B:	Resets inner forestay/babystay.
M:	Resets mainsail boom preventer.
Crew:	Tidy up and return to standard positions.

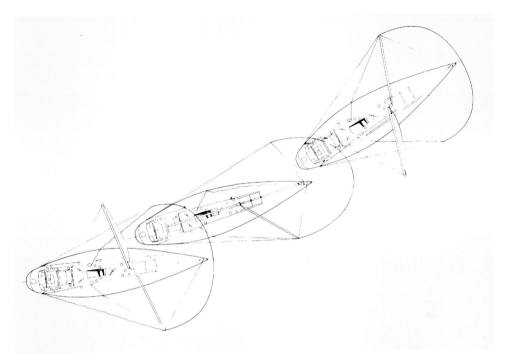

TWIN POLE GYBE – PORT TO STARBOARD

This method offers greater control over the spinnaker when sailing short-handed or in heavy weather.

T/H: Make decision to gybe.
W: Calls warning 'Prepare spinnaker gybe.'
M/B: Set up second spinnaker pole and attach topping lift.
S: Squares first spinnaker pole to 45° off headstay.
C: Sets new spinnaker guy up on primary winch.
B: Takes new lazy guy forward and places in beak of second spinnaker pole.
C: Raises second spinnaker pole on topping lift to same height as first.
P: Sheets in new spinnaker guy to bring new pole back 45° from headstay.
M: Releases main boom preventer.
N: Pulls mainsail in to centre line and cleats off main traveller.

P: Squares spinnaker aft as **H** bears off straight downwind.
W: Calls 'Gybe-ho' and **H** turns bow 15° on starboard gybe.
T: Releases port running backstay.
N: Gybes mainsail and adjusts traveller.
T: Winches in the starboard running backstay.
M: Trips the first spinnaker pole from inner end.
C: Lowers spinnaker pole topping lift.
P: Eases foreguy for new course.
P: Takes up on after guy.
S/G: Trim spinnaker sheet.
B/M: Stow first spinnaker pole.
M: Resets mainsail boom preventer.
Crew: Tidy up and return to standard positions.

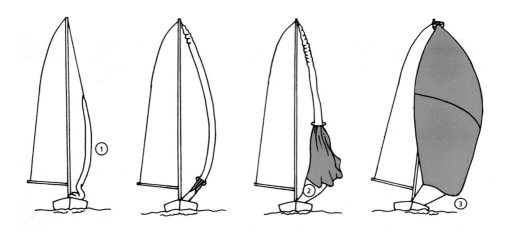

CRUISING CHUTE – SETTING

This is a simple form of spinnaker that sets like a loose luffed genoa and is often supplied with a 'snuffer' or sock. If not, then the sail should be stopped with rubber bands or wool prior to hoisting.

1:	Cruising chute in snuffer.
2:	Cruising chute tack line attached to bow.
3:	Sheet attached to clew.

T/H:	Make decision to hoist cruising chute.		**B:**	Hoists 'snuffer' to top of mast.
W:	Calls warning 'Hoist cruising chute.'		**P:**	Tails sheet.
M/B:	Bring up cruising chute and attach tack line, halyard to head and sheets to clew.		**G/S:**	Grind winch until **P** calls 'Stop.'
			N:	Slackens backstay for running/reaching.
W:	Calls order 'Hoist.'		**C:**	Flakes down genoa halyard ready to run.
M:	Jump hoists halyard at mast.		**W:**	Calls 'Drop' genoa.
C:	Tails halyard around deck winch and when fully hoisted, calls 'Halyard made.'		**C:**	Casts off genoa halyard.
			S:	Releases port genoa sheet.
			M/B:	Gather in genoa and fold.
			N:	Slackens backstay for running/reaching.
			Crew:	Tidy up and return to standard positions.

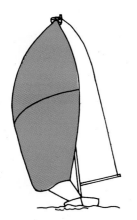

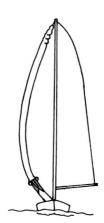

CRUISING CHUTE – TAKE DOWN

T/H:	Make decision to lower cruising chute.		**C:**	Lowers spinnaker halyard.
W:	Calls 'Chute takedown.'		**M&B:**	Gather chute, disconnect halyard, sheets and tack, and pass down hatch.
M:	Flakes out spinnaker halyard at mast.			
P:	Releases spinnaker sheet.		**Crew:**	Follow standard routine for setting genoa, then tidy up and return to standard positions.
B:	Pulls snuffer down from masthead to envelop chute.			
W:	Calls 'Drop.'			

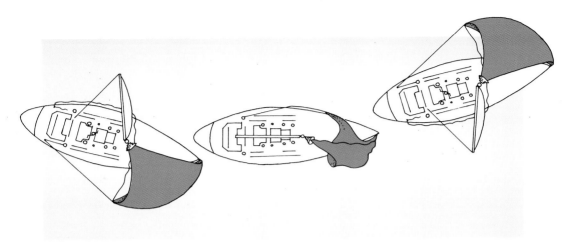

CRUISING CHUTE – GYBE – PORT TO STARBOARD

Standard gybing technique – same as gybing a headsail.

T/H: Decide to gybe.
W: Calls warning 'Prepare spinnaker gybe.'
B: Removes inner forestay/babystay (if fitted).
N: Pulls mainsail in to centreline and cleats off main traveller.
S: Square spinnaker aft as **H** bears off straight downwind.
M: Releases mainsail boom preventer.
W: Calls 'Gybe-ho' and **H** turns bow 15° on starboard gybe.

T: Releases port running backstay.
N: Gybes mainsail and adjusts traveller.
T: Winches in starboard running backstay.
P: Trims spinnaker sheet.
B: Resets inner forestay/babystay.
M: Resets mainsail boom preventer.
Crew: Tidy up and return to standard positions.

Satellite pictures and computer analysis have brought us a long way from the days of monitoring the weather with a sprig of seaweed nailed up in the companion-way. Meteorology, like navigation, is now a subject of such complexity that race crews invariably have computerised weather routeing patterns to second-guess approaching weather systems and suggest the best course through. There are also onshore experts who provide a more personalised service.

One of the experts is the Massachusetts based forecaster Bob Rice who Peter Blake and Robin Knox-Johnston entrusted to keep them in favourable winds during their successful attempt to win the Jules Verne round the world record aboard the catamaran *ENZA New Zealand*. Fellow crew member David Alan-Williams explained 'Wherever we were in the world, his forecasts were uncannily accurate. One bulletin we received when we were deep in the Southern Ocean, some 2,000 miles from land, was so accurate that we decided that he had to come onboard for New Zealand's America's Cup campaign. He forecast that a front would come through within 45 minutes and correctly predicted both the exact wind strength and direction. It was so good that we called Bob up on the satellite phone to tell him he had been wrong. The front had come through after 42 minutes!'

Rice's forecasts became a key element in *Team New Zealand's* successful challenge for the America's Cup in 1995 where he proved that he could be just as accurate with his predictions over a five-mile strip of water off San Diego as he had been across the entire Pacific.

Valuable weather information is readily available straight from the Web:
www.noaa.gov/

Here, we confine ourselves to the key rules to understanding weather patterns drawn up by David Houghton, a former director of the Meteorological Office, Bracknell and for many years the weather guru for Britain's Olympic yachting teams.

Sea breezes

This daytime phenomenon on sunny days results from the fact that the land heats up faster than the sea to create a pressure differential. This convects the airflow in a circular motion towards the shore. When conditions are ideal, this airflow commences around mid-morning, building up from a faint breeze to a force 3-4 and sometimes 5-6 by mid-afternoon, before weakening again at sunset. This cycle is so regular in some parts of the world, like the Tropics, that you can almost set your watch by it. Indeed, fishermen in these latitudes use the last of the land breeze (a night wind, opposite to a sea breeze, where the air drains away from the fast cooling land towards the more even temperatures of the sea) to sail out to their fishing grounds, and then return with the sea breeze later in the day.

The direction of the sea breeze is often perpendicular to the coastline at first, but the effect of the earth's rotation gradually veers this by as much as 50° during the course of the day in northern latitudes, and backs by a similar amount in the southern hemisphere. Only near the equator does this rotation have little effect.

There are many occasions, however, when the sea breeze does not develop as expected despite the warming effects of the sun. A sea breeze requires two essential elements in order to develop in strength. The first is an offshore component to the upper wind, for if this is blowing onshore it inhibits the sea breeze circulation from developing. The second

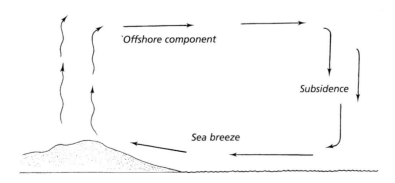

A classic sea breeze scenario wth the cooler air over the sea drawn towards the warmer land which convects the air in a circular motion.

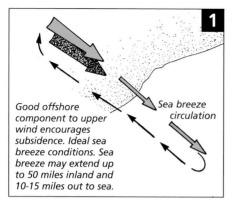

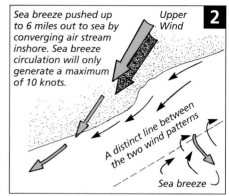

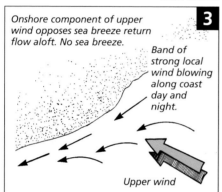

Good offshore component to upper wind encourages subsidence. Ideal sea breeze conditions. Sea breeze may extend up to 50 miles inland and 10-15 miles out to sea.

Sea breeze circulation

Sea breeze pushed up to 6 miles out to sea by converging air stream inshore. Sea breeze circulation will only generate a maximum of 10 knots.

Upper Wind

A distinct line between the two wind patterns

Sea breeze

Northern Hemisphere

Onshore component of upper wind opposes sea breeze return flow aloft. No sea breeze.

Band of strong local wind blowing along coast day and night.

Upper wind

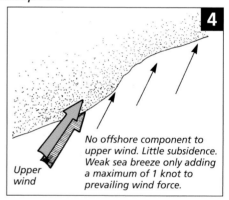

No offshore component to upper wind. Little subsidence. Weak sea breeze only adding a maximum of 1 knot to prevailing wind force.

Upper wind

Sea breeze pattern for the Northern Hemisphere.

element is a downdraft, or subsidence of air, offshore, to complete the circulatory sea breeze pattern. If this is broken by converging airstreams running parallel to the coast, then this too will prevent the sea breeze from developing. The diagrams for northern and southern hemispheres relate to any coastline. A sea breeze depends, not on compass bearing, but on whether the prevailing upper wind stems from the left – or right – hand quadrant of someone looking along the coastline with their back to the wind.

Conditions shown in quadrant 1 offer the best sea breeze possibility, since the upper wind provides a good offshore component and subsidence is encouraged. At night, however, it will be necessary to set a course well off the coast to avoid being becalmed, unless there is the likelihood of a local land breeze draining down through the valleys.

The prevailing winds in quadrant 2 provide an offshore component, but the converging airstreams expanding upwards close inshore, diminish subsidence. In these conditions the sea breeze is likely to develop as far as 5 miles out to sea and may not reach the coastline at all. Taking a south facing shoreline in the northern

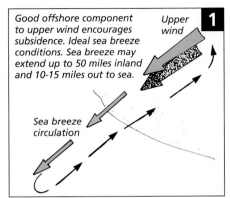

1 Good offshore component to upper wind encourages subsidence. Ideal sea breeze conditions. Sea breeze may extend up to 50 miles inland and 10-15 miles out to sea.

Upper wind

Sea breeze circulation

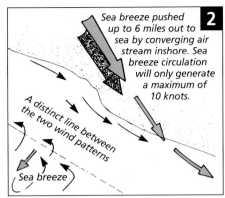

2 Sea breeze pushed up to 6 miles out to sea by converging air stream inshore. Sea breeze circulation will only generate a maximum of 10 knots.

A distinct line between the two wind patterns

Sea breeze

Southern Hemisphere

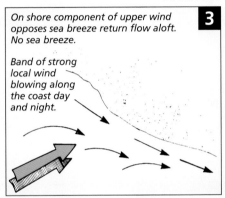

3 On shore component of upper wind opposes sea breeze return flow aloft. No sea breeze.

Band of strong local wind blowing along the coast day and night.

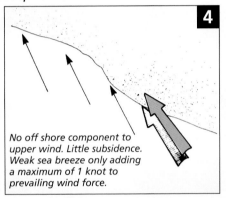

4 No off shore component to upper wind. Little subsidence. Weak sea breeze only adding a maximum of 1 knot to prevailing wind force.

Sea breeze pattern for the Southern Hemisphere.

hemisphere as an example, a south westerly sea breeze will develop out to sea while a north easterly wind will prevail close inshore, with a discernible line of cloud often dividing the two areas.

The upper wind in quadrant 3 counters the offshore component to a sea breeze. However, what often prevails is a strong band of wind close to the coastline, which navigators often mistake to be a sea breeze. It is not: this phenomenon is created from a convergence of airstreams close inshore, which will be there at night as well. This phenomenon was highlighted during a race along England's south coast

as the fleet returned from the Royal Sovereign light tower back towards the Solent. Many of the leaders headed out to sea as dusk fell – the correct strategy in a sea breeze situation – only to run out of wind completely. Those who persevered inshore on the other hand enjoyed a continuing breeze throughout the night and found themselves at the top of the leader board when they finished at Cowes.

The upper wind in quadrant 4 does not provide an offshore component, but with some subsidence, a sea breeze component is often observed, adding 1 or 2 knots to the prevailing wind.

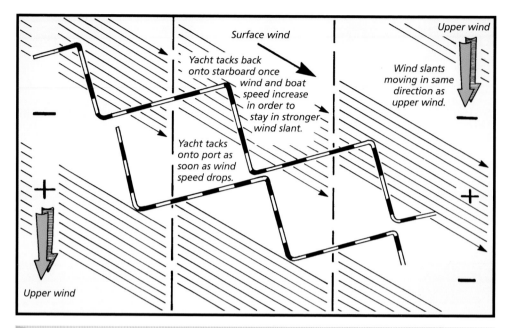

Surface wind

Yacht tacks back
onto starboard once
wind and boat
speed increase
in order to
stay in stronger
wind slant.

Yacht tacks
onto port as
soon as wind
speed drops.

Upper wind

Wind slants
moving in same
direction as
upper wind.

Upper wind

Wind slants in the Northern Hemisphere.

Wind slants

Adlard Coles noted many years ago that when the breeze was dying it often paid to tack onto port (or starboard in the southern hemisphere) to find fresher winds. The rationale for this is that surface winds are rarely uniform in strength but divided into bands with the distance between points of minimum and maximum velocity (which can differ by as much as 30%) varying from 0.5 to 6 kilometres. Acting as a component on this surface airflow is the gradient wind above, which causes these bands (though not the wind direction) to drift down the component of the wind at any time. Thus, when winds appear less strong than they should be, it pays to tack or gybe towards the next band of stronger air, then return to the original course once the anemometer starts to rise, in order to remain within the influence of this stronger band for as long as possible. The distinctive cloud lines seen in the Trade belts provide the best indication of this banded nature to the wind. Here the bands move across the ocean at between 0 and 1 knot, but even where the low stratus cloud is solid, the wind strength remains far from uniform.

The weight in the wind

One crew racing in the Key West Series off Florida found it best to put in a flattening reef when apparent wind speed reached 18 knots, and changed down from the heavy No. 1 genoa whenever the anemometer exceeded 22 knots. When this same crew came to race in the English Solent later that season, they were very surprised to find that sail changes had to be made much earlier than they had been off Miami, a phenomenon also noticed by crews from Australia and others from warmer climates.

Some people put this apparent change in the weight of wind down to variations in the density of the air, but the difference in pressure exerted on a sail by warm and cold air varies by no more than 5% – a change so small that it can go unnoticed.

The problem has baffled the best brains and led to the defeat of more than one America's Cup challenge, for sails cut to excel on northern European waters have not provided anything like the same performance during Cup races off Newport, Fremantle or Auckland. Initially, the need for fuller, more powerful sails was put down to the notorious 'Cup Chop', for the seas can become badly confused by the wash from the armada of spectator boats that turn out to watch these America's Cup matches. But this was really only a part of the story.

The major factor is the change in the spectrum of turbulence between warm and cold airstreams or, correctly speaking, stable and unstable airstreams. The latter airflow breaks down earlier, to increase the heeling moment on a sail at the expense of forward power. Yachts travelling from warmer climates to compete in European events are well advised to have their sails cut flatter to encourage this airflow to stick over a greater percentage of the sail, while yachts from Europe racing in events like the Sydney Hobart or Bermuda races require fuller, more powerful sails to compete on level terms with local boats.

Low pressure systems

These circulate in an anticlockwise direction around their centre in the northern hemisphere and clockwise in southern latitudes. The first signs of their approach are sudden changes in the direction of the wind and swell, coupled with a falling barometer reading, the latter being most pronounced if the centre of the low is within 200 miles or a vigorous front or trough is approaching. A marked increase in wind strength will also be apparent, together with the approach of high cirrus clouds and layers of

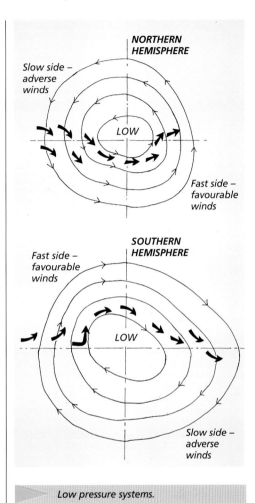

Low pressure systems.

cirrostratus cloud in the upper atmosphere, which sometimes has the effect of providing a halo round the sun and moon.

When running with, or beating against, the prevailing winds, the safest fast passage is to steer a course through the semicircle nearest to the Equator, whichever hemisphere you are sailing in, for the winds will be more favourable in this sector. These are the telltale signs:

1. If the winds begin to head you when sailing with the prevailing weather, you are on the favourable side of the low's centre, for the winds will not head further than abeam.

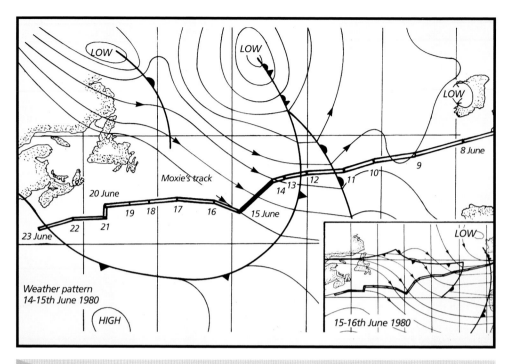

Phil Weld's winning course across the Atlantic in the 1980 OSTAR and the prevailing weather pattern.

2. If the winds show any initial signs of freeing, however, then you are on the wrong side of the low away from the Equator, for the airstream will turn to headwinds later.

3. Where no change in the direction of the wind is noted, the centre of the low is likely to pass very close, often leaving you almost becalmed as the eye of the storm passes overhead.

Those who have sailed well to the south in an attempt to follow the shortest track across the Southern Ocean during round the world races, and disregarded the depressions that sweep unchecked across these wastes, have paid a high price. They have run into strong headwinds on the wrong side of these lows, while those to the north continued on their chosen course, reaching at high speeds to gain 200-300 miles or more with the passing of each storm.

The late Phil Weld proved that these same tactics pay dividends when sailing against the prevailing weather patterns when he won the 1980 *Observer* single-handed transatlantic race with his 15.5m trimaran, *Moxie*. From his study of the June weather patterns in the North Atlantic, he drew up a plan not to sail above the 45th parallel after crossing 35°W. Instead, he steered the rhumb line course for the first week, then dipped to the southwest to avoid the risk of bad weather. This strategy gave him the opportunity to skirt round on the sunny side of the lows that battered others into submission further north, and to close-reach most of the way across the Atlantic at an average of more than 200 miles a day. The American was rewarded by finishing first and breaking the solo transatlantic record by a remarkable two day 14 hour margin.

High pressure systems

There are two types of high-pressure system. The first type consists of the permanent warm highs like those over the Azores, the South Atlantic, the Indian Ocean, Bermuda and Hawaii. These can remain stationary for days – and sometimes weeks, before moving about on seemingly erratic and unpredictable courses, often covering large distances in short periods of time. The second type are the cold anticyclones that get sandwiched between two moving depressions. Strong, even gale force winds can be generated within these 'windy' highs, especially during the winter when the surrounding depressions are lower and thus more vigorous than in the summer months. These cold anticyclones generally follow the same path as their escorting lows, making their approach easier to forecast.

In early Whitbread Round the World races, the Azores and South Atlantic Highs regularly trapped yachts for up to five days at a time. The mistake they made was to concentrate on the centre of the high, rather than its overall movement.

The central ring of this, and all warm anticyclones, can be likened to a pot of boiling water bubbling indiscriminately, each rising bubble representing the exact centre, and making it impossible to forecast. Instead, navigators need to concentrate on the overall position of the high, for this dictates where it is on its track east or west. The Azores High does in fact move on a regular track from an extreme westerly point on the African coast and back again, without changing its overall direction, before reaching one side or the other. By watching its movement for two weeks or more before reaching the area, one can see quite clearly which way it is moving and set a course accordingly. During the return leg of one Whitbread Race, the Azores High was centred at its

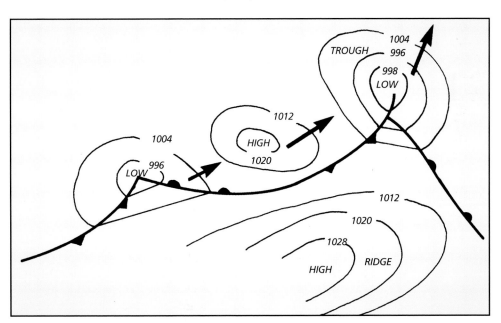

Typical cold anticyclone in Northern Hemisphere sandwiched between two moving depressions. Strong, even gale force winds can be expected within these 'windy highs' especially during the winter months.

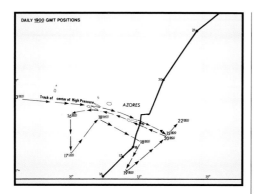

The erratic movement of the Azores High. Whitbread Round the World Race sailors learned to concentrate, not on the exact position of its centre, but to look at the High's overall position to determine its track east or west

shut, which they did, though others who tried to follow ran slap into its path and lost five days as a result.

The South Atlantic High is another to have trapped many notable names in the past and will doubtless continue to baffle yachtsmen in the future. There is a course of action one can take to evade the calms. High pressure systems revolve in the opposite direction to the lows, turning clockwise in the northern hemisphere and anticlockwise in the south. The secret is to maintain a course within the windward air stream to maintain the maximum apparent wind and thus boat speed. This is achieved by passing to the north of the centre in the southern hemisphere and to the south of it in the northern hemisphere, tacking away if the centre of the high threatens to sweep overhead or down towards it if the centre starts to move away.

most westerly extreme, so the crew on the leading yacht knew that it was only a question of time before it began its path eastwards. The race was therefore to squeeze past before this weather gate

Classic trade wind sailing conditions. It is warm, enjoyable days like this that help you to forget the times when the conditions are less favourable.

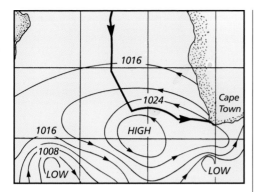

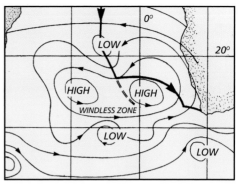

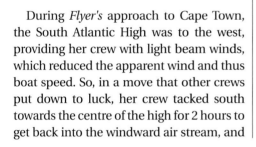

Flyer's *course to negotiate the South Atlantic High gained her 2.5 days on her intermediate rivals.*

If the high splits in two, never be *tempted to sail through the middle towards the running winds on the other side, for you will only be becalmed as a result.*

During *Flyer's* approach to Cape Town, the South Atlantic High was to the west, providing her crew with light beam winds, which reduced the apparent wind and thus boat speed. So, in a move that other crews put down to luck, her crew tacked south towards the centre of the high for 2 hours to get back into the windward air stream, and as a result, gained more than 2 days over their nearest rivals, who all ran out of wind completely.

If the high splits in two as often happens, the same tactics apply. Never be tempted to sail through the middle in an effort to get into the running air stream on the other side. You will be stuck there for a week!

food

After being on board a yacht for any length of time, the simplest of foods become like manna from heaven – quite literally. Ask almost any round the world racing crew what they have missed most during their time at sea and the answer is invariably the same – 'the taste and smell of fresh bread!'

Nowadays, long life dough mixes are readily available and some cruising yachts with sufficient power capacity carry bread makers rather than devote valuable freezer space to such low priced commodities. Another alternative is to vacuum wrap bread, replacing the oxygen with an inert gas, which can keep loaves fresh for up to six weeks, but more about that later.

Certainly, variety is key to a complaint-free life at sea. During the first, pioneering Whitbread Round the World Race in 1973, Chay Blyth had learned that Indian cuisine can provide all the nutritional requirements that the body needs. Since he likes curry himself, he stocked *Great Britain II* almost entirely with his favourite dehydrated mixes and rice. His fellow paratroopers were not impressed, and at

Cape Town, the first stopover port, he faced a potential revolt if this Indian fare was not replaced with more standard rations. The incident highlighted just how important food is at sea. During long voyages, meals can be the sole highlight in a life regimented by strict watch times, and eating and sleeping routines.

Catering for a weekend trip or five-day passage calls for little imagination or the exercise of much culinary skill. Food can always be prepared at home and stored on board as precooked meals to be served cold or simply reheated. Alternatively, the crew can rely on convenience package foods. The problems of providing a varied diet afloat arise only when planning a food itinerary for several weeks at sea. The Global Challenge is a typical long distance race where food requires a great deal of forethought, not only because each 3000-6,000 mile leg takes up to six weeks to complete, but because crews need the very best diet if they are to remain in peak physical and mental condition. Large cruising yachts are invariably big enough to accommodate a deep freeze without its weight and the extra power required to run it adversely affecting performance. On smaller yachts or those involved in racing, however, space is invariably at a premium and the extra weight is considered an unacceptable burden. So what are the alternatives to traditional package soups and plates of 'Russian Roulette' – the mixed contents of unmarked rusty cans, whose labels have long since disintegrated in the bilges?

One alternative to the deep freeze is to have a well-insulated icebox charged with dry ice before leaving port. This will keep meat deep-frozen for three weeks in the Atlantic and up to 5 weeks in colder latitudes. Freeze-dried and other dehydrated foods are not exactly popular, but do provide a practical solution, especially if the yacht is equipped with a desalinator to provide fresh water on tap. That was not the case back in 1973 and when Chay Blyth's crew of paratroopers arrived in Cape Town desperately short of water and vowing never again to darken the door of an Indian restaurant, those parched tongues served as a lesson to all future marathon sailors never to rely on just one type of food. If dehydrated products are to serve as a main supply, carry some tinned food as a back up. In an emergency, the contents can be cooked in their own juice, helping to supplement any shortfall in water supplies.

Freeze-dried food

The subject of food afloat received little in the way of research until the late 1970s. when Conny van Rietschoten was among the first to experiment with freeze-dried packaged food. At that time, the leading brand name was the US company, Mountain House Foods, which had developed a wide range of products. The *Flyer* skipper spent a week at their Oregon headquarters with an expert dietician from Martinaire, Holland's largest air caterers, sampling this dehydrated food

One thing the sea gives all onboard is an appetite! Freeze-dried food may not be haute cuisine, but the plates are always licked clean.

for themselves. Because freeze drying is an almost instantaneous process – the substance is frozen before the water content is evaporated away under vacuum – food processed in this way retains its flavour and nutrients better than if treated to the old methods of dehydration. What appealed to them most, however, was the fact that these stores provide an 80% weight saving over natural products and even more over canned food. This means that the powdered stores can be placed almost anywhere in the yacht without adversely affecting trim, while the fresh water required to mix with them is stored in tanks directly above the keel, where it adds to stability.

The two men spent three days munching their way through plate after plate, tasting all manner of dishes from Shrimp Creole to Mexican Omelettes before drawing up a list of requirements for final testing afloat prior to the second Whitbread Race. This freeze-dried fare proved a great success, with the varied dishes finding favour with all on board. *Flyer's* meals were planned as three set menus a day, rotated on a seven-day cycle to ensure that food was not only appetising but provided the correct balance of calories and vitamins. Each meal was made up from a mixture of freeze-dried and deep frozen supplies, supplemented by fresh fruit, eggs and vegetables for the first three weeks at sea, together with '*Jack Mie*' – French long-life bread. It was a compliment to the cook that this 12-man crew actually put on weight during the seven-month voyage, but being totally untrained in the culinary arts, he was unable to provide sufficient imagination or variety to the set meals, with the result that, even with this high class food, the crew became bored with the seven-day cycle during the months that they were at sea.

This problem was solved in the 1981 Whitbread Race when Van Rietschoten signed up Patrick Antelme, a Parisian chef, within the crew of his second *Flyer*. Despite little experience afloat, his culinary skills turned the blandest food into appetising dishes. This time there were no set menus. Instead, each meal became a surprise, made up to suit the day and conditions, with Patrick adding spices and the odd drop of spirits in the best French tradition to improve flavouring. Using this method there was less chance of a curry dish coinciding with orders from the skipper to ration drinking water!

Much of the Mountain House freeze-dried food is very appetising though there were one or two unpopular dishes, and stocks of these were sold off to other crews. This proved there is no accounting for taste in life, because they liked it and were queuing up to buy more at the following ports! The list of food stores consumed by *Flyer's* crew includes comments and cooking tips from Patrick.

It can be seen from this that the diced ham proved too salty for most palates, the dried onions remained hard and the macaroni cheese found few friends. The butter was not liked as a spread and simply boiled in the pan when you try to fry with it. Its only use was as a garnish sprinkled over vegetables and mashed potato. Good quality margarine covered other requirements and was chosen because, unlike butter, it will spread easily whatever the ambient temperature. The cottage cheese proved to be rather bland, but Patrick livened up the flavour by adding garlic, chives, tarragon and onions, which then went down very well on crackers. Carrots too had a taste all of their own that was not universally liked and the slices had to be hidden away in 'home made' soups. Another dislike was the dried milk and these supplies were

The Flyer *crew was among the first to rely on freeze-dried foods to sustain them during long ocean passages. It was a credit to the products, as much as the cook, that crew members actually put on weight during their 27,000 mile circumnavigation.*

replaced with safety instant milk from Domo-Holland, which has an 18% fat content and is produced as food-aid. Complaints about the Shrimp Creole were concerned not so much with taste, but the fact that all felt they had been short measured. The Pacific Shrimp was found to provide better value per plateful.

Popular items included pineapple, peaches and pears which, when mixed with sultanas and a drop of rum or vodka, made up a delicious fruit salad. Mexican and cheese omelettes soaked in milk instead of water went down well at breakfast time. And, as for the spinach, Patrick swore that this was better than the real thing!

From *Flyer's* list, it can be seen that many of the freeze-dried products can be mixed with a certain amount of salt water, providing a valuable saving on fresh supplies carried onboard. When preparing the vegetables, Patrick mixed 0.5 litres of salt water with every two litres of fresh, though one observation he made during the voyage was that sea water in the Indian Ocean tasted less salty than in the Pacific, forcing him to vary these ratios slightly.

FLYER'S STORES (for 16 crew x 5 weeks)

Deep frozen meat
(delivered to the yacht ready frozen)
4 x 16 chicken legs
2 x 16 boneless fillets of hake
6 x 5kg beef stewing steak
4 x 4kg pork stewing steak
10 x 16 sirloin steaks
3 x 3kg minced meat
4 x 16 veal scallops

Mountain house freeze-dried food
(typical list of contents air freighted to each port of call)
M = Mixed with dried milk
F = Mixed with fresh water
S = Mixed with 2 litres of fresh and
    0.5 litres of salt water
F-7 tins spaghetti with meat
Made a good lunch when mixed with tomato ketchup.
F-8 tins chicken chop suey
Perfect product when mixed with vinegar and soya sauce.
F-9 tins shrimp creole
Not nearly enough shrimps included.
F-10 tins sausage patties
Can be prepared in many ways.
F-7 tins diced ham
Not popular. Too salty. We sold our stocks to other crews!
S-7 tins green peas
Perfect vegetable. Can be used to make delicious soups.
S-21 tins green beans
Excellent product.
S-10 tins carrots
For soups and salads. Also good in a creamy sauce.
S-9 tins corn
Excellent in salads when mixed with a dash of olive oil.
S-18 tins spinach
Tastes better than the real thing!
F-10 tins mushrooms
Used in soups and sauces but good in salads too.

F-13 tins pineapple
F-7 tins peaches
F-6 tins pears
Mixed with a dash of rum or vodka together with sultanas, these ingredients make up a delicious fruit salad.
M-6 tins cheese omelette
M-3 tins mexican omelette
Ready meals.
M-9 tins cottage cheese
An interesting addition for potatoes and sauces. Can also be mixed with tarragon, garlic, chopped parsley, chives and pepper to produce an excellent spread for crackers.
M and S-6 tins instant mashed potatoes
Economical and good. Can be used to thicken soups.
S-7 tins hash brown potatoes
Delicious when tossed in a pan.
F-5 tins powdered butter spread
Only suitable as a garnish – instant mash etc.
F-7 tins pacific shrimp
Expensive but excellent product. Can be used in a cocktail sauce.
F-12 tins noodles and stroganoff
Just add vodka and chopped onions!
F-3 tins chicken salad
Not popular.
F-6 tins tuna salad
Just add anchovies and fresh lettuce.
F-2 tins macaroni and cheese
Not popular. We sold our stocks to other yachts.
F-6 tins banana chips
Rich in vitamins.
Can be added to curries and chop suey.
F-2 tins orangeade mix with vitamin C
Well liked.
F-6 tins granola with milk and raisins
Not popular.
F-2 tins butterscotch pudding
F-6 tins chocolate pudding
F-1 tin Banana cream pudding
Mixed with a dash of rum or brandy, they

make a tasty sweet.
M-1 tin cocoa mix
Makes a delicious creamy beverage when mixed with milk.
F-1 tin dry milk
Not popular.
F-25 tins Domo Safety Instant Milk from
More popular than Mountain House.

General food supplies *(for each leg)*
15kg margarine (unsalted)
5 x 28oz tins of bamboo shoots
3 x 600ml soya sauce
48 x 170g salted black beans
3 x 600g cod's roe
10 x 125g tins of tuna in tomato
10 x 100 tea bags
35 x 1kg refined sugar
3 x 5 litre pure refined sunflower oil
6 x 500g honey
2 x 2.5kg tins of custard powder
3 x 375g gherkins
10 x 800g tins of sauerkraut

2 x 900g tins of plums
4 x 450g tins of Seville oranges
1 x 5 1litre vinegar
20kg of cheese
3 x jars Marmite
3 x jars Vegemite

Dried fruits
4 x 500g apple rings
4 x 500g apricots
4 x 500g prunes
4 x 500g currants

Fresh fruit and vegetables
1 crate apples (export)
1 crate oranges
5kg bananas

Veg consumed during first week at sea
green cabbages
potatoes
tomatoes
cucumbers
green peppers

The key to having good food on board is to select the best ingredients. Here, Challenge crews are given a lesson in butchery during their stop-over in Buenos Aires. Fresh meat, when vacuum wrapped, will last for two weeks or more on board.

The Global Challenge yachts have neither a freezer nor the space to store bulky food items, and crews rely almost exclusively on freeze-dried and boil-in-the-bag fare. For several of these races, McDougals worked closely with the crews to develop a series of nutritional and interesting menus and the following lists the favoured freeze-dried packaged ingredients and their nutritional values.

Product	Serving (as consumed)	Sugars	Carbs	Fibre	Kcals	Sodium
Indian Paste – Korma	50g	4.60g	8.85g	1.70g	139.35	1.475g
Indian Paste – Tikka Masala	50g	1.15g	4.95g	1.30g	95.50	1.36g
Indian Paste – Madras	50g	2.70g	9.30g	1.30g	219.75	1.00g
Minced lamb with Sauce	200g	2.27g	12.51g	0.78g	187.02	1.01g
Minced Chicken Pie Filling	200g	3.45g	11.02g	0.48g	186.29	0.81g
Shortcrust Pastry	114g	1.20g	55.51g	2.47g	541.40	0.46g
Suet Mix	114g	0.73g	38.62g	2.07g	367.77	0.76g
Plain Muffin Mix	180g	58.42g	106.32g	2.38g	607.64	0.71g
Plain Cookie Mix	88g	27.17g	56.64g	1.41g	368.59	0.33g
Tomato Soup	340g	12.16g	22.56g	1.28g	108.79	1.11g
Thick Chicken Soup	340g	4.82g	15.92g	0.37g	98.33	1.19g
Spring Vegetable Soup	340g	1.06g	11.15g	0.54g	51.14	0.74g
Minestrone Soup	340g	5.17g	20.90g	0.89g	92.14	1.034g
Chocolate Delight	226g	31.32g	43.09g	1.45g	238.22	0.38g
Strawberry Delight	226g	33.01g	43.57g	0.01g	237.67	0.42g
Butterscotch Delight	226g	33.39g	43.57g	0.07g	237.93	0.43g
Peach Delight	226g	33.18g	43.52g	0.01g	238.02	0.42g
Banana Delight	226g	33.37g	43.48g	0.04g	237.75	0.42g
Refresh Orange	400g	33.26g	36.17g	0.06g	152.69	0.189g
Refresh Grapefruit	400g	31.80g	34.80g	0.06g	149.74	0.24g
Flapjack	120g	32.46g	74.26g	4.01g	516.83	0.21g
Original Cheesecake Mix	160g	13.95g	29.89g	0.33g	615.42	0.31g
Cherry Cheesecake Mix	180g	21.12g	37.58g	0.43g	633.73	0.30g
Sponge Mix	114g	29.64g	62.45g	1.31g	371.97	0.54g
Scone Mix	114g	8.70g	58.74g	2.60g	344.21	0.76g
White Bread Mix	114g	2.89g	53.52g	2.59g	270.60	0.51g
Crumble Mix	114g	36.84g	80.62g	1.97g	538.00	0.25g
Brown Bread Mix	114g	2.40g	48.94g	5.82g	258.12	0.54g
Bolognese with Minced Beef	200g	7.98g	16.80g	2.39g	148.49	0.66g
Curry with Chicken	200g	7.84g	17.697g	1.09g	158.11	1.030g
Chilli Con Carne	200g	5.68g	15.99g	3.08g	152.92	0.55g
Sweet & Sour Chicken	200g	13.63g	19.75g	2.14g	165.69	0.57g
Vegetable Curry	200g	11.00g	24.60g	4.10g	132.14	0.90g
Minced Beef with Sauce	200g	3.40g	10.06g	0.80g	189.03	0.67g
Chunky Chicken Pie Filling	200g	3.45g	11.02g	0.62g	186.24	0.82g
Curry with Beef	200g	10.13g	17.36g	1.32g	154.57	0.67g
Macaroni	120g	1.74g	30.04g	1.74g	150.61	0
Pasta Spirals	120g	1.74g	30.04g	1.74g	150.61	0
Short Spaghetti	120g	1.74g	30.04g	1.74g	150.61	0
Pasta Shells	120g	1.74g	30.04g	1.74g	150.61	0
Pasta Tri Colour Spirals	120g	1.74g	30.04g	1.74g	150.61	0
Complete Mashed Potato	200g	0.27g	24.58g	2.35g	124.94	0.38g
Sliced Onions	114g	17.30g	17.30g	3.33g	78.56	0.03g
Complete Custard Mix	226g	23.10g	36.46g	0	183.46	0.12g
Instant Custard Mix	200g	16.03g	22.35g	0.14g	153.76	0.11g

Vacuum wraps

Vacuum wrapping can extend the life of fresh food considerably, and by replacing the oxygen with an inert gas such as nitrogen or carbon dioxide, can do wonders for bread, crackers, biscuits and even cakes. Working with the Department of Scientific and Industrial Research in Auckland, the *Flyer* crew experimented with preserving fresh bread this way and found that it lasted the full four weeks it took them to round Cape Horn and reach Mar del Plata in Argentina. The secret to this success was to have a Cryovac machine on hand to package the bread almost immediately after it came out of the oven.

Even fresh meat merely vacuum wrapped in a similar manner can be carried on-board for two weeks or more if stored at a temperature of 7°C, and for four weeks when the thermometer remains below 4°C. Vacuum packed cuts are now common enough on supermarket shelves, and the packaging process is also favoured by many restaurants, since the meat

An early experiment with vacuum packing showed that the life of fresh bread could be extended to 4 weeks, and meat to between 2-4 weeks, depending on the storage temperature. Fragile items such as bread, biscuits and crackers are protected this way by replacing the air with an inert gas during the packaging process.

matures slowly, improving the taste. Most butchers are now equipped with one or more of these vacuum chambers and, from my experience, are pleased to package other commodities too. The possibilities are almost endless. Biscuits, for instance, can be protected against damp, large cheeses can be cut up into more manageable sizes and kept fresh, and bulky items like lifejackets, spare sleeping bags or clothing can be reduced down to a fraction of their size.

Ready meals

For longer periods at sea, fresh meat can always be salted or smoked to extend its life, but those with a palate for more common flavours can now rely on modern science and the retort pouch. Developed for America's space and military needs, these sealed packs made up from aluminium foil laminated with layers of polypropylene or polyester, keep prepared dishes edible for three years or more. No preservatives are used and the pouches merely have to be heated up in boiling water for eight minutes before serving. One manufacturer is Stevens-Lefield from Glasgow, Scotland, who offer such delights as Lamb Portsonachan, Beef Casserole, Carbonnade of Beef, Ragout of Veal, Chicken Supreme, Turkey Marengo, and venison, together with mince and onions, and beef burger with beans for those wanting less sophisticated dishes.

Some manufacturers package meals complete with vegetables: Right Away Foods of Edinburgh, California, produce such dishes as Chicken a la King and Pork with Scalloped Potatoes, all reduced down to the size of bars of chocolate. Their range of appetisers, entrees and desserts, originally developed for the US Armed Forces, are freeze-dried to remove 90% of their water content, then compressed into wafers at pressures as high as 3,000psi before being packaged in an inert gas to give them a five year shelf life.

Back Country Foods based at Invercargill, New Zealand, produce true outward bound food. Several Global Challenge crews commissioned them to package the freeze-dried food in 'crew size' portions which then gave them the option of emptying the contents into an insulated box and simply adding boiling water. The menus are quite good and the company had a good understanding of what the crews required.

It is these developments that are of most interest to blue water sailors and offshore racing crews because they take up little space and require minimal preparation – a particularly important factor in heavy weather. Beware of the portions listed on the front of these packages though. Many suggest two servings, but from my experience, there is only enough for one – especially after a hard watch on deck!

The 'Boil in the Bag' type food supplied by the UK firm Westler/Wayfarer is limited in choice, but has found favour with Global Challenge crews, providing ready hot meals when it would normally be unsafe to cook. These foods have the advantage of not needing any rehydration and can either be emptied out of the packet into a pot or the foil bag can be dropped into boiling water and heated for 7-8 minutes. The company also supplies some menus such as beef stew and dumplings complete with self heating kits to avoid the danger of boiling water. Another plus is the fact that in extreme conditions, this type of food has the same nutritional value when eaten cold straight from the packet. This boil-in-the-bag option proved so successful that some Global Challenge crews limited themselves to just this food during the Southern Ocean legs, simply because it is so easy to prepare.

The idea of self-heating food cans has been around for some time. The Armed Forces have long been issued with double cans containing a pyrotechnic substance in the bottom to heat the ready-prepared food stored in a second integral container, but at around £10 a meal, they proved too expensive for the retail market.

However, one company has developed a cheaper way of achieving the same result by using a chemical heating system instead of gunpowder. These 'Hotcans' are certainly a marvellous convenience, especially for single-handed sailors. One merely has to punch two holes through the top of the can with the spike provided to burst an annular polythene container in the outer can that allows the water and non-toxic chemicals to mix and form an exothermic reaction. The inner can is then opened with a ring-pull tab and such delights as Irish stew, beef casserole and turkey curry are stirred occasionally for 10-12 minutes until hot. The one drawback is that each tin weighs 1 kilo, half of which is accounted for by the container and its chemicals, which in many cases is just too heavy to be carried on board for anything more than emergency rations in bad weather, or for when someone forgets to replace the gas bottle!

High energy foods

High protein diets are now an essential preparation for anyone taking part in short offshore or inshore racing. Cereals, milk, eggs, fish, toast, butter, jams, meat, game, poultry, fish, cheese and such vegetables as peas and beans are the foods to concentrate on. They should be supplemented on the water by glucose or barley water soft drinks, and Mars Bars or Milky Way snacks. After eating a hearty breakfast, always leave enough time for the crew to eat and drink their fill 45

Main Meals	Code	No of Cases
Vegetable Curry	693	25
Chicken Casserole	697	23
Chili Con Carne	691	34
Beans & Bacon in Tomato Sauce	623	23
Beans & Sausages in Tomato Sauce	624	22
Lancashire Hot Pot	625	35
Beef Stew & Dumplings	626	12
Sausage Casserole	627	24
Chicken Pasta & Mushrooms	611	34
Chicken Dopiaza Curry	696	24
Spicy Vegetable Rigatoni	699	37
Meatballs & Pasta in Tomato Sauce	694	34

Sweet Meals	Code	No of Cases
Chocolate Pudding with Chocolate Sauce	698	51
Treacle Pudding	600	9
Spotted Dick & Custard	692	58

Hot Food Kit*	Code	No of Cases
Beef Stew & Dumplings	605	
Chicken Casserole	610	
Meatballs & Pasta in Tomato Sauce	615	
Spicy Vegetable Rigatoni	620	

Hot Food Kit: Consists of one Pouch, Self Heating Bag and Cutlery/Condiment set
Packaging: ■ Main Meals 6 x 300g per case ■ Sweet Meals 6 x 200g per case
Shelf Life: Three years from date of manufacture
Storage: Unopened pouch in cool, dry conditions

minutes before the race start, and have cheese sandwiches, Mars Bars and drinks ready prepared below to sustain them during the race whenever the situation allows.

Dietitians

Sport at the highest levels is now as much about science as it is about playing the game. Sporting universities have specialist courses for sports trainers to study the finer points of psychology, fitness and diet. Such expertise has been sought by professional round the world crews and Olympic teams since the late 1980s. It is not surprising that some Global Challenge crews have also gone down this route to acquire an edge over their competitors.

The Challenge Business also organises a series of short Challenge Races following classic courses like the Fastnet and Round Britain. For these 1-2 week races, each crew is given the freeze-dried ingredients and set menus to follow each day. In addition, skippers are given a fixed budget to cover beverages and snacks which they buy for themselves.

Water supplies

Drinking water is the most essential supply on a long voyage, and it would be very unwise to rely on collecting rainwater en route. Many yachts built for blue water sailing are now fitted with a desalinator to turn salt water into fresh, but these have not always been reliable so it is essential to carry a minimum reserve of five cups per day per person. These desalinators can produce upwards of 25 litres an hour at the expense of around three litres of fuel, but if they break down beware, because the hand-operated back-ups require a huge amount of effort!

When taking on fresh supplies from an unknown source, it is essential to check the quality of water. At the Rio de Janeiro stopover during the 1978 Whitbread, Van Rietschoten became so alarmed at the foreign objects floating in his glass of water that he had *Flyer's* tanks drained, cleaned and refilled with bottled mineral water. The problem was still prevalent two decades later when the Global Challenge called there, and at least one crew decided to follow the same course.

Fresh food

Fresh produce, chosen with care and stored correctly, can remain edible for very long periods and provide a worthy compliment to essential packaged supplies. Eggs for instance, when bought fresh from the farm, will last for six weeks or more, even when sailing through the Tropics. They will last much longer in colder climes as Naomi James found during her single-handed circum-navigation, when her supply remained edible for four months. Do not expect the same length of life from eggs bought from a supermarket, however, which can be held up in transit for weeks before reaching their point of sale. In the past, people have gone to the extraordinary lengths of varnishing the shells or boiling the eggs for a minute to coagulate the white but, like Sir Alec Rose, who set out on his single-handed adventures in *Lively Lady* back in 1967 found, this extra effort adds nothing to their lifespan.

Large potatoes, carefully selected and washed before being stored in black polythene bags in the dark of the bilge, also last well. *Flyer's* crew was still tucking into their 50kg stock five weeks after leaving the Hamble River during their shakedown transatlantic crossing, having had to discard not more than 500g en

The smell of freshly baked bread on board each morning is a sure way to get crew out of their bunks and eager to tackle the day ahead.

Day	Lunch	Dinner	Pudding
Day 1	Sausage Casserole	Chicken Dopiaza Curry	Chocolate Pudding
Day 2	Meatballs & Pasta in Tomato Sauce	Chili Con Carne	Chocolate Pudding
Day 3	Chicken Pasta & Mushrooms	Beef Stew & Dumplings	Spotted Dick & Custard
Day 4	Vegetable Curry	Lancashire Hot Pot	Chocolate Pudding
Day 5	Beans & Sausage in Tomato Sauce	Spicy Vegetable Rigatoni	Strawberry Delight
Day 6	Bacon & Beans in Tomato Sauce	Chicken Casserole	Spotted Dick & Custard
Day 7	Sausage Casserole	Chili Con Carne	Chocolate Pudding
Day 8	Meatballs & Pasta in Tomato Sauce	Spicy Vegetable Rigatoni	Treacle Pudding
Day 9	Beans & Sausage in Tomato Sauce	Lancashire Hot Pot	Spotted Dick & Custard
Day 10	Chicken Pasta & Mushrooms	Chili Con Carne	Chocolate Pudding
Day 11	Bacon & Beans in Tomato Sauce	Lancashire Hot Pot	Strawberry Delight
Day 12	Meatballs & Pasta in Tomato Sauce	Chicken Dopiaza Curry	Spotted Dick & Custard
Day 13	Vegetable Curry	Chicken Casserole	Chocolate Pudding
Day 14	Chicken Pasta & Mushrooms	Spicy Vegetable Rigatoni	Spotted Dick & Custard

route. Lettuces, too, can be made to last for long periods if roots are retained and the plants stored in open boxes on a mattress of damp paper or cotton wool. In time, the outer leaves shrivel up, but the hearts remain edible for several weeks.

One yacht with a six man crew which circumnavigated the globe without benefit of fridge or freezing facilities was the late Sir Francis Chichester's 55ft (17m) *Gipsy Moth V*, which took part in the Parmelia Race to Australia, before returning to Europe via the Spice Race a year later. For that latter event, the skipper, Tony de Sousa Pernes, was not only faced with victualling the yacht with sufficient fresh food to last each six week leg, but had to find enough room to store it all in the cramped quarters below. She was still laid out for single-handed sailing, just as Chichester had planned her, for solo transatlantic sailing. Space was limited to the lazarette and a spare single cabin, neither of which was well ventilated, but the voyage proved that fresh produce, when chosen with care, can last much longer than one expects, even when stored in less than ideal conditions.

At the finish of the 7,000 mile second leg to Rotterdam, Tony wrote down the list of stores taken on board at Cape Town, making useful comments on the food that proved to be particularly good – and bad.

GYPSY MOTH STORES
Fresh fruit and veg
(ordered specifically 'green', good quality produce)
6 x 15kg potatoes
3 x 10kg onions
1 x 10kg squash
12 x large cabbages
4 boxes tomatoes *(3 green, 1 semi)*
8kg sweet potatoes
12kg butternuts *(small pumpkin)* x 12kg
2 boxes green peppers *(3.5kg per box)*
15 bunches carrots
3 sacks lemons *(approx 30 per sack)*
1 box najtjes *(mandarins) (approx 60)*
Excellent, should have been x 3.
5 sacks oranges *(approx 20 per sack)*
Ordered small, but received extra large, which were often dry and stringy.
1 box quinces *(approx 30)*
Very long lasting and popular as stewed fruit and custard.
4 sacks grapefruit *(approx 25 per sack)*
10kg bananas *(approx 90)*
1 box pineapples *(approx 24)*
Good quality, but we left them approx 8-9 days and most were lost because of unseen rot from inside.
3 boxes apples *(approx 96 per box)*
Granny Smiths, packed between shaped polystyrene and individually wrapped in blue paper – excellent and still have some left. One box Star King was eaten first but began to go off early on.
1 tray avocados *(24)*
12 x lettuce
12 x cucumber
12 x celery
12 x cauliflower
Ordered but quality not good, and no time to purchase elsewhere.

Bread
12 x wholemeal loaves
Went mouldy after ten days, but 'doctored' or toasted.
6 x ryebread
Lasted longer than wholemeal but went mouldy just the same.
20 x sliced brown
Contained soya flour, wheat germ, honey. Double wrapped and lasted five weeks.
12 x pumpernickel loaves
Excellent value and lasted almost indefinitely.

Cheese
1 x whole Gouda
1 x whole Edam
7kg of Cheddar
5kg of processed cheese
2.5kg left over at end of voyage.
12 x small tins of various cheeses

Meat
(all smoked or pickled except for packets of bacon.)
12 x packets of bacon
1 per breakfast
2.5kg leg of lamb
2 x 2kg joints of ham
3 x chip beef (5kg in total)
24 x various salami
Various tinned meats

Fish
(all tinned – all good, but tuna was a favourite.)
Mackerel
Sardines
Pilchards
Tuna

General food supplies
36 dozen eggs
3 dozen left, none bad.
80ltrs x long life milk

12 dozen x 200ml fruit juices
Various tinned fruits
Very little used.
Various tinned vegetables
Tomatoes particularly useful.
Various tinned soups
8kg x rice, white and brown
Very useful.
Dried fruits and nuts
Dried beans and pulses
Pasta

Drink
1.5 cases Red Wine
1.5 cases White Wine
1 case Gin
1 case Whisky
6 bottles Vodka
2 bottles Sherry
Had a drink almost every evening before
supper and a bottle of wine with special
meals or to recover from a bad day's run.
Good and plentiful!

Cooking

One major advantage with convenience package meals is that they require minimal preparation equipment, which saves valuable weight and space. A two-burner gas stove will suffice even for a crew of twelve.

One labour saving device is the pressure cooker trays stacked inside so that two or more dishes can be cooked simultaneously. This did not enable the cook to produce roasts, but beef, pork and chicken stews stay hot in the cooker for the second watch without needing reheating. This pressure cooker is also a great gas saver, for meals take less time to cook than in open pans. It can also used to boil water safely.

Gas consumption and pressure can vary with conditions. *Flyer* used 6.5 bottles of butane gas during the 36 days it took to sail from Portsmouth to Cape Town, while 8 bottles were consumed on the second 30-day leg through the Southern Ocean to Auckland – a 22% increase. 18% of this extra consumption was caused by the drop in temperatures (while 2 litres of water took only 3 minutes to boil at the Equator, the same task took 12 minutes down in the *Roaring Forties*) and the remaining 4% was lost because the last of the gas in each bottle refused to vaporise. In colder climes, propane gas is a better proposition because it has a lower boiling point (-42°C against -10°C for butane) and has 4.5 times the pressure that butane gives in the 1°-5°C conditions of the Southern Ocean.

Storage

The sight of a human chain passing down endless supplies of tinned food from shore to yacht is a common dockside scene before the start of any long distance event. Lids have to be coded with an indelible pen before labels are ripped away and the tins are often also treated to a protective

Keep a plan of where everything is stored, and tick off the list as stocks are consumed. Heavy items should be stowed as close to the centre of the boat as possible.

coat of varnish before being finally stowed below. It is a boring, time-consuming chore that is totally unnecessary! Canned supplies will survive a circumnavigation simply packed in heavy-duty polythene bags sealed at the neck with tape to protect them against water slopping about in the bilges.

The key is to make, and keep, a plan of where everything is stored, tick off the list as stocks are consumed, and write out a decipher list for the code markings so that everyone can understand the system. Because of the 80% weight saving in freeze-dried food, these stocks can be stored with more fragile items like biscuits, ketchup etc in a net strung up under the cabin sole. Eggs are best stored in polystyrene boxes stacked in a large plastic crate, which can then be jammed between the polythene bags filled with food cans.

Traditional canned food should always be stored as close as possible to the centre of buoyancy of the hull so as to have the least effect on trim. It may seem obvious enough, but remember to keep tins well clear of the compass. One crew sailing back across the English Channel after a race to France were more than surprised to spot Portland Bill as their first landfall after spending a fruitless hour or more searching the horizon for the Isle of Wight. It took them even longer to realise that the 40-mile discrepancy in their navigation was due, not to bad arithmetic, but to the stock of beer that had been thoughtlessly stowed below in readily accessible cupboards close the bulkhead mounted compass!

And finally, a word about keeping the food on the plate, especially in heavy weather. It was Dan Byrne, a crusty American single-handed sailor competing in the first Around Alone Race back in 1982 who struck on the idea of eating out of a dog's bowl. A man who liked his food as much as sailing, he became increasingly frustrated at continually scraping up his food off the bulkhead or cockpit floor every time his yacht was hit by a wave. To start with, everyone laughed at the idea, but now dog bowls have become standard issue on almost every long distance yacht.

clothing

11

Imagine yourself in the Roaring Forty latitudes mid way between Cape Horn and New Zealand. The headwinds are Force 8 from the southwest and sea and air temperatures are down to 1°C. But with the wind chill factor, this brings the effective temperature down to -14° C. That's cold – teeth-chatteringly cold; a chill that gnaws through the bone within minutes unless you are fully protected.

Your hands and face are most susceptible. Russell Pickthall, my brother, suffered frostbite to one side of his face and never recovered any feeling, after removing his balaclava and oilskin hood for five minutes, while working on an emergency sail repair. The first he knew of the problem was a burning sensation on his right cheek and ear lobe – and by then it was too late!

Back in the 1970s and early 80s, waterproofs were far from watertight and early Whitbread crews used to wear a set of PVC oilskins under their ocean racing suits simply to keep dry. This, coupled with the sheer bulk of fleeces and other undergarments needed to keep warm, not only restricted movement but left everyone bathed in sweat after any burst of activity – a clamminess that promptly chilled them the moment they took a rest. Incessant head colds or worse, flu, was the inevitable result, and feet became so cold that it could take two weeks or more ashore before they lost their numbness.

Conny Van Rietschoten is a man who feels the cold badly, so before embarking on his second Whitbread race in 1981, he commissioned Musto to test new material technology and ideas for his crew. This led to the development of the three-layer system of clothing that has since been adopted by most manufacturers. Two decades later, the Musto clothing now worn by all Global Challenge crews is far advanced on the originals worn by the *Flyer* crew, but the principals of the three-layer system remain the same.

Foundation garments

Washing clothes during a race is not practical, and with storage space limited on many yachts to one small shelf per man, there is no room for large stocks of underwear. Back in 1977, crews experimented with throwaway paper undies, but many found them uncomfortable. Now, trans-ocean crews

Thermal conductivity related to air	
Polypropylene	6
PVC	6.4
Polyester	7
Wool	7.3
Acrylic	8
Polymide 6 and 66	10
Viscose	11
Cotton	17.5

Density table	
Fibre	Specific gravity
Polypropylene	0.91
Nylon	1.14
Acrylic	1.17
PVC	1.37
Polyester	1.38
Wool	1.32
Cotton	1.50

Staying cool and keeping warm are two sides of the same coin as far as thermal insulation is concerned and these comparison tabes show that polypropylene not only has the lowest conductivity among fibres available, but the lowest density also, providing the most bulk – and thus warmth – for the least weight.

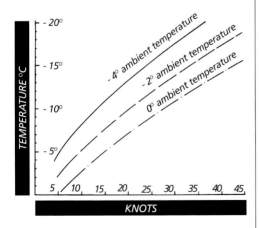

The effect that the wind has on the ambient temperature - reducing temperatures from 0°C-15°C when there is a 45 knot gale blowing.

carry six pairs of cotton pants for a 4-6 week crossing and make them last the distance by periodically turning them inside out!

Polypropylene knitted undergarments have also been long-term favourites, but because of this material's limitations regarding weaving and dyeing, manufacturers have made great strides in bringing polyester up to match the polypropylene performance. These man-made fibres are both light and buoyant, but where they score best is with their low conductivity and density, as shown in the tables above. Of equal importance is their unique wickability, keeping the body warm and dry by drawing perspiration away from the skin by capillary action into the outer garments.

Staying warm and keeping dry are really

two sides of the same coin as far as thermal insulation is concerned and the comparison tables show that these materials not only have the lowest conductivity among common fibres available, but the lowest density as well, to provide bulk – and thus warmth – without weight. Musto's latest foundation garments, which are available as tee shirts, long-sleeved shirts, polo necks, long-johns and socks, together with a balaclava and hat, are produced from the latest polyesters which are treated with an anti-microbial finish to reduce bacteria build up and thus odour. The balaclava and knitted hat are extremely important because 25% of body heat is lost through the head. Socks in the same materials have the same effect on feet and have the added benefit of drying out between watches, despite the inevitable build-up of salt.

Once in port, all this clothing can be washed thoroughly to remove body oils and salt from within the fibres, but do make sure you follow the washing instructions on the labels. If the wash is too hot, then they finish up as dolls' clothes!

Mid layer

The intermediate layer is designed principally to provide warmth without weight, but by giving them a waterproof shell, they can double as outer garments too. Warmth has nothing to do with the fabrics or yarns; it is all about trapping dry warm air. Water transmits heat 30 times faster than air, so by starting with a non-absorbent yarn like polyester or polypropylene, half the battle is won already. Cotton, by comparison, can absorb up to 100% of its own weight in water, and with this moisture next to the skin, body heat is sapped out 30 times faster than with a dry fabric. Polyester fleece, such as the Polartec 200 brushed

fabric, maximises air space with only a minimal weight penalty to trap a large volume of air, which your body heats up. Providing your outer shell is stopping all the drafts, it is this air layer that forms the dry warm boundary around your body. Comparison tests carried out by The Shirley Research Institute in Manchester showed that Thinsulate, a 3M product made from a 35/65 mix of polyester and polyolefin fibres not only has twice the thermal properties of polyester, but absorbs less than 1% of its own weight in water. This was the material that the *Flyer* crew tested successfully in the first mid-layer clothing experiments.

Many top-of-the-range mid layer garments are now shelled and seam taped with a breathable and waterproof Gore-Tex material. These work remarkably well on all fronts. When you go off watch and take your foulies off below and sit on wet sails or rub up against condensation, you are protected by the waterproof outer layer. They also make very good sleeping garments, and when the call comes down

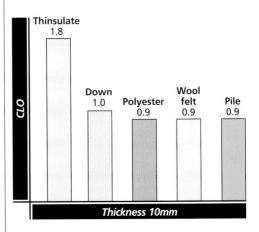

Thermal comparison table showing that thinsulate provides twice the insulation properties of other common materials. The unit of thermal resistance used in evaluating clothing warmth is the CLO. Each unit represents the approximate warmth of a wool business suit.

Clinging on for dear life. This Global Challenge crew are caught on camera putting the latest waterproof clothing through the severest test.

for all hands on deck, you can rush straight up without worrying about getting wet. Just as important, they are windproof too. Finally, having a fully breathable middle layer of clothing means that any moisture is continuously wicking through, making them an integral part of the three-layer system.

Some manufacturers design their intermediate clothing as one-piece garments, but this is not really practical at sea, since you then have to strip everything off whenever nature calls. Life is much easier if these layers are made up as separate tops and bottoms with an overlap to provide double the insulation around the rump and kidney area.

Foul weather gear
Each leg of a Global Challenge race represents 2-3 seasons' sailing for most other sailors, so foul weather gear

produced for these circumnavigations not only has to be waterproof, but extremely tough. The *Flyer* crew was equipped with two sets of foulies – a lightweight suit for use in the relative warmth of the Atlantic, and a heavy duty set which had the addition of closed-cell buoyant foam in the jacket and trousers, for the harsher conditions experienced in the Southern Ocean. PVC and other materials, which have a waterproof membrane coated on the outer surface, were discarded because of their lack of resistance to wear against the harsh non-slip deck finishes. They also tested the first generation of Gore-Tex breathable materials but found the salt clogged up the pores and reversed the material's wickability. They finally opted for a standard Oxford neoprene-proofed cloth. Two decades on, the American manufacturer has overcome this problem and most oilskin producers, including Musto, now make their top-of-the-range suits in Gore-Tex. The secret behind this breathable yet waterproof material lies in a film of PTFE, laminated on the inside of the cloth, which is full of microscopic pores 20,000 times smaller than a drop of water yet 700 times larger than a molecule of water vapour – hence the one-way traffic.

Musto paid a lot of attention to the design of the hood/collar, cuffs and trouser seals to keep the water out when crews are standing knee-deep in the scuppers changing a sheet, or standing up to green water breaking down the deck. The feedback they received from the *Flyer* crew, and successive Global Challenge teams, helped enormously to perfect their HPX range which, with their anti-spray hoods and latex seals, have revolutionised sailing clothing. This range includes an offshore smock as a practical alternative to the standard front-zippered jacket, which can be difficult to do up in extreme conditions. The smock has no zips or flaps, but rather an inner neck seal which not only stops spray penetrating down the front, but those waves that sneak up behind and dump water down the back of your neck! This, combined with boot gaiters to seal ankles, now gives offshore crews almost dry-suit levels of performance.

Survival suits

After the 1989 Whitbread Race when two crew were washed overboard from the cruising division yacht *Creighton's Naturally*, oilskin manufacturers were asked to develop a suit that would give crew members a minimum of two hours survival time and a better chance of being found alive. Musto's answer was the Ocean One-Piece Suit, a dry suit now made from Gore-Tex, with an Ocean hood and collar system to give crews sailing in extreme conditions a lightweight breathable suit with all the Ocean features that they are happy to wear on deck when the going gets really tough. It extends survival time over two-piece gear from 15 minutes to more than 2 hours in cold Southern Ocean conditions, and has become standard issue not only for Global Challenge crews, but the preferred choice for Volvo and Vendee Globe sailors too.

Boots

Sea boots came in for some critical testing during *Flyer's* preliminary trials. Not only do these need to have good non-slip soles but they also need to dry quickly between watches. Standard rubber sailing boots with cloth inner linings are not a great success in this respect and their rubber sole does not give sufficient insulation against the cold. The final choice was for the extremely hard-wearing leather-lined Chameau sea boots matched with furry Actylmer socks, which were both warm and fast drying. Leather is an excellent insulator and several manufacturers now make leather sailing boots which are infinitely better than their cheaper rubber counterparts. which tend to perish. These, worn in conjunction with polyester socks, serve the purpose admirably.

Gloves

Leather sailing gloves, on the other hand, are fine until they get wet, when they afford little or no protection against the cold. This does not matter in temperate conditions, but down in the Southern Ocean the cold renders them useless. The *Flyer* crew tested all manner of hand warming ideas from ex-naval mittens with inflatable cuffs to the latest in race wear. Mittens proved too restrictive for anything other than steering, and the leather just did not stand up to rough handling. What they ended up using were oversize cotton-based industrial gloves dipped in PVC, or ordinary rubber gloves worn over a thin pair of polypropylene knitted liners to provide the warmth. This was a tip learned from the lobster fishermen at Marblehead who have found nothing better to protect their hands against the chilling wind and spray, while allowing sufficient freedom of movement to perform most fiddly tasks on deck.

Two decades on and hand protection remains an issue. The Global Challenge crews find that Gore-Tex mittens work well when steering, but have to be taken off to do anything else. Waterproof liners are now available to wear inside fingered gloves, but water still finds a way inside, so the simple solutions found by the lobstermen still reign.

Safety harnesses

Persuading a top racing crew, hand picked for their agility, to tie themselves down habitually every time they come on deck, is a problem. In reality, it is only in the worst conditions that anyone gives this any real consideration, unless the skipper or watch-leaders are continually pointing out the dangers. If a crewman has to don a harness and life jacket separately, then the inconvenience reduces the probability of wearing one when it matters most. Many manufactures now produce a combined harness and gas inflated lifejacket that is worn over foulies, and the Global Challenge yachts have a standard rule that these should be worn whenever oilskins are donned. However, these same Challenge circumnavigatons highlighted so many design shortcomings (there was a 70% lifejacket failure rate during the first race) that Andrew Roberts and his team instigated a rigorous testing programme which has led to the development of their own design. This overcame problems of the bladder splitting on the folds, fatigue failures where the gas bottle connects to the rubber, and the position of the automatic inflation device, which had a habit of setting itself off whenever a wave doused the crew.

medical matters

12

The medical preparation for offshore and trans-ocean voyages requires the same attention to detail as all other aspects of Safety of Life at Sea (SOLAS). Careful thought to crew health, welfare and morale pays handsome dividends, for not only is a healthy ship a happy one to be aboard, but it can have a direct effect on the yacht's performance, which is often the ultimate goal. Here, Dr Campbell Mackenzie RD* FRCP (Edin), the chief Medical Advisor to the Challenge races and a veteran of the first event, provides detailed advice.

Ocean racing is a contact sport that has been likened to playing rugby continuously, day after day. The body can experience multi-directional gravity forces of up to 10G, and this, coupled with the power of solid water racing down the deck can lead to serious injuries. The sea is a hostile environment and major traumas and fatalities are not unknown. However, participants know the risks, which are invariably part of the adventure and lure of competing, and the adrenaline rush that comes with any excitement often provides that extra stimulus. As Laurie Smith, a consummate ocean racing skipper, once said, 'If you're not frightened you're not driving the boat hard enough!'

Down-time is a term used when sails or

rigging fail, but it applies equally to crew members forced off watch through injury or illness. Their loss on deck places an added strain on the watch system, which in turn leads to sleep deprivation and fatigue all round, and an inevitable drop in boat speed. The old adage: Perfect Preparation Prevents Pathetic Performance is good advice in the prevention and management of injuries and illnesses on board, and in a world where weight, or the lack of it, is all important, a gram of prevention is easily worth a kilogram of treatment. Fortunately serious injury or illness at sea is rare, and with careful preparation, the medical chest should be considered a compulsory passenger rather than a participant – just like the life-raft!

Crew selection and preparation
The oceans are no longer the realm solely of the fit, experienced, professional male yachtsman. Amateur events like the

When planning medical cover for a race or extended voyage, several factors will influence your decisions, including:

The category, route and length of the race/voyage:
- Whether it is inside or outside helicopter range
- Whether it is mainly upwind or downwind

The type of yacht – mono or multihull:
- Number of crew ie fully crewed, short or single-handed

Crew selection based on medical and psychological screening and standard medical fitness criteria

Crew preparation: advice on basic fitness training and other health issues, medical insurance and appropriate immunisation programmes

Selection of a dedicated medic within the crew;: their role, course training, certification and medical indemnity

Pattern of injuries and illnesses and their management

Communication:
- Medical support ie medical officers (MOs) afloat and ashore for advice
- Search and rescue (SAR) to arrange evacuation of casualty if necessary

Documentation: medical log, treatment charts, referral forms and recommended medical handbooks

Medical kit: composition, packing, storage, deployment and replenishment at stopovers

Special requirements ie single-handers, females, older crew and ports of call

Global Challenge, Clipper Races, the Blue Water Rally and Atlantic Rally for Cruisers (ARC) offer women and even disadvantaged crews of mixed ability an equal opportunity to share the challenges of trans-ocean sailing. Each group brings with it potential problems for the medic, who may need to look at keeping a tin of penetrating oil alongside the packs of paracetamol in order to keep prosthetic limbs in working order.

The importance of careful crew selection cannot be overemphasised, for choosing the 'right stuff' in a crew will minimise medical problems later. This need not rule out the disadvantaged, for though one might be forgiven for thinking that disabled crews might bring with them a higher incidence of medical problems, this is not always born out in practice. The tenacity of the *Time and Tide* disabled crew to prove themselves at least equal to other teams during the 1996 BT Global Challenge was a revelation to many. It was a performance that remains a counter to the creeping legislation that now challenges the selection policies which allowed this Corinthian spirit to flourish.

Skippered by the admirable James Hatfield, himself a survivor of major heart surgery, the *Time and Tide* crew was made up of amputees, cancer and cerebral palsy sufferers, and others who had to deal with deafness or blindness. They finished a remarkable fifth from last on the two toughest legs around Cape Horn and across the Southern Ocean to the Cape of Good Hope. Statistically, they suffered no more injuries or illnesses than the rest of the fleet.

Time and Tide's participation did produce one memorable emergency PAN-PAN signal after one of their number suffered a badly fractured leg, and caused considerable concern within the medical shore support team. It was only after several progress reports began to mention 'gaffa' tape and WD 40 that they realised that Hatfield and one of his team of amputees were having a bit of fun.

Any selection process should include a simple Yes/No medical questionnaire listing past injuries and illnesses, and serious question marks should be placed on anyone who suffers from such infirmities as unstable heart disease, asthma, epilepsy, or diabetes etc. The Maritime and Coastguard Agency (MCA) which follows the gold standard outlined in the Merchant Shipping Notice (MSN) 1765 or its update, now requires all yacht skippers to hold a valid ENG 1 certificate which could well be extended to all the crew in the future. This system, which has the benefit of MCA backing and legal standing, does have some flexibility, and an MCA examining doctor can discuss borderline cases with the yacht's medical officer. This questionnaire approach avoids unrevealed medical problems and the cost and disappointment these can lead to should any crew have to be taken off the yacht at a later stage.

A good standard of basic fitness can also minimize injuries and illnesses. During the work up before any voyage, crew members should be encouraged to exercise three times per week for about 40 minutes at optimum heart rates for their age. This should include a blend of cardiovascular, aerobic and anaerobic work to build strength and stamina. If they can achieve their optimum Body Mass Index (BMI) or ideal weight and stop smoking, then these are added benefits. Harken have designed a mini-gym incorporating winches, pedestals, sheets and halyards, but ordinary circuit training is sufficient. We discourage road running or jogging, particularly among older groups, because of the impact 'wear and tear' on hips and knees. Speed walking,

Table 1: Useful personal items.

- Head torch
- Ear plugs
- Battery razor
- Eye mask
- Baby wipes/tissues
- Battery fan
- Ski goggles
- Deodorants
- Small mirror
- Sun hat
- Foot powder/spray
- Tiny Swiss knife
- Sunglasses
- Odour eater insoles
- Camera
- Binoculars
- Body powder/lotion
- Sewing/manicure kit
- Spare glasses/lenses
- Chewing gum/mouth spray
- Personal CD
- Spare teeth
- Sun block/after sun
- Diary/palmtop
- Mini hot water bottle
- Insect repellent
- Dictaphone
- Hand/foot warmers
- Hobby/game kits
- Personal documents
- Small flask
- Current medications
- Small watertight box for spare batteries etc.
- Small medical kit

cycling or rowing are far more beneficial. Training at extremely low temperatures is now in vogue, and for those heading to Arctic or Antarctic regions, this can provide a taste of what is to come.

Crew members should have a full dental check up to prevent trouble later, and also have ears cleared of wax. It is also essential that crew obtain insurance cover against accident and illness, since treatment and repatriation is very expensive. In order to maintain morale and make life more tolerable at sea a suggested list of 'comfort' items is provided, though some items may be banned because of the extra weight!

The stopover ports where exotic diseases may be prevalent will dictate any immunisation programme, though it is worth remembering that weather, injury or damage can lead to unscheduled visits en route. During the first Global Challenge race, several crew members took off from Rio de Janeiro, their first port of call, to explore the Brazilian rain forests, without taking prophylactic anti-malarial drugs. Their yachts did not carry drugs to treat malaria, so they not only put their own lives in jeopardy, but the race as well.

Care, common sense and a responsible attitude is required from all on board. In the next Challenge race four years later, an outbreak of meningitis within the fleet was averted by prompt diagnosis, prophylactic antibiotics and immunisation, though sadly not before the much-respected sailmaker, Peter Vroon, had succumbed to the disease. This was a salutary lesson in the importance of pre-race immunisation, which should include tetanus, typhoid, hepatitis, meningitis etc. The fleet medical officer or any family doctor will have available immunisation schedules for the countries visited en route.

Crews must be encouraged to be responsible for their own health. Self-inflicted conditions such as dehydration, constipation and sunburn are all too common. The best advice is to drink copious amounts of fluids and pack a 500ml water bottle in your oilskins along with the torch and knife, and drink a bottle every six hours. Keep your urine clear, bowels open, bum and crutch free of salt, breath sweet and your body odourless and you will be doing everyone a favour – including the medic!

Importance of the sailing medic

Anyone experienced in accident and emergency, trauma or sports medicine and certificated in Advanced Trauma Life Support (ATLS) and/or sports medicine, conflict and catastrophe, or travel medicine will make an ideal medic. They can be nurses (medical, dental or veterinary), dentists, ambulance staff, paramedics or police, and since there is little difference between a winch gorilla and a real gorilla, the same applies to veterinary surgeons and vets. Someone with expert medical knowledge will diagnose sickness and the full extent of injuries at an early stage, ensuring a quick recovery time, and the presence of a doctor provides peace of mind – for the skipper at least! The sailing doctor is your insurance policy which, with luck, you will never need to claim on. In addition to the skipper holding an MCA's medical certificate, other crew members should have elementary first aid certificates from either their national authority, Health and Safety or the MCA.

Non-MOs should attend a five-day MCA authorised back-to-back course on Medical First Aid At Sea (MFAAS) and Medical Care Aboard Ship (MCAS) and obtain certification. The latter is the equivalent of the old Ship Captain's Medical Certificate. Some training schools include an ocean yacht module and use a mobile skills laboratory to teach advanced skills such as: airway management and resuscitation, setting up intravenous fluid drips, insertion of chest drains, cricothyroidotomy (a tube in the neck of a casualty with an obstructed airway to allow them to breathe) nasogastric tubes and urinary catheters.

As well as his/her obvious duties, the sailing medic is also responsible for the health, hygiene and welfare of the crew. They should ensure that each crew member has a health and dental check-up, and complete an insurance-type questionnaire. If a women thinks she may be pregnant, that too needs to be tested. The medic needs to know past social and medical history. Any documentation such as a GP's notes, immunisation records and health insurance should be filed away and kept confidential. If any crew members suffer from recurrent dislocations or have suffered from severe knee injuries resulting in unstable joints, kidney stones, had major heart surgery or other illnesses such as epilepsy or diabetes, a decision has to be made on whether they should sail or not. If they do, then the medic must ensure that there are adequate facilities on board to treat them if problems recur.

The medic must also act as confidante on board, defusing potential flare-ups, anticipating health problems and keeping the crew generally fit and well. He/she must get to know everyone's strengths and weaknesses, look out for troubles that can bubble up in the emotional 'pressure cooker atmosphere' of a yacht, and confide in the skipper on a 'need to know' basis about any health problems. He/she must keep comprehensive records of all medical and related problems in the form of an accurate, readable medical log and drug register, and replenish the medical kit at each stopover. The medic is also responsible for the maintenance of uncontaminated fresh drinking water and its replenishment, as well as ensuring that the food is adequate and fit to eat.

Personal and yacht hygiene are also important. Both the galley and heads require antiseptic dispensers, which can reduce the incidence of food poisoning and other 'nasties'. These areas also need to be inspected on a regular basis for cleanliness. Crew members often need to be 'reminded' to bring along a small personal pack that can include mouth fresheners, deodorant, odour eaters or foot sprays, baby wipes, skin cream, lip salves and sun block. The one big lesson I learned from sailing around the world with crews in Chay Blyth's first Global Challenge is the importance of warning young bucks (and wenches) of the dangers of casual sex, as well as discussing the treatment of more mundane infections. Condoms are a must-have.

The role of the medic is to prevent illness and injuries, as well treat them to the best of his/her ability. If in doubt *seek medical advice*. It is writ large for a reason. There may be more specialist advice or even assistance available from other vessels in the vicinity who will be alerted with a PAN PAN call. If there is an INMARSAT satellite phone on board, a telemedicine link will also provide immediate advice.

Medics require gravitas and must inspire confidence, which, while not quite spelling competence, does at least help. Above all the medic must have a genuine desire to fulfil the role and accept the responsibility that goes with it.

Patterns of injuries and illnesses and their management

If the selection process has been properly enforced, common illnesses such as heart problems, unstable diabetes, epilepsy or asthma should not be encountered. Analysis of the medical logs from several round the world races shows a distinct pattern of injuries and illnesses. Table 2 lists the number, with percentages, of problems logged in a fleet of 12 yachts, each with a crew of 12. Predictably almost 50% of injuries were minor lesions, abrasions, contusions and lacerations.

While skin problems usually predominate on yachts, surprisingly perhaps, gastro-intestinal, genitourinary and respiratory conditions were also troublesome. Since this was an amateur race, one could anticipate a higher incidence of medical problems, since the crew were less experienced and thus more prone to accidents, and ages ranged from 21-60. However, because of the natural selection that invariably took place, ie older crew are often less exposed to the more dangerous roles such as foredeck or

Table 2: Injuries sustained on 12 yachts during round the world race.

Illnesses (Number)	386 %	Injuries (Number)	299 %
Gastro-intestinal/Genitourinary	22	Abrasions and contusions	36
Skin	21	Burns	16
Respiratory	19	Fractures	11
Seasickness/Hypothermia	16	Lacerations	11
Central nervous system (CNS)	4	Musculo-skeletal	10
Dental	4	Head injuries	7
Eyes	4	Miscellaneous	9
Miscellaneous	10		

mast, it is difficult to read any correlation between these injuries and the sex, age and position of those afflicted. Nor did seasickness seem to have any effect, but further studies are needed.

Injuries occur most commonly during extreme conditions, particularly during sail changes. One of the worst incidents occurred during the 2001 BT Global Challenge Race. One crew member suffered multiple fractures and another lost a finger aboard *Veritas* while crossing Bass Strait. A solid wave swept over the yacht, lifting Robert Brooke and Charlie Smith from their perch on the weather rail and threw them across the deck. The wave was so powerful that it also washed the yacht's satellite dome overboard. Brooke recalled 'swimming' by the instrument panel and landed heavily on the port side. Smith, a stocky, 31 year old professional

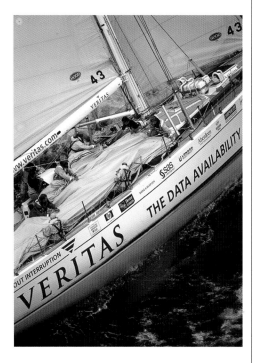

The *Veritas* crew re-pack a sail. Problems began when a huge wave washed down the deck, sweeping Robert Brooke and Charlie Smith off their feet to leave them badly injured.

rugby player, bent the stainless steel railing between the two cockpits before landing in a tangled mess in the 'catch-fencing' surrounding the wheel. Once the rest of the crew had gathered their wits, they found Smith with his feet pointing in grotesquely, unnatural angles, and the 61 year old Brooke bleeding profusely, having lost the smallest digit from his left hand.

Smith was dosed with morphine and skipper Will Carnegie took the wheel to steady the yacht as the crew splinted Smith's legs together and carried him below, howling in pain. Laying him out on the cabin sole, they then cut away his clothes to reveal the full horror of his injuries. Smith had suffered a compound fracture of his right femur and his left leg was fractured in two places. He had also broken an elbow. Medic Stephen Filery, who had 30 years' experience as a policeman, was concerned that some of his ribs and vertebrae were also broken, or badly bruised. An evacuation was essential and the crew made an immediate PAN PAN call for assistance. However, conditions were too severe to organise an airlift, and Will Carnegie was advised to motor the 70 miles to Port Eden on Australia's south east corner. Race Control back in the UK secured advice from Australian physicians who kept in touch with Filery by radio, and paramedics were waiting on the dockside when *Veritas* finally arrived in port. The two crew members were then airlifted to Canberra Hospital, where they both made a full recovery.

Having circumnavigated the Southern Ocean myself, at what often appeared to be at periscope depth, one could be forgiven for thinking that at times you have joined the submarine service. Certainly, one has to challenge the wisdom of sitting out on the weather deck, or sending people onto the foredeck in

Table 3: Danger areas and scenarios relating to injuries.

Situation	Injury
Foredeck in heavy weather	Ligaments/knees and ankles
Winches, sheets and halyards under load	Trapped fingers and rope burns
Winching	Back injuries
Spinnaker and main boom	Head injuries
Main sheet track	Forearm and hand injuries
Wheel (spinning)	Forearm, patella injuries
Helming	Shoulder and wrist strain
Bunk – falls from	Ribs, shoulder dislocation, collar bone fracture
Engine room	Harness, clothing caught in moving parts
Galley	Burns
Overboard	Head injury, hypothermia and drowning
Anywhere else eg mast/cockpit	Bruising, cuts, abrasions, strains, head and back injuries, blunt trauma to abdomen
In port	Alcoholism, drugs, accidents, infectious diseases, ie STDs

Table 4: More serious incidents and their outcomes.

Race	Illness/Injury	Action
1992/93	Amputated fingers	Landed at stopover
	Crushed vertebra	Landed at stopover
	Internal derangement knee	Landed at stopover
	Intractable seasickness	Landed at stopover
	Man overboard (suicide)	At sea
1996-97	Renal calculi	Evacuated at sea
	Appendicitis	Evacuated at sea
	Bleeding peptic ulcer	Evacuated at sea
	Traumatic pancreatitis	Continued race
	Meningococcal meningitis	On shore
2000-01	Femur fracture and compound Pott's fracture	Diverted to port
	Amputated finger	Diverted to port
2004-05	Fractured dislocation of hip	Diverted to port
	Generalised oedema (drug reaction)	Diverted to port
	Abdominal trauma (perforated gut)	Evacuated at sea
	Humerus fracture	Diverted to port

these conditions. Crews need to be aware of the danger areas and scenarios relating to injuries, shown in Table 3.

While only one death is reported in this series, other races have had fatalities, usually following man overboard incidents. Serious accidents at sea are reassuringly rare, and most can be coped with on board, though situations like the one on *Veritas* highlight the importance of researching before departure what medical facilities are available en route.

Management of medical problems

The findings highlighted in Tables 3 and 4 make it possible to anticipate likely problems and plan medical strategies. Problems, no matter how trivial, can feel a damn sight more serious when one is cold, wet, miserable, sick and apprehensive and sitting on a yacht that is banging and crashing about. A great deal of medical management boils down to common sense coupled with firm reassurance, pain relief and a deep seated belief in the healing powers of nature.

There is only a certain amount of treatment that can be administered in the confined conditions on a yacht, which is limited further by the extent of the medical kit and experience of medic. However, just as control tower staff can talk a lay person into landing an aircraft, so radio-communications from a medical shore support team can guide a medic through quite elaborate practical procedures. The mantra must always be *seek medical advice*. This is paramount to the successful management of medical problems and is only a radio/telephone link away.

Help can often be obtained from medics on other vessels in the vicinity who will be alerted to the problem by a PAN PAN call. Most race organisers man a Race HQ 24 hours a day and have their own MOs on call. They also have a crisis plan in place so that the skipper knows exactly whom to contact, irrespective of the yacht's position. Arrangements can also be made to obtain medical cover from specialist remote medical centres such as the Accident and Emergency Department at Derriford Hospital in Plymouth, UK, which administers to the British Antarctic Survey Medical Team and the Global Challenge yacht races.

In an emergency, yachts can meet and transfer a medic with specialist knowledge. This has been undertaken in both the Whitbread Round the World Race when a crewman aboard the French yacht *33 Export* broke his femur, and during the Clipper Race when a crew member mangled a foot. Fortuitously, there was an orthopaedic surgeon on another yacht within the fleet, and he was transferred across. He was unable to do very much but his arrival brought relief to the faces of both casualty and crew, and morale on board improved measurably.

Finally a decision has to be made as to whether the patient's needs would be best served by retaining him/her on board or evacuating them to a ship or shore. It is vital for all the crew to be taught how to transfer a casualty from yacht to helicopter or other vessel.

Singlehanders

Provided that they don't fall overboard, singlehanders seem eminently capable of looking after themselves because they have to be more careful. Notably, Ellen MacArthur wears a crash helmet when climbing the mast and gives more consideration to padding and protective clothing. Serious medical problems such as stitching a wound are difficult to self-treat, and are performed better with a skin stapler. We also recommend carrying a large shaving mirror to visualise areas of the body that are difficult to see.

Female crew

The fairer sex have their own requirements. It is often convenient to stop periods for the duration of the voyage using hormone treatment, and contraception has to be considered. A pre-voyage pregnancy test should be carried out because a miscarriage or ruptured ectopic pregnancy could be life threatening in mid-ocean. Just in case, *The Ship Captain's Medical Guide* shows how to deliver a baby!

Female sailors invariably carry their own medication, but if they are prone to monilial infections these should be eradicated before sailing. Most medical kits include the 'morning after pill' for stopover slip-ups. Cystitis and urinary tract infections can be prevented by a high fluid intake and regular urinating with a full bladder, particularly before turning in. These infections respond well to a course of antibiotics.

Older crew

Older crew members can have problems with vision, hearing and more importantly a loss of balance. Males over 50 should probably take 75mgs of aspirin to prevent coronary artery occlusion, particularly on cold passages. Older men can also have prostatic problems and if a catheter cannot be passed to relieve retention of urine, then a large bore needle can be pushed into the bladder supra-pubically in the midline after infiltrating with local anaesthetic.

Ports of call

After a hard voyage, sailors always anticipate the run ashore with relish. Tensions are relieved and the crew need to unwind, but some advice will avoid trouble. First the skipper should brief the crew beforehand. The medic will also want to join in the fun, so some medical cover should be arranged. Crew members should stay in groups, and not flash money and valuables about. Exotic food, alcohol, sex, drugs, tropical diseases and poisonous wildlife could all jeopardise the chance of rejoining the yacht to continue the voyage. Lastly, remember where the yacht is moored!

Textbooks and documentation

The medical log is a legal document and incidents must be recorded meticulously. If an electronic log is used, a printed back up must also be kept. Each crew member should have a page in the log containing all relevant medical details, including immunisation status and blood group.

Litigation is becoming more common in relation to illnesses and injuries at sea, and a well kept log, backed up by the ship's log or incident report, can become an invaluable defence. A drug register lists all the scheduled medicines used such as morphine and diazepam (Valium) with the date, patient's name, dose and frequency. This must be signed by both skipper and medic. Vital indicators such as temperature, pulse, respiration, blood pressure and urine output charts are useful particularly if the patient is being landed, or evacuated. Specific Glasgow Coma Scale (GCS) charts are useful for recording the course of an unconscious patient. Referral forms containing all the relevant information about the problem help the medic before radio communication is established with the shore support team or referral centre. Remember to omit the casualty's name when on air to preserve confidentiality. From these logs, the medic can compile a deficiency list so that items used and out of date drugs can be replaced.

The Ship Captain's Medical Guide from Her Majesty's Stationery Office (UK) or a copy of The International Medical Guide for Ships must be carried onboard, but several other manuals are also worth considering. These include:

The Sea Survival Manual
By Frances and Michael Howarth
Adlard Coles Nautical

The St John's First Aid Manual*
Dorling Kindersley

Kurafid, the British Antarctic Medical Handbook*
BOE Publishing

Your Offshore Doctor
by Dr Michael H Beilan
Sheridan House

Advanced First-Aid Afloat
by P F Eastman
Cornell Maritime Press

Marine Medicine
by Eric Weiss and Michael Jacobs
Adventure Medical Kits

The Essentials of Sea Survival
by Frank Golden and Michael Tipton

Human Kinetics

Performance enhancing drugs are banned in all forms of sport, including ocean racing, so medics and competitors must also be aware of those listed in:

Drug Control within the Sport of Yacht Racing – A Guide for Competitors
International Sailing Federation

The British National Formulary
Pharmaceutical Press

This lists the doses of all drugs and their side effects, and clears confusion between approved (generic or non-proprietary with a small letter) and proprietary drugs (with a capital letter) ie diazepam is Valium.

* Available on CD

The medical kit

Putting a medical kit together is rather like victualling a yacht: the more often you do it, the better balanced it becomes. The MCA outlines what is the ideal for each category of vessel, based on distance offshore, in their MSN 1768 and later updates, which provides a good basis for the kit. All MCA notices, including those on medical matters, can be downloaded from their website: www.mcga.gov.uk

The old Code of Practice for the Safety of Small Commercial Sailing Vessels has been replaced by the Maritime Guidance Notes (MGN) 280(M). Within the wealth of SOLAS material for vessels up to 72ft (24m) there is information about medical stores in Annexe 2 and Annexe 3 available from www.mcanet.mcga.gov.uk

The MCA is sympathetic to the needs of yachts and if, for instance, a medic has good reason to omit certain items from the category A kit such as body bags or Neil Robertson stretchers, the MCA will usually give their blessing when requested. It is also permissible to supplement the kit and substitute drugs or items of a similar type. One medic took the initiative of including a bottle of Laphroaig whisky until the skipper accused him of providing a 'Club Class' service and complained about the excess weight!

The International Sailing Federation, the governing body of the sport, also publishes the lists for two types of medical kit: Type A for offshore and Type B for inshore sailing. These recommendations, which race organisers invariably make compulsory for events, relate to a crew of six for one week, so that stores can be adjusted to the size of crew and duration of the voyage. Another useful reference is The Offshore Sailing Regulations by Alan Gibbs, published by Adlard Coles Nautical.

Table 5, listing recommended supplies, has been developed over three decades of top flight yacht racing and takes both the 'gospel' MSN 1768 and ORC stipulations into account. Separate columns indicate what supplies are required for weekend passages, voyages lasting between 3-7 days, and ocean crossings that take yachts out of the operating sphere of the air/sea rescue services. Drugs are listed under their generic names with some of the better known commercial brand names in brackets. Most drugs and medicaments have a limited shelf life, and each will need to be checked and replaced where necessary before embarking on a voyage.

It is important to have a portable immediate response kit for coping with emergencies on deck, which can then double as the medical grab bag to go in the life raft. Pelican cases or other large waterproof holdalls are the favoured containers and should be stored in a dedicated position on board.

Common items need to be readily available. It also makes sense to pack the medicines in relation to illness, and colour code them accordingly. Hence, a 'tums and bums' container will have all the drugs for the gastro-intestinal tract, the remedies for the gut (including anal suppositories) and an 'anaphylactic shock box' will contain injectable adrenaline, hydrocortisone and antihistamines with skin wipes, syringes and needles to administer them. This avoids the need to rummage around in the main kit box for a combination of medicines and equipment when speed is of the essence.

Injuries and illness
First Aid
First Aid is a misnomer on a yacht. Instant aid it may be, but the medic may have to provide ongoing care for many days or weeks before outside help is available.

Sailing is a high risk sport, and driving a yacht 24 hours a day in all weathers increases the likelihood of injury. Accidents at sea can be fatal, with the deck-sweeping boom and flaying spinnaker pole the most lethal. Crew members must recognise the danger areas including up the mast or when working around it, a fast spinning steering wheel, as well as loaded winches and ropes. Below decks, the galley and engine space are real fire hazards. There is also the danger of falling overboard.

First Aid is based on the principles of the 4 Ps:
- Preserve life
- Prevent further injury
- Provide a diagnosis
- Promote a recovery

It may not be possible to prevent death but in many cases, victims have died unnecessarily, simply because basic first-aid was not applied immediately to stop bleeding or aid breathing.

Preserving life relates to the prompt treatment of the 5 Bs:
- **Breathing** – Secure airway and protect cervical spine, followed by CPR
- **Bleeding** – Stop bleeding and support the circulation
- **Blackouts** – Estimate level of consciousness and nerve disorders
- **Broken bones** – Undress the patient and examine for other injuries
- **Burns**

If breathing has stopped, seconds saved are vital. Never waste time straightening limbs, moving the victim below decks, or in the case of drowning, even waiting to get the victim back on board, before providing artificial resuscitation. When there are several casualties as there were aboard *Veritas*, triage or prioritising treatment is essential. The first rule of First Aid is to attend the silent casualty first, *continued on page 188*

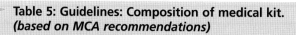

Table 5: Guidelines: Composition of medical kit.
(based on MCA recommendations)

REQUIREMENTS				
Time at Sea			**MEDICATIONS**	**USE**
2 days	3-7 days	1+weeks		
			Antibiotics for infection	
		x	AMOXYCILLIN	Chest and urinary infections
		x	FLUCLOXACILLIN	Skin infections
x	x	x	ERYTHROMYCIN	Skin infections
x	x	x	CIPROFLOXACIN	Infections, various
		x	DOXYCYCLINE	Chest and urinary infections
		x	METRONIDAZOLE	Serious infections
		x	METRONIDAZOLE (supps)	As above
		x	CEFTRIAXONE	As above
		x	FLUCONAZOLE	Vaginal thrush
			Analgesics for pain	
		x	BUPRENORPHINE (Temgesic) (tablets, buccal and injection)	Severe pain
		x	NALOXONE (injection)	Antidote to opioid overdose
x	x	x	PARACETAMOL	Mild pain, fever, sunburn
x	x	x	ASPIRIN	As above
x	x	x	IBUPROFEN	Moderate pain
		x	DICLOFENAC (suppositories)	Severe pain and renal colic
x	x	x	IBUPROFEN (gel)	Rub on sprains/strains
			Acute Anxiety/Fits/Sleeplessness	
	x	x	DIAZEPAM (tabs,inject and rectal)	Anxiety and fits
		x	NITRAZEPAM	Sleeping tablets
			Ears	
x	x	x	OTOMIZE (ear spray)	Infections, ear canal
			Eyes	
		x	ACICLOVIR (eye ointment)	Herpes
x	x	x	CHLORAMAPHENICOL (ointment)	Conjunctivitis
		x	CIPROFLOXACIN (eye drops)	Corneal ulcers
		x	HYPROMELLOSE (eye drops)	Artificial tears
x	x	x	HYDROCORTISONE (eye/ear drops)	Allergic red eye
		x	AMETHOCAINE minims	Eye anaesthetic
		x	FLUORESCEIN minims	Eye stain

Table 5: Medical kit continued.
(based on MCA recommendations)

REQUIREMENTS				
Time at Sea				
2 days	3-7 days	1+weeks	**MEDICATIONS**	**USE**
			Nose	
		x	EPHEDRINE nose drops	Decongestant
		x	KARVOL caps	Inhalation from handkerchief
			Mouth and Throat	
	x	x	BONGELA	Mouth ulcers
		x	STEROID PELLETS	Mouth ulcers
x	x	x	THROAT LOZENGES	Sore throats
		x	PHOLCODINE SYRUP	Cough
		x	AMPHOTERCIN LOZENGES	Oral fungus infection
			Anaphylactic shock / Allergy and Asthma	
x	x	x	ADRENALINE (1:1000 injection)	Anaphylactic shock
		x	HYDROCORTISONE (injection)	As above and asthma
	x	x	PREDNISOLONE	As above and asthma
x	x	x	CHLORPHENIRAMINE	Allergy
		x	CHLORPHENIRAMINE (injection)	Severe allergy
	x	x	SALBUTAMOL (inhaler and spacer)	Allergy and asthma
		x	AMINOPHYLINE (injection)	Severe asthma
			Stomach and Gut (tums and bums)	
x	x	x	GAVISCON	Indigestion
	x		OMEPRAZOLE	Severe peptic ulcer pain
x	x	x	CINNARIZINE	Seasickness
x	x	x	SCOPOLAMINE (patches)	As above
			PROCHLORPERAZINE (tablets, injections, suppositories)	Severe vomiting
		x	DOMPERIDONE (tablets and suppositories)	As above
x	x	x	LOPERAMIDE	Diarrhea
	x	x	BISACODYL	Constipation
		x	GLYCERINE (suppositories)	As above
	x	x	ANUSOL (suppositories and ointment)	Piles
x	x	x	DIORALYTE	Salt and fluid replacement
		x	CYCLIZINE (injection)	Opioid induced vomiting

REQUIREMENTS				
Time at Sea				
2 days	3-7 days	1+weeks	**MEDICATIONS**	**USE**
			Skin preparations	
x	x	x	E 45	Dry skin
x	x	x	HYDROCORTISONE (cream)	Skin rashes
x	x	x	ZINC (cream)	Gunwhale bum
		x	FUCIDIN (ointment)	Infected skin
	x	x	MICONAZOLE (cream/ powder)	Foot and crutch rot
		x	MALATHION	Head and pubic lice
	x	x	FLAMAZINE	Burns
x	x	x	ACICLOVIR (cream)	Cold sores
	x	x	STERZAC (powder)	To dry wet rashes
x	x	x	VASELINE	General uses
x	x	x	CALAMINE (lotion)	Sunburn rash
		x	MAGNESIUM (paste)	Draw boils
		x	COLLODION FLEXIBLE	Splinting toes
		x	TINCT BENZION	Stick down dressings
		x	CLOTRIMAZOLE SPRAY	Fungal infections
x	x	x	CHLORHEXIDINE (solution)	Skin disinfectant
		x	'NEW SKIN' (spray)	Cover wounds
x	x	x	SUN BLOCK	Skin and lips
			Anaesthetic agents	
x	x	x	LIGNOCAINE (injection)	Before suturing/stapling
		x	BUPIVICAINE (injection)	Nerve blocks
		x	LIGNOCAINE (gel)	Passing urine catheter
		x	ETHYL CHLORIDE (spray can)	Before incising boils
			Cardiac agents	
x	x	x	ADRENALINE (1:10,000 injection)	Stimulate heart
		x	ATROPINE (injection)	Quicken pulse rate
x	x	x	GLYCEROL TRINITRATE (spray)	Increase heart circulation
		x	AMIODARONE	Stabilize heart rate
		x	FRUSEMIDE	Fluids on lungs
		x	ASPIRIN	Stop further thrombosis
		x	SOTALOL	Stabilize heart rate

| REQUIREMENTS | | | | |
| Time at Sea | | | | |
2 days	3-7 days	1+weeks	**MEDICATIONS**	**USE**
			Intravenous fluids	
		X	WATER for injection	For injectable drugs
		X	NORMAL SALINE	Shock and dehydration
		X	HAEMOCEL	Artificial blood
		X	MANNITOL 20%	Head injuries
		X	GLUCOSE 50%	As above/low sugar
			Miscellaneous	
		X	GLUCAGON (injection)	Low sugar in diabetics
	X	X	SYNTOMETRINE (injection)	Uterine bleeding
		X	MORNING-AFTER PILL	Possible pregnancy
		X	QUININE or MEFLOQUIN	Malaria

*NB: Data sheets on dosage and side effects accompany drugs or can be found in the British National Formula or its equivalent.

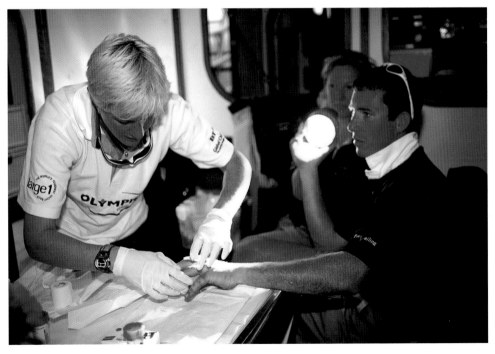

The dinette is turned into an operating table as the medic attends to a hand wound during a Global Challenge Race.

Table 6: General hardware and software supplies advised.

____ REQUIREMENTS ____			
Time at Sea			
2 days	3-7 days	1+weeks	**GENERAL SUPPLIES – HARDWARE**
x	x	x	HEAD TORCH
			Strapped inside lid of instant response bag/box
x	x	x	TUFF SCISSORS
x	x	x	POCKET RESUSCITATION MASK
x	x	x	CRICO-THYROTOMY KIT
	x	x	STETHOSCOPE
	x	x	BP MACHINE AND LARGE CUFF
		x	DIAGNOSTIC SET
x	x	x	FLEXIBLE PROBE, DIGITAL THERMOMETER: WIDE RANGE
		x	GUERDAL AIRWAYS
	x		NASO-PHARYNGEAL AIRWAYS
		x	LARYNGEAL MASK AIRWAYS
		x	BAG AND MASK
		x	SUCKER
	x	x	ARTERY FORCEPS
		x	NASO-GASTRIC TUBE
		x	RECTAL TUBE
		x	LARGE BORE NEEDLE AND 50ml SYRINGE
		x	CHEST DRAIN AND HEIMLICH VALVE
		x	IV GIVING SET AND CANNULAE
x	x	x	SYRINGES AND NEEDLES (various)
x	x	x	SAM SPLINT
		x	FRACTURE SLINTAGE SYSTEM
	x	x	FRACTURE STRAPS (Velcro)
		x	PELVIC IMMOBILISER
		x	FRACTURE CAST MATERIALS
	x	x	ADJUSTABLE CERVICAL COLLAR
x	x	x	THERMAL PROTECTION AIDS (TPAs)
		x	SUTURE INSTRUMENTS AND SUTURES
	x	x	SKIN STAPLER AND REMOVER
x	x	x	SKIN CLOSURE STRIPS
	x	x	DERMABOND SKIN GLUE
		x	URINARY CATHETERS AND BAG
		x	URINE TESTING KIT
x	x	x	SURGICAL GLOVES (sterile and non-sterile large)
x	x	x	EYE IRRIGATION BOTTLE
	x	x	DENTAL KIT

REQUIREMENTS			
Time at Sea			
2 days	3-7 days	1+weeks	**GENERAL SUPPLIES – HARDWARE**
X	X	X	SAFETY PINS
		X	PREGNANCY TESTING KIT
X	X	X	EYE MAGNIFYING GLASS AND LOOP
X	X	X	PEN TORCHES
X	X	X	SCALPELS AND BLADES
X	X	X	TONGUE DEPRESSORS
		X	NASAL TAMPONS
			GENERAL SUPPLIES – SOFTWARE
X	X	X	FIRST AID PLASTERS (assorted)
X	X	X	EYE PADS AND PATCHES
X	X	X	SLINGS (triangular bandages)
X	X	X	STERILE GAUZE
X	X	X	FIELD DRESSINGS (assorted)
X	X	X	TUBAGRIP AND APPLICATOR (assorted)
X	X	X	STERILE DRESSING PACKS
X	X	X	PLASTER OF PARIS (or equivalent)
X	X	X	ELASTOPLAST (roll)
X	X	X	CLING FILM
X	X	X	SLEEK ROLL (or Gaffa tape)
	X	X	BURNS KIT
X	X	X	CREPE BANDAGES (assorted)
	X	X	CLING AND CONFORMING BANDAGES (assorted)
X	X	X	MELONIN DRESSINGS
X	X	X	MICROPORE TAPE (assorted)
X	X	X	COTTON WOOL
X	X	X	COTTON BUDS
	X	X	RIBBON GAUZE
		X	CONDOMS
	X	X	INSTANT ICE PACK

For consideration on extended/remote voyages:
- LIGHTWEIGHT OXYGEN CYLINDER
- NEW INTEROSSEOUS FLUID ADMINISTRATION KIT
- FEMORAL FRACTURE SPLINT ie DONWAY
- IV KETAMINE AND MEDAZOLAM for 30 minutes anaesthetic
- TOURNIQUET BANDAGES
- QUICK CLOT POWDER
- AUTOMATIC EXTERNAL DEFIBRILLATOR for marine use
- STRETCHER/SCOOP/LITTER to remove injured persons from the deck

NB: Pack medical kit according to body systems ie all eye materials in one see-through bag or box

continued from page 181

since they may have an obstructed airway. Those who are screaming in pain have clear airways! Others are then dealt with in order of priority given to the seriousness of their injuries.

Remember, you are only a radio-telephone or telemedicine link away from expert advice. Failing this, then a PAN PAN call could well bring professional assistance from other vessels in the area.

Cardio-pulmonary resuscitation(CPR)

Absence of breathing and cardiac arrest

The most serious emergency of all is airway obstruction and the cessation of breathing. This is often the result of becoming unconscious from near drowning, hypothermia, severe pain, head injury, electric shock, poisoning or a severe heart attack.

Since the outcome following cardiac arrest is dramatically improved by the use of a defibrillator to shock the pulse back into a normal rhythm, the RYA and other national authorities have begun to introduce Automatic External Defibrillators (AEDs) into their CPR programme. These idiot-proof machines are now carried on airlines, and supermarkets are being equipped with them for lay people to use. There is a marine version available and crews planning extended voyages should give serious consideration to carrying one, along with oxygen. All the latest information on CPR is available from www.erc.edu

Treatment: The medic and other crew members will have been trained to provide basic resuscitation, including the use of an AED. Speed is essential, as the brain will suffer irreversible damage within 3-5 minutes without oxygen or a blood supply. If an AED is not available then the Resuscitation Council now recommends applying 30 chest compressions followed by 2 mouth-to-mouth breaths (30:2) instead of the old CPR method of 2 breaths first then 15 compressions ie (2:15).

Airway blockage

If a foreign body such as food blocks the larynx and airway (known as a café coronary because it mimics the condition) then treatment must be just as immediate because the casualty will die if the blockage is not removed.

Treatment: Double the victim forward over your forearm and administer five sharp blows with the heel of the hand between the shoulder blades to encourage coughing. If this fails, proceed immediately with the abdominal thrust, or as it is sometimes referred to, the Heimlich maneouvre. Place your arms around the victim from behind so that your clasped hands can be brought sharply upwards and inwards at the level of their solar plexus in order to mimic a cough. If that also fails, then you will need to perform a cricothyroidotomy to remove the blockage. This was famously performed on an airline passenger by a doctor inserting a penknife and the casing of a 'biro' pen into the neck, but we recommend using the equipment in the medical kit!

Once the casualty has recovered, place a hard collar around their neck if you suspect any damage to their spine, then roll them onto their side in the recovery position to keep their airway clear and prevent inhalation of vomit. Now the casualty has to be thoroughly re-examined in what MOs call a secondary survey by groping the body all over to detect any other injuries or painful areas and check that the casualty can move all limbs. To do this, all areas have to be exposed even if oilskins and clothing have to be cut away.

Remember, of course, the need to protect the casualty from the environment.

Bleeding

Many areas of the body can bleed profusely, so it is important to estimate how much blood has been lost. Some of it can be hidden internally as in a fracture of the femur or pelvis, or a torn spleen when it is possible to lose 2-3 pints. Since the average person has only 9 pints of blood circulating around their body, shock can set in after the loss of only $1^{1/2}$ pints.

In the Ocean Challenge races, crew members are screened as universal blood donors to ensure a compatible supply of blood in the event of a major emergency. This is because, in the absence of surgery, fresh blood is the only way to treat internal bleeding because it encourages blood clotting.

Treatment: Bleeding can be stopped by applying direct pressure to the bleeding site with a large field dressing, or over the main feeding artery on what are known as pressure points, ie the femoral artery in the groin. Although tourniquets are frowned upon, they can be life saving if applied properly and for not too long. The blown up cuff of the blood pressure (BP) machine can double up as a tourniquet. A new development is the emergency bandage, which incorporates a dressing, pressure and tourniquet effect. Some are impregnated with a clotting agent and can be self-administered.

Where there is major blood loss, an intravenous line should be inserted and fluids and plasma expanders given. It is better to anticipate shock and insert a line into a vein while they are easily seen. Nobody will come to any harm by having a litre of intravenous solution given to them. If the bleeding is internal, then another crew member will be required to donate fresh, compatible blood.

Bleeding from the nose can be stopped by nipping the soft part between thumb and forefinger. If that does not work, pass a nasal tampon or gauze up the nostril. Bleeding under the nail can be very painful and is best relieved by pushing a red-hot paper clip end through the nail to relieve the pressure.

Shock

Shock of any form is usually obvious with the patient becoming ashen-grey, cold, clammy and sweaty. Their pulse will be difficult to feel at the wrist and often feeble, even over the carotid in the neck, if blood pressure falls below 60mmHg. Breathing will become rapid and shallow, and the patient may behave irrationally and complain of blurred vision before becoming unconscious.

Anaphylactic shock results from an acute allergy associated with such things as bee or wasp stings, or particular foods like shellfish and peanuts. The diagnosis is pretty obvious with the patient wheezing, feeling faint, becoming pale and sweaty, or sometimes feeling that their throat is constricted, leading to total collapse. Their condition will respond dramatically to adrenaline and hydrocortisone. Any pre-voyage health screen will have shown this up and people with known allergies should carry their own adrenaline in easily administered 'Epipens'.

Cardiac shock follows a heart attack when the pumping action of the heart fails. This requires immediate AED or CPR.

Neurogenic shock can occur when a victim has suffered severe head or spinal injuries. More rarely, shock can also be brought on by blood poisoning.

Fainting is a minor example of shock and results from the loss of circulation to essential organs. The most common causes include: severe pain, major trauma, severe bleeding either externally or internally from the gut, fractures or damaged organs such as the spleen. It can also follow serious burns.

Treatment: In all cases, follow the ABC rule: Airway, Breathing and Circulation.

The patient should be laid flat on their back with legs extended and raised 30% to drain blood from the limbs into the central circulation. Severe pain is best treated with morphine or an equivalent drug, given intravenously if circulation is poor. Bleeding should be stopped if it is external by using a pressure bandage, or in extreme cases by applying a tourniquet to the limb. Ultimately, intravenous fluids may be required since rectal fluids made up of electrolyte replacement solution are really only capable of combating dehydration. The British Antarctic Team once performed a crew-to-crew cross-transfusion, but artificial blood is carried in the medical kit.

Fractures

Fractures can affect any bone in the body but commonly involve limbs, occasionally ribs, and less commonly skull and pelvis. Fractures cause extreme pain and tenderness around the damaged bone, and often a 'grating' feeling is felt when the bone ends move on each other. The limb can also become very swollen. Dislocations are obvious because when compared with the opposite side of the body, the joint looks to be out of line.

Nerves and blood vessels close to the bones are easily damaged, either by the fracture or clumsy handling afterwards. Damage to arteries may also lead to poor blood supply to the distal limb, causing

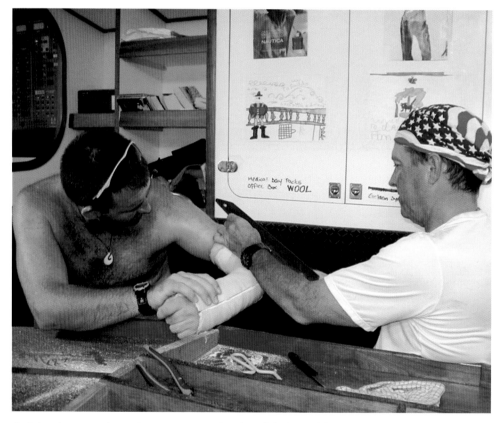

An injured crewman has a plaster cast removed on board during a Global Challenge race.

paleness or blue colouring and coldness, which, if left untreated, can lead to gangrene. Any damage to the nerves will lead to a tingling numbness, which can result in total loss of sensation. Fractures of the femur are rare on board a yacht but have occurred when crew have been washed down the deck with great force and crashed into rigging, wheel or stanchions.

Treatment: Limb fractures are often difficult to diagnose from a sprain, but are both treated using the **PRICE** principle:

- Painkilling drugs (not aspirin as it makes the fracture site bleed more)
- Rest
- Ice, immobilisation (splinting)
- Compression
- Elevation

Pelvic fractures are particularly shocking since bleeding is excessive. Immobilisation using a SAM belt or several slings will stabilise it and reduce bleeding. If a bone is misaligned then it should be straightened under cover of an analgesic or nerve block. This is very important in fractures of the ankle when the circulation to the foot may be compromised. Most importantly if the fracture is compound or open, with the bone breaking the skin, then a sterile iodine impregnated dressing must be applied and antibiotic cover given.

The most useful painkillers are the non-steroid anti-inflammatory drugs (NSAIDs) ie Brufen, which is available in gel form to rub on minor strains and sprains.

Splinting can take several forms and in emergency situations, can be as basic as sail battens strapped up with 'gaffa' tape. Inflatable versions compress the fracture site, thus reducing bleeding and pain.

Rib fractures cause a great deal of localised pain but are usually uncomplicated, unless a lung is punctured, causing air to enter the chest ie pneumothorax. This is serious and immediate help or advice should be called for. If the lung is under any sort of tension, a large bore cannula followed by a chest drain will have to be inserted. This emergency operation was carried out on a passenger aboard an airliner by a doctor using a coat hanger and a urinary catheter. DO NOT STRAP RIBS, NOR GIVE MORPHINE as it suppresses respiration further.

Head injuries

Head injuries caused by booms and sheets sweeping the deck and even exploding winches, can vary from simple scalp wounds to severe fractures of the skull, and result in internal haemorrhaging, loss of consciousness and concussion.

Treatment: Put a cervical collar on any suspected cervical spine injury. Very little can be done for skull fractures other than keep a continuously running Glasgow Coma Scale. This is measured by assessing eye opening and limb movement on command, plus verbalisation. If one adds pulse and respiration rate, blood pressure, and urinary output, a good idea of seriousness of the injury can be obtained.

'Raccoon' or blackened eyes, bruising behind the ear over the mastoid process, or clear fluid running from the nose or ear suggests a serious skull fracture. Compression inside the skull, diagnosed by a dilation of the pupil can be fatal. Intravenous application of Dextrose 50% or Mannitol 20% could buy some time. If it is not possible to land or transfer the patient and get them specialist care, then they will either survive or succumb, and little can be done if there is internal bleeding, other than conservative management.

Late sequelae can occur after a few weeks with the patient suffering loss of memory. More seriously, a residual

Simple faint	Heart attack
Head injury	Pulmonary embolus*
Cerebral-vascular stroke	Tension pneumothorax
Hypovolaemic shock	Severe pain/trauma
Anaphylactic shock	Post epileptic fit
Gassing eg CO	Insulin excess eg diabetics
Alcohol/drug overdose	Choking/asphyxia
Drowning/near drowning	Hyperthermia
Lightning strike	Hypothermia

*Secondary to economy syndrome ie thrombosis in deep leg veins.

Treatment: The principles of **DRABC** and the recovery position apply.

1. Check for **D**anger to yourself.
2. Shout and shake casualty for a **R**esponse.
3. Clear the **A**irway by tipping the head back to bring the tongue forward and checking for foreign bodies in the mouth or throat.
4. Look, listen and feel for **B**reathing.
5. Feel for the presence of a **C**irculation by palpating for a pulse in the neck over the carotid artery.

Some attempt should be made to assess the depth or level of consciousness (LOC) so that improvement or worsening of the condition can be recorded. AVPU is a simplified version of the Glasgow Coma Scale and stands for:

■ **A**lert and normal.
■ **V**ocal – responds to shouted commands.
■ **P**ain – only responds to painful stimuli.
■ **U**nrousable – completely flat.

collection of blood can cause pressure on the brain, ie a subdural haematoma. Whatever the case, reference to a neuro-surgical unit at the first available opportunity is essential.

Spinal injuries

Whenever a crewman has fallen heavily or suffered unconsciousness from a blow to the head, it is quite possible that they will have sustained a neck fracture. DO NOT MOVE THE PATIENT. If they are conscious, ask where the pain is and test whether they can move their toes, legs and hands. If there is severe localised pain, difficulty with moving a limb, numbness or any tingling sensation felt in the legs or arms, a spinal fracture should be suspected.

Treatment: The first task is to protect the cervical spine by straightening and extending the neck under light traction with a hand on either side of the head, before establishing an airway. Do not allow the head to flex. A cervical collar can then be fitted to reduce the chance of permanent spinal cord damage and paralysis. If the patient has to be moved, then one person must take responsibility for steadying the head and neck. Rest and pain relief using non-steroidal anti-inflammatory drugs with firm reassurance is the only treatment available on a yacht.

Loss of consciousness

Blackouts and unconsciousness are

always alarming, especially when accompanied by fits. The commonest causes and relevant treatments are listed in Table 7.

Burns

Burns can be caused by wet and dry heat, cold, friction, electricity, chemicals and radiation, ie sunburn. Thermal burns occur all too often in the galley, which is why some skippers wisely insist that chest trousers be worn when cooking. Another danger zone is around the engine. Rope burns can be avoided simply by wearing sailing gloves. Thermal burns are classified as partial or full thickness, the latter after the initial pain has gone and the area becomes painless to the touch and will require skin grafting later. The wind chill factor experienced in the Southern Ocean can burn the skin just as badly. Just five minutes of exposure can lead to permanent loss of feeling. The face and hands are especially susceptible.

Treatment: The principle is to cool the area with copious amounts of cold water until the pain is relieved. This can take up to 20 minutes. You can then remove clothing, provided it is not adhering to the skin, and all rings and jewellery. The wound can now be covered with a non-adherent dressing such as specially prepared burn bags or even kitchen cling film, which allow the burn to be seen and monitored. These dressings should remain in place for three days. Painkillers may also be required. It also helps to elevate the area if possible to reduce blood circulation. Do not break blisters or put any creams on the burn. If signs of infection occur, then oral antibiotics will be needed .

The 'rule of nine' is used to assess the size of the burn by percentage, ie an arm is 9%. However, the best method is to use the hand, which is 1%, and work out roughly the area burned. Burns of over 9% can lead to shock, which is best overcome by drinking up to three litres of fluids a day. Infected burns have to be covered with Flamazine ointment and antibiotics.

Sunburn, sunstroke and hyperthermia

Sunburn is a punishable offence in the Royal Navy and is easily avoided. Sunstroke follows prolonged exposure to the sun and is caused by lack of fluids and a severe rise in body temperature (from 37°C to 40-42°C). Victims usually feel very hot and dehydrated. If treatment is not immediate, they may also become delirious and even comatose. Prevention is all-important. Adopt the Aussie 'Slip, Slap, Slop' regime. **Slip** on a long sleeved T-shirt, **Slap** on a hat and **Slop** on plenty of Factor 30 sun cream. For added pro-tection, apply sun block particularly on lips, ears, bald spots and on the tops of feet, and wear good sunglasses to protect the eyes.

In hot latitudes, the body can overheat and excessive sweating can cause dehydration, faintness and exhaustion. If the process is not halted, the body's temperature regulating mechanisms will fail and the body temperature can rise above 40°C.

Treatment: This is aimed at keeping the patient cool and making them drink as much water as possible. In severe cases, it will be necessary to cool the patient artificially by covering the body with wet towels and allowing a cool breeze to flow over them. A course of aspirin administered every four hours will deaden the pain, and hydrocortisone cream will decrease inflammation. Heat stroke victims may also require an intravenous solution such as Dioralyte.

Open wounds and infections

Treatment: First stop the bleeding by direct pressure, examine for any foreign bodies, see if any other structures have been damaged, ie nerves or tendons, and thoroughly clean with a bactericidal agent and sterile swabs – having washed your hands first! If the cut requires closure then there is a choice of dumbbell, steri-strip sutures, biological skin glue, staples or suturing; the latter require local anaesthetic infiltration around the wound. Cover the wound with sterile dressings and watch out for infection around the edges of the wound, particularly a spreading redness known as cellulitis when it is redressed every day or two. Antibiotics may be necessary. Wounds on the face can be covered with 'new-skin' sprays, which dispense with the need for dressings.

Hypothermia, immersion and exposure

Hypothermia occurs when the body temperature drops to 35°C, but impaired body function can occur when the temperature drops below 37°C. The condition usually occurs following immersion, and the speed of onset depends on the sea temperature, length of time in the water and wind chill factor. Other contributory factors include the BMI (fat layer), sex, age, health and fitness, state of hydration and the amount and type of protective clothing and life jacket worn.

A one-piece survival suit not only increases survival times considerably, but also insulates the body better than oilskins against wind chill when working on deck. Graphs relating to time immersed, against the temperature of the water, predict survival rates. Hypothermia can occur within minutes of someone falling in water even as high as 20°C. In parts of the Southern Ocean where the waters are between 1-2°C, death can still occur within 20-30 minutes even with a one-piece survival suit. Thus, recovery routines following a man overboard incident have to be performed rapidly.

Hypothermia can also develop in a crew member sitting immobile on deck with insufficient clothing to combat the wind-chill factor. In these cases, the onset can be insidious. The condition is also common in people with little fatty tissue and those suffering from exhaustion or the effects of seasickness. Victims can appear confused or drunk, with slurred speech and a staggering gait which, if not treated promptly, can progress to a state of semi-consciousness, coma and eventual death. For practical purposes, a casualty has a body that feels as cold as marble. Even their armpits will be profoundly cold. A patient's temperature should be taken rectally with a low-reading thermometer. As a guide:

37-35° C: Feels cold and shivers.
35-33° C: Confused and disorientated.
33° C or less: Unconsciousness, coma leading to death.

If someone goes overboard, they should try to stay calm, and adopt the **HELP** pose – Heat Escape Limiting Position. To avoid cold shock, do not move until breathing and heart rate settle down, and then think positively about being rescued.

All those who go down to the sea in ships should see the instruction film *Cold Water Casualty* produced by the Institute of Naval Medicine, which is shown on most respectable medical courses.

Treatment: Treatment is based on a slow passive re-warming of the body core to avoid a severe drop in blood pressure and loss of circulation. If the patient is conscious, lay them flat and undertake CPR. Oxygen can be given provided the cylinder is not very cold. In these cases, it needs to be 'chambered' like a wine bottle.

Remove wet clothing and wrap the patient in a sleeping bag and/or thermal foil blanket. The optimum treatment is to place a conscious casualty in a bath kept at $40°C$, but not many yachts have this facility.

In other situations, re-warming is best achieved passively with the heat being generated from the core of the body rather than the surface to avoid a catastrophic fall in blood pressure. It will help if a warm crew member can lie with the victim in the spoons position, ie normal chest to cold back. The cabin can also be warmed up with the help of a heater or by running the engine. Consider 'airway, insulation and warming'. A loose scarf rested over the mouth and nose can help, provided the airway in not compromised. Hot water bottles (glass, spirit, or lemonade bottles with a screw cap, filled with warm water will suffice) placed on either side of the groin to warm the large femoral artery and vein, just below the skin, can also be considered.

DO NOT administer alcohol, rub the skin, or place the victim in a shower, as these actions will only lead to a further drop in blood pressure and possible cardiac arrest.

In profound hypothermia, the patient may appear dead, but do not assume this until they are warm and dead. Casualties must never be left alone for the first 48 hours because fluid in the lung from inhaled water can sometimes cause what is known as secondary drowning, which is difficult to treat.

Other cold injuries such as frostbite are rare, but non-freezing cold injuries such as trench immersion or cockpit foot are seen. Tight sea boots coupled with the wet and cold, can damage the nerves and blood supply to the feet, which may remain numb permanently.

Skin problems, boils and abscesses

Salt water rashes, prickly heat, or sweat rash and boils, together with foot and crotch rot are all too common if skin care is not practised.

Most crews develop some skin problems when at sea for extended periods. This can start out as 'gunwale bum' caused by salt water, sweat and friction from oilskins, which then spreads throughout the crew to produce a contagious 'yacht pox'. It looks rather like acne and leads to recurrent skin sepsis that can seriously affect the running of any vessel, This happened aboard *Heath Insured* during the first Global Challenge race, and her crew continued to suffer from it until they reached port and professional medical care.

Prevention: Daily personal hygiene is important. Liberal use of baby wipes to the nether regions and armpits, followed by a dusting of a medicated powder such as cicatrin or sterzac will reduce the incidence. The most prevalent areas are on the bum, and wherever salt impregnated oilskins rub on the skin, ie wrists and neck. Hot showers every three days, using medicated anti-bacterial soak or hibiscrub from a dispenser in the heads, together with a regular change of underwear will help. One useful preventative on long voyages is to use throwaway paper underwear.

Foot rot or tineapedis from fungal infections can also be a problem, and the smell from this, coupled with bad breath and body odour will lower morale. Feet should be kept clean, dry and dusted regularly with Daktarin powder. Socks should also be changed daily. Sailing boots and trainer type yachting shoes can become extremely malodorous and need to be washed out, have odour eaters inserted, and sprayed on a regular basis with shoe freshener.

Treatment: Carry lots of nappy rash cream. Bad boils should be allowed to come to a point, then frozen using an ethyl chloride spray and lanced with a scalpel. If cellulitis develops give antibiotics.

Oilskin chafe over the elbow can inflame the small pad, ie bursa, which can fill with pus and be extremely debilitating. This happened to Pete Goss during the Southern Ocean stage of the 1996 Vendee Globe solo round the world race. He had to incise his wound with the aid of a shaving mirror, while under radio guidance from a shoreside doctor. Goss survived the ordeal, but early aspiration with a syringe and needle, then binding and a course of antibiotics is a simpler, less painful course of action.

Eyes, ears and mouth

Treatment: A foreign body in the eye can be removed by irrigation, moving the top lid over the bottom or by flicking it out using a cotton bud. Sometimes the upper lid needs to be turned inside out and if nothing can be seen, then the eye may have to be stained with fluorescein to highlight the foreign body. The eye should then be covered.

Salt-caked eyelids can become chronically inflamed (*blepharitis*) but usually respond to warm, saline bathing. If the problem persists, Cloramphenicol eye ointment can be applied.

Eye infections like conjunctivitis, which is an inflammation and infection of the white of the eye (sclera), is best treated with antibiotic eye ointment but not covered. One unusual case of conjunctivitis was caused by the slime from a flying fish, which struck the helmsman in the face during a Global Challenge race. Helmsmen should wear ski goggles or masks to protect eyes from flying spray – and fish! Artificial tears will cure dry eyes.

Swimmers' ear, an infection of the

The best way to avoid eye infections is to wear goggles.

external auditory canal, is best treated with eardrops and the use of cotton buds to clean the tract.

Cold sores are very common on board and are best treated with acyclovir ointment such as Zovirax. Mouth ulcers respond well to Bongela.

Toothache

Dental problems should not occur if pre-voyage check-ups have been done. The dental kit will allow fillings to be replaced and crowns stuck back on. An abscess is easily diagnosed by tapping a spoon on the affected tooth – the patient will yell when you make contact with the right one!
Treatment: Dental abscesses are treated in a similar way to any deep-seated infection with a course of three antibiotics – flucloxacillin, metronidazole and ciprofloxacin.

Seasickness

The sailor's curse, this is an appaling disability suffered by some during the first few days of any voyage. You feel terrible. You start thinking that you are going to die

– then worry that you are not! The condition is aggravated by cold, wet conditions, tiredness, apprehension and strong smells and tastes. There have been several accounts of crews vomiting for weeks, losing 10kg in weight and becoming dangerously dehydrated, even when taking medication. The problem is that any medication taken orally usually comes back up long before it has had time to be absorbed into the body.

Sickness affects people to varying degrees. Some feel queasy just contemplating a row around a boating lake. Others find they become affected only for a short period. Many succumb only when conditions get rough, and the lucky few remain immune whatever the weather or sickening antics of those around them.

Chronic sufferers should be discouraged from joining a yacht for extended voyages, since they can become a danger not only to themselves, but those around them. Alcohol can also be a contributory factor. There is no doubt that boozing before a sail can disturb the balance organ and make seasickness more likely.

Dr Chris Price, a crew member aboard *Pause to Remember,* made a study of the condition while participating in the 1996/7 Global Challenge. In his report, he wrote:

The subject of seasickness is close to many hearts. My own observations not only come from a medical background but a fellow sufferer, for some of what I say is essentially from personal experience.

Motion sickness (MS) can be defined as an acute onset of vomiting secondary to an inner ear disturbance attributable to motion. This is a considerable over-simplification as it has been well established in naval research that fear, anxiety, fatigue and even boredom can aggravate, if not initiate the condition.

Symptoms usually develop within 30-60 minutes of motion onset, but in some cases can be almost instantaneous. Sickness is often, but not always precipitated by loss of horizon. A first sign might be feeling hot and sweaty or experiencing symptoms of indigestion. In addition, seasickness can manifest itself as lethargy, dizziness and/or a headache.

Another research group studied the malaise during the first Global Challenge race in 1992/3 and concluded that people displayed a great variability in their response to motion. Some were sick and some were not. Most crew volunteers were symptom free after the first ten days of each leg – which might seem a long time to sufferers! In the study, seasickness was greatest when sailing into wind, and least when sailing downwind, though a select few were more prone to sickness when experiencing downwind motion. In addition the study found that motion sickness declined with repeated exposure to conditions. Those that were sick on the first leg of the race from Southampton to Rio were sick again on the next leg to Hobart, but the recovery time shortened.

A separate study by the Human Movement and Balance Unit found that female crew were more susceptible to MS for three days before menstruation and up to day five. This group also found that severe motion conditions can trigger migrainous headache in crews who do not usually suffer migraine.

On a lighter note, a quarter of crews who competed in the 1992/3 Global Challenge Race experienced instability and balance problems when returning to land. My personal experience of this was that such symptoms soon gave way to ones prompted by alcohol intoxication, and that one's brain soon loses its capacity to make any sense of it at all, anyway!

Prevention: *Different remedies work for*

different people, but on the basis that prevention is better than cure, here are a few tips that may help:

- *Start any medication the night before you set sail.*
- *Avoid too much alcohol and strong tastes the night before.*
- *Avoid fatigue and keep warm.*
- *Stay on deck. Get any navigation done before setting out and concentrate on specific tasks.*
- *The Southampton study found steering, general deck duties and lying down hindered sickness.*
- *The study also found that cooking, writing and eating were the most contributory factors.*
- *Keep drinking water – even if you see it again later. This will counter dehydration.*

Treatment: Royal Naval research has demonstrated that Hyoscine products are as good as anything but the related scopolamine delivered from patches stuck behind the ear can also be effective and last for three days. However, wash hands after handling the patch, for they can cause eye contamination. A wide variety of anti-histamine drugs can help but do cause drowsiness. For many sailors, Stugeron is the drug of choice. In resistant cases, injectable or buccal Stemetil or even rectal Motilium suppositories may be needed. Some sailors swear by acupressure wristbands and others on ginger extract. The answer is 'whatever works for you' and it may include a combination of drugs.

Sufferers often want to stay up on deck and in fresh air, but they tend to get cold and wet, and with continuing vomiting, this only increases their heat loss. They are then in danger of developing hypothermia. Far better to return them to their bunk, and leave a bucket to hand. If they

Seasickness can be totally debilitating. A survey among 223 Challenge crew members conducted for Yachting World *magazine during a transatlantic leg, revealed that 62% suffered from it. 78% of these were among the 20-24 age bracket. By contrast only 33% of older crews aged between 60-64 were inflicted, suggesting that the incidence rate decreases with age. Also, more women experienced sickness than men – 73% against 62% for males.*

do stay on deck, then victims should be kept occupied or encouraged to fix their gaze on the horizon, which can help them to regain their inner equilibrium. They should also be clipped on to prevent them from falling overboard and have a buddy keep an eye on them.

On landing ashore, the unsteadiness of 'mal de debarquement' is more amusing than harmful. People just think you have been drinking!

Sleeplessness

Watch-keeping plays havoc with sleep patterns and some crew members, who have not developed the ability of the singlehanded sailor to catnap, have difficulty in adapting to this loss of sleep. This leads to loss of vigilance, irritability and consequent inefficiency. During circumnavigations, the continual changing of time zones and periods of light and dark are a contributory factor. It is worth identifying whether a crew member is an owl and likes to stay up late at night, or a lark and prefers to get up early in the morning, and to modify the watch keeping rota in order to accommodate them.

Fatigue can cause enormous problems for singlehanders in particular. The need for sufficient sleep cannot be over emphasized. Recent research has shown that it is the brain which takes priority over the body. It is amazing how the body can continue functoning when power or cat-napping for 10-15 minutes every hour, as Ellen MacArthur did during her record breaking solo circumnavigation – though she did complain about extreme tiredness throughout the voyage!

Treatment: When sleeplessness becomes an issue, the cycle can be restored by standing down from the watch, turning in and taking a sleeping tablet. Skippers are the most common sufferers because they invariably 'float' between watches and attempt to stay up indefinitely.

As a guide, one should sleep for at least two hours at a time in order to have a complete sleep cycle and guarantee recovery. Ideally, crew should sleep in multiples of two hours for three periods, and given a minimum of six hours once every twenty four.

Chest problems

The Ship Captain's Medical Guide contains excellent spreadsheets with all the important causes of pain in the chest and abdomen with the differing diagnoses based on signs and symptoms.

Heart attacks are not common but Cornelis van Rietschoten, skipper of *Flyer*, was struck down during the southern ocean stage of the Whitbread Round the World Race. Thanks to the immediate attention from a doctor on board, he not only survived, but the team went on to win the race!

Angina pectoris, meaning heart pain, occurs when the blood supply to the heart muscle becomes temporarily inadequate for the work that the heart is doing. The condition can be relieved by rest or the administration of nitrates. Success with the latter will confirm the diagnosis. If the pain is not relieved, then it is possible that they are suffering from coronary thrombosis, where one or more blood vessels to the heart and the muscle are no longer functioning. This is a full blown heart attack. It is best to assume that angina pectoris will progress to a heart attack and treat it as such. The symptoms are a severe central constricting chest pain that can radiate down the left arm and into the neck. Faintness, shock and un-consciousness are other telltale signs.

The main concerns are:

1. Trauma involving the ribs with either damage to the left sided spleen or right sided liver with bleeding.
2. Traumatic pneumothorax, when air gets into the pleural space from broken ribs which, if under tension, can be fatal. This requires immediate relief by passing a large bore needle through the second intercostals space in the mid-clavicular line on the affected side and probable insertion of a chest drain later.
3. Heart attack with severe cramp in the heart muscle, ie angina pectoris, which can presage occlusion of a coronary artery and death of heart muscle ie a myocardial infection.

Treatment: It is important to get the patient into a comfortable position in bed unless shocked, to reassure them and administer morphine for pain relief, as well as oxygen if it is available. It is also customary to give aspirin in a small dose to thin the blood and prevent extension of the clot. With older crew it is suggested that clot-busting drugs should be included in the medical kit. Occasionally, cardiac arrest will occur and then full CPR will be required.

Abdominal problems

Constipation and the often accompanying piles are time honoured sea going diseases. They can be very distressing but when the bowels eventually open it is the nearest thing a man will come to knowing what childbirth is like! To avoid these problems in the first instance simply drink plenty of fluids *at all times.*

Treatment: Relieve constipation with glycerine suppository or a sliver of soap placed up the rectum. Piles are best treated by washing the bum regularly using baby wipes (not rough toilet paper), ointment and suppositories.

Diarrhoea

Outbreaks of diarrhoea and vomiting are often encountered soon after stopovers. Treatment relies on hydration, anti-emetics to stop vomiting, and anti-diarrhoeals such as Stemetil and Imodium to reduce bowel actions. Occasionally, an antibiotic like ciprofloxacin may be needed.

The most serious conditions include appendicitis, gall bladder infection and pelvic inflammatory disease in women, accompanied by infection and fever. It is no longer necessary to remove appendices unless performed at least six months before a voyage because this condition will respond to conservative management.

Blunt trauma to the abdomen, apart from damaging the liver and spleen, can lead to a ruptured gut or torn pancreas. Table 4 (page 177) highlights two cases who were dangerously ill with peritonitis. The intestinal obstruction that afflicted a Volvo Ocean Race crewmember was most likely caused by large quantities of freeze dried food, constipation from a poor intake of fluid and profound dehydration.

Treatment: The conservative management is the same in each case. Rest the gut by sucking gastric contents from the stomach via a nasogastric tube, maintain hydration with intravenous fluids (2 litres per day) and give two broad-spectrum antibiotics, one by injection and metronidazole added per rectum. This regime will sustain the patient for 3-5 days until evacuation. In extreme cases, extra intravenous fluids may have to be organised either by air drop or from other vessels in the area.

Backache, bruises, strains and sprains

These are the most common problems for the medic. Back problems and boats do not go well together, though interestingly, many of these injuries occur off watch when crew members are in light, non-protective clothing.

Treatment: The most useful treatments in the medical kit are oral non-steroidal anti-inflammatory drugs, sprays and ointments for applying to the affected areas. The medic should learn and practise basic strapping techniques for fingers and joints and ensure that the yacht has a supply of elastic supports for the lumber region, knees, elbows and ankles.

Cystitis and urinary tract infections

Maintaining a high fluid intake can prevent infections in the urine. This is a more common disease in women who have a shorter urethra and are notoriously bad at maintaining their fluid balance. In the Royal Navy, Chief Petty Officers working in the sick bays have a pet phrase:

'Keep it clear laddie' ie drink enough fluid to keep the urine pale and copious. The onset is often sudden, and marked by a 'burning' sensation when passing water. It is also associated with an ache over the pubis, which may radiate up and down from the loin, indicating an ascending infection into the kidney substance (pyclonephritis). There may also be evidence of a fever.

Treatment: Drink lots of fluids, coupled with a course of painkillers and antibiotics. Trimethoprim is the drug of choice and should be taken for 5-7 days.

Sexually transmitted diseases (STDs)

Venereal diseases have long been a problem among sailors. Alcohol fuelled runs ashore after long periods at sea can lead them to losing their inhibitions and much more. The advent of AIDS and the threat of contracting HIV has emphasised the importance of warning crew members against casual sex and always using condoms. Any request for an HIV test will alert the medic to the possibility of other more common STDs such as non-specific urethritis (NSU), gonorrhea (GC), and syphilis, which mercifully is now much less prevalent.

The telltale signs for any form of urethritis or gonorrhea is a discharge from the penis a few days after intercourse, accompanied by a burning sensation on passing water. Any lesion on the penis or an unexplained rash after intercourse can also be venereal in origin. Female crew members can be infected too, but the signs and symptoms are far less obvious.

Treatment: The medical chest carries a wide range of antibiotics to treat STDs and these should be marked appropriately. Crabs or pubic lice indicate sexual activity and should be treated with malathion, which is also useful in treating scabies and head lice.

Conclusions

This rather daunting chapter on problems at sea should not curb enthusiasm for sailing the oceans. Countless yachts have completed gruelling round the world races without any trouble, and some well known single-handers have carried little more than a few plasters and a tub of Vaseline! Nevertheless, a well trained medic, a comprehensive medical kit, and an experienced shore support team will give the crew the security and confidence that if anything should befall them, then the best treatment will be available.

Whether your yacht is going around the world, or overnight to Cherbourg, the need for checks and a crew safety briefing are just the same. The skipper is responsible for the safety of the vessel and her crew.

Around the buoys

It doesn't matter if it is around the buoys, or simply working to be first to reach port in a cruise in company, competition sharpens skills and injects fun in what can otherwise become a somewhat monotonous voyage for those crew members with little to do on board.

Preparation and practice are the keys to performance, but it is pre-race planning that most often determines winner from also-ran. There is rarely little to divide the top ten yachts at any major regatta as far as performance is concerned, and the silverware invariably goes to the crew that has done the most to bone up on likely weather patterns and local conditions as well as put in that final practice time that makes teamwork needle sharp.

Luck plays its part too, but over a series

of races or a long distance course, this element has a habit of balancing out. Those who do their homework before racing – charting tidal streams, spotting wind bends and other local trends – are likely to minimise the bad breaks and turn good luck to its fullest advantage.

Checklist

- Liferaft/flares and other compulsory safety equipment
- Lifejackets for all crew
- Safety harnesses for all crew
- First-Aid kit
- Oilskins for all crew
- Food and water
- Engine fuel
- Tool box
- Sails
- Battens, including spares
- Spinnaker/jockey poles
- Sheets and guys
- Anchors and warps
- Winch handles
- Spare shackles and snatch blocks
- Sail ties and seizing wire

Navigator's checklist

- Latest weather forecast
- Charts
- Chart work implements – parallel rule, plotter, dividers, pencils, erasers etc
- Binoculars
- Hand-bearing compass
- Course, any sailing instructions and waypoints plotted
- Time of high and low water
- Working radio frequencies noted

Offshore races

Knowledge of local winds, lobster pots, shallows, strong eddies and other useful local pointers can often be gleaned from local sailors at the yacht club bar. However, this is no substitute for the hours put in to sailing around the course area to build up your own detailed picture.

Take with you a tidal atlas and local charts to pick out prominent landmarks and buoys and check the tidal streams against their predictions. Where courses are likely to be sailed round fixed navigation marks, check their shape and distinguishing marks to ensure easy recognition when racing. Never rely solely on charted positions and descriptions, for this information is not infallible and vital minutes can be lost when all eyes have to be diverted to search for an elusive mark camouflaged by the surrounding coastline. If the mark was checked beforehand, then all on board will have the confidence to continue driving the

yacht without loss of concentration, knowing that they are going in the right direction, even though the buoy may not be sighted until the last moment.

Unless the course area is set several miles offshore, the land will invariably influence the wind. Check its direction when leaving harbour and again at the course extremities for any variations. A sail along the coastline may also reveal bends in the airflow, particularly where there are folds in the landscape. In many sailing areas, the wind direction is known to swing progressively through the day. It is essential that you know this when it comes to deciding which side of the course is likely to be favoured during the beat, reach and running legs.

Back at the mooring, sit down with the crew to analyse your findings:

- Did the tide turn as predicted?
- How strong was the stream?
- Were there any back-eddies close inshore that might prove beneficial?
- Did sea conditions vary greatly around the course?
- Were any significant changes to the wind noted?

The more practice put in around the course, the better. If new crew members are coming on board for the first time, the accepted sail changing routines have to be explained and rehearsed. Just one slip can cost several boat lengths, which may in turn be all that divides first from second, or worse!

Anchor a fender close to a fixed mark so that the helmsman and tactician can practice their starting routines. A series of timed runs to the line, crossing at full speed just as the imaginary cannon fires, does most to help equate distance against boat speed, and once that judgement is proved right, the confidence this instills does most to ensure a first rate start.

Final preparations

Morale onboard can be given a severe jolt if, minutes before the start, an essential chart, sail, or even the sailing instructions, are found to have been left ashore. Whatever the level of competition, a checklist run through before leaving the mooring is essential if last minute panics are to be avoided. That list will be several pages long for an ocean race, and is best checked through the days preceding the start. However, for short offshore races, a standard list can be prepared which, if heat sealed in plastic, can be ticked off with a chinagraph pencil and wiped clean for re-use after each event.

Pre-race checklist:

- Undersides are clean and smooth Rudder, keel and propshaft clear of weed. Special attention should be made to the leading and trailing edges of the foils, for even the smallest imperfections have a marked effect on drag
- Mast and rigging is set up correctly with all locking pins, links, blocks and halyards in position
- Check rig for any signs of metal fatigue
- Race entry instructions have been complied with
- Sails
- Battens (including spares)
- Spinnaker and jockey poles
- Sheets and guys
- Windex
- Class pennant and protest flag
- Winch handles
- Anchor/kedge anchor and warps
- Spare shackles, snatch blocks, seizing wire, sail ties
- Safety harnesses, lifejackets, first-aid kit, foul weather gear
- Food and water
- Fuel and tool box

Navigator's pre-race checklist

- ■ Latest forecast
- ■ Course and sailing instructions
- ■ Last minute check on official notice board for late changes to sailing instructions
- ■ High and low water times
- ■ Charts
- ■ Two stopwatches synchronised with official timepiece
- ■ Radio frequencies noted for official messages, eg recalls after start
- ■ Hand bearing compass
- ■ Binoculars
- ■ Chart work implements

Out on the course

Plan to be out in the race area at least 1 1/2 hours before the start to check the position and bearing of the first mark and note any variations in the wind. After

Team briefing: 40 minutes before the start is the time for the arfterguard to brief the crew to ensure that everyone knows what their role is.

reconnoitring the first mark, check the direction of the wind every five minutes during the sail back to the starting area. Its direction often oscillates at regular intervals – information that may be crucial when it comes to deciding which end of the start line is favoured. When a permanent change is noted, this sometimes signifies a wind bend rather than a swing in direction; the clues come from watching other yachts in the area. If they are heading at differing angles to the wind a bend in the airflow is likely, especially if the course is set close inshore, dictating that the weather mark should be approached from the favoured side. Also, check the wind gusts to see if they are heading or freeing. On squally days the cat's paws on the water heralding their arrival will be the clue for going about to gain most from the freeing tack.

Final checks

40 minutes before the start

While the navigator/tactician is busy planning his strategy for the first leg, the remainder of the crew will be clearing the decks ready for battle. Mainsail and genoa have to be set and other headsails likely to be chosen to match any change in the conditions, placed at the ready. Spinnaker sheets and guys must also be reeved. After hoisting the main and genoa, the first task is to match their set and shape to the conditions, putting in a few tacks to check sailing angles and sharpen teamwork. If performance or pointing ability is less than expected, incorrect sail shape is the most likely cause, unless of course the keel or rudder has picked up weed. When there is a swell, sails need to be set with greater fullness to power the yacht through the chop. If the shape is too flat, performance will be sluggish and the yacht will make excessive leeway.

One word of caution though – if winds are light during these manoeuvres, stay in the vicinity of the starting area, keeping a constant eye on the committee boat for signs of any change to the course.

Once the yacht is fully prepared, the time is ripe to hand out the high protein food and drink so that it is absorbed within the body before the start, to provide that extra pep and energy when it is required most. While eating these rations, use the time to brief the crew on possible strategy as well as check that everyone is fully aware of their duties on board, so that no one is left in the dark when the gun fires. This is also the time to hand over any sails and equipment that will not be required to a nanny or spectator boat.

20 minutes before the start

By now the committee should have finalised the course. After making another check on wind direction to compare with those earlier readings, start line strategy must be planned. Merely luffing head to

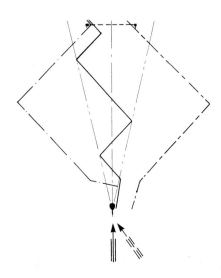

A good race is run by minimising risks. Always keep a middle course up the first beat, monitoring the performance of those on either flank to gauge any advantage.

wind at a point midway between committee boat and outer distance mark to gauge any bias in the line is not enough to decide which end of the start line is favoured. Other factors must also be taken into account.

- Is the current more favourable at one end than the other?
- Are sea conditions rougher at the offshore end of the line?
- Are the gusts stronger at one side of the course?
- Can the first mark be laid in one tack?
- Does the start timing coincide with an expected oscillation in wind direction?

Only when all these questions have been answered can an intelligent assessment be made.

First leg strategy

A race series is won by minimising risk, not by taking miracle-seeking flyers to one side of the course, particularly on the first beat. Unless tide or wind clearly favour one side, it invariably pays to take a middle path up the first beat, while monitoring the performance of those on either flank to gauge any advantages.

If the weather forecast or your own observations indicate that a wind shift is likely, beat up to the mark in a sector 10° towards the favoured side, tacking on the oscillating shifts as they occur. If, after completing half the distance to the weather mark, it is apparent that conditions on one side of the course present a significant advantage it will not be too late to cross over. The lead will doubtless be held by another yacht, but having made a good start and played the percentages you will still be in a challenging position to take the lead later in the race – which is more than can be said for those that gambled on the opposite side of the course!

The start

Accurate timing, clear air and boat speed are the ingredients for a perfect start, but achieving this in the highly charged atmosphere of a big fleet takes practice and a degree of aggression that many helmsmen lack. A moment's hesitation or sign of timidity as other yachts converge on the line, all fighting for pole position during the closing seconds before the gun, is a sure passport to the second row. You will be left with the unenviable task of fighting a path through the choppy wake and wind shadow cast by those ahead. During this final count-down, the crew must be in their positions with someone posted in the bow to warn the helmsman of oncoming yachts hidden from view beneath the genoa, especially after the five-minute gun when the racing rules come into play.

The bowman is also best placed to sight the line during those closing seconds before the start, so it should be his task to ensure that the yacht does not cross early, especially if a Five or One Minute Rule is in operation, earning instant disqualification for line jumpers. The tactician, not the helmsman, should keep an eye on the time, quietly calling out a 15 second countdown during the final five minutes, and at five second intervals during the last minute. It is also sensible to have a second crew member monitoring the time, just in case a mistake is made or the tactician's watch fails at a crucial moment.

Timed run

One of the oldest and most precise methods of hitting that line on cue is the timed run start. This is based on the assumption that a yacht sails at the same

The start of a Global Challenge race from Cape Town. In short offshore races, timing at the start is all important, but in long distance transocean events, being ten seconds late at the start makes no difference over an ocean leg. Far better to have a clear air position and hold to your long term course strategy.

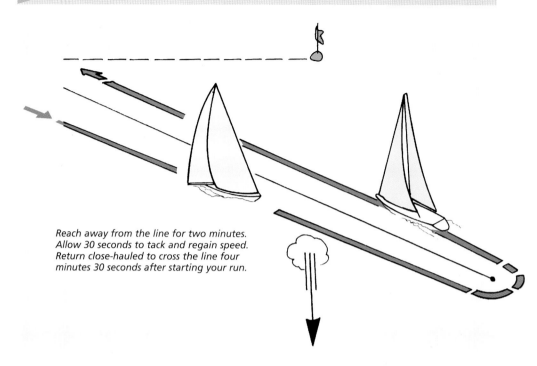

*Reach away from the line for two minutes.
Allow 30 seconds to tack and regain speed.
Return close-hauled to cross the line four
minutes 30 seconds after starting your run.*

speed on a broad reach as it does when close hauled. Having pinpointed the favoured position on the line, the strategy is to sail off on a reciprocal course to the final close-hauled approach for a set time. A two-minute run is often best because it does not take you too far from the line. Allow a further 30 seconds to tack and regain speed and two minutes later you will have your bows on the line. That's the theory anyway!

By practising a series of timed runs in the 20 minutes before the start, the helmsman can get an accurate idea of how much time he needs to allow for tacking in that day's conditions, as well as gauge any effect that the current has on his timing. If a number of yachts are beginning to gather to weather during the reach away from the line, their blanketing effect has to be taken into account by adding an extra 15-30 seconds for the final approach. If a wall of yachts builds up ahead, the knowledge that they will either have to bear off or free sheets to avoid being over the line early, gives you the confidence to keep speed up, driving to weather of any that luff. Never bear off to clip under the stern unless you yourself are early, and then only if you are sure of breaking

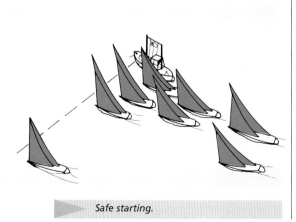

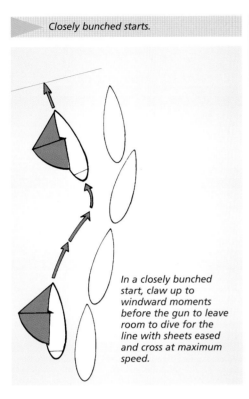

In a closely bunched start, claw up to windward moments before the gun to leave room to dive for the line with sheets eased and cross at maximum speed.

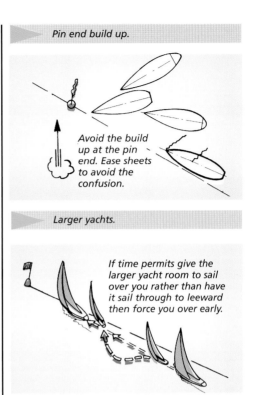

Pin end build up.

Avoid the build up at the pin end. Ease sheets to avoid the confusion.

Larger yachts.

If time permits give the larger yacht room to sail over you rather than have it sail through to leeward then force you over early.

through to leeward, otherwise you will both be late for the line and trapped in the dirty air cast by others. During this final approach, it is imperative to protect your position against yachts to windward. If a larger yacht sailing up from astern threatens your position by blanketing your wind at the start, a hard, purposeful luff when there is still time for it to escape under your stern, will show that you mean to protect your weather position. With the final seconds ticking away fast, the chances are that the helmsman will want to avoid a skirmish, and take the easier course offered to him.

If other yachts are approaching the line on a parallel course, claw up to windward as far as possible during the final seconds, to leave a gap to leeward in which to dive with sheets eased slightly, and hit the line at maximum speed. Never have sheets pinned in hard during the the first minute

of the race. Speed through the water is far more important than pointing ability when striving to get ahead of the fleet into clear air. Only when that is achieved should sails be progressively inched in to achieve that optimum tacking angle.

Port end start

When conditions favour a port end approach to the line, those attempting a timed run on starboard tack are likely to be overwhelmed by the rest of the fleet reaching down the line. It is far safer to sail down the line on starboard with the fleet protecting your weather position that point up in the final seconds before the gun. To avoid the build up of yachts that invariably arrive at the pin end, ease sheets 1½ minutes from the start to distance yourself from the inevitable confusion that occurs, for a gap will almost certainly appear ahead, allowing you to build up speed again before hardening up to cross the line.

It is imperative to protect your weather position while reaching down the line during the closing minutes before the start by luffing up early to discourage any yachts from sailing past to weather. However, when larger yachts threaten your position in a tightly bunched situation, the decision to luff must be weighed against the chances of being forced over the line early by this or other yachts to leeward. Timing is the critical factor. If there is still a minute or so to run before the start, it is often better to encourage the yacht to pass to windward by first bearing off, then luffing up into clear air from under their stern, rather than have them duck under and force you over the line early.

A well timed port tack start close to the pin may work well in club races where competition and numbers are low, but it is a courageous act that many would regard not worth the risk in a highly competitive fleet – and, in this game of percentages, undue risk is to be avoided if consistent winning is the ultimate aim.

Likewise, when the line is heavily biased to port or starboard, it is far safer to avoid the bottlenecks at the favoured end by planning your start a little way down the line to be sure of clear air, especially where smaller yachts are concerned.

However good your starting technique, bigger brethren will inevitably overwhelm your position once the gun has fired.

Smaller boats are always at a disadvantage immediately after the start. However bad the disturbed air, though, it invariably pays to stick with your original plan, tacking in phase with the shifting wind, and taking advantage of any yachts ahead and to leeward, to fend off potential interference from other competitors on port tack.

Off-wind starts

This is when timing becomes critical, for, unlike a windward start, it is impossible to slow down if wind or current threaten to push you across the line early – and beating back against the tide to answer that recall without any rights on the oncoming fleet is a move that no one relishes.

A down wind start calls for a number of practice starts during the final 20 minutes before the gun fires to perfect timing and team work and to get the spinnaker set and pulling on cue. Racing yachts have an almost level performance when it comes to running dead down wind, so the first across the line in clear air, free from the blanketing effects of the fleet behind, is more likely to hold that advantage to the next turning mark.

If a compass bearing taken along the

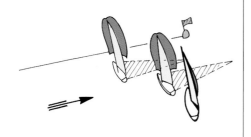

Leeward end starts.

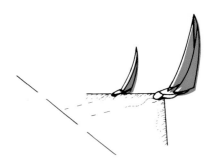

Smaller yachts and starting tactics.

Playing the shifts.

line before the start is monitored during the final approach this knowledge gives the helmsman confidence to be very close to the line when the gun fires, especially where a mid-line start is called for. Clear air is the most essential aspect of all good downwind starts, however, so when making a timed run (beating away from the line and returning on a broad reach) the spinnaker should never be hoisted until the last moment to allow total freedom to luff others who may threaten your wind or exploit an opening in the line of yachts. The spinnaker should be hoisted only when the chance of a premature start is extinguished. It is the afterguard that must make this call once they have gained a clear air advantage, but the crew will have the pole set and the spinnaker ready to hoist. They will be at their stations ready to perform a fast set. If there are any hitches at this stage, then any positional advantage gained will be lost.

Reaching starts

In level boat or one-design racing, the golden rule is to start at the leeward end of a reaching start line, for yachts at the pin-end will be sailing a closer and thus faster course to the wind than their opposite numbers to windward. Also, by having the apparent wind further forward, the yacht to leeward is less likely to be affected by the wind shadow cast by other yachts around them. The exception to this rule comes when sailing a small yacht in a mixed fleet for, however good a start, the larger yachts quickly break through, blanketing the wind. The only way to avoid this is to start on the weather side of the fleet, sailing high to maintain clear air before setting a course directly for the next mark once the threat from larger yachts has receded. The only problem with this tactic emerges when the first leg to a starboard hand mark is short, and the large yachts take up station at the windward end of the line in the hope of gaining an overlap advantage at the turning mark. The smaller yacht is then blanketed wherever it starts but some advantage can be gained from the situation by accepting a 'tow' – riding the stern wave of a leading yacht – to pull you through the fleet. This is particularly effective when the apparent wind is between 70^0 and 110^0 aft of the beam.

Around the Course

First beat strategy

The first few minutes after any start should be spent extracting maximum speed from the yacht and getting the crew settled down to the task in hand. Never put in a tack unless you are completely blocked ahead, for far more ground will be lost manoeuvring in the confused wind and wave conditions immediately after the start than by bearing off a few points, easing sheets, and driving clear of the wind shadow cast by competing yachts. Unless conditions change dramatically, never be drawn from your original strategy. If port is the freeing tack and you are on a collision course with another yacht on starboard, give way. It is better to lose two boat lengths bearing away under its stern than tack to leeward and lose the initiative to choose your own course.

The tactician must keep a constant eye on the compass or VMG meter, monitoring the changes and calling for a tack whenever the wind heads more than 5°. The wind plays all manner of tricks and you must learn to differentiate between shifts that head momentarily before returning to their previous direction and more stable changes. The simplest way to avoid being tricked into tacking is to hold a one-minute moratorium after the shift occurs. This not only gives time for the wind to settle, but warns the crew to be ready for a fast tack when the decision is made.

Unless the yacht is equipped with multi-function instrumentation, write the mean compass headings for each tack on self-adhesive plastic sheets stuck on either side of the deck, close to the compass, with a plus sign against the port figure and minus sign against the starboard heading. This gives the helmsman and his tactician a visual reminder that when the compass heading reads above the mean starboard figure (and below on port tack) the yacht is enjoying a freeing wind.

Remember that a gusting wind generally veers in the northern hemisphere thus lifting yachts on starboard, but backs in the southern hemisphere to favour those on port tack. Therefore, crews with the foresight to cross over to the favoured tack as the cat's-paws approach are likely to enjoy an immediate advantage over those who wait for the compass to tell them of the change. In these circumstances that one-minute tacking rule can be dispensed with – but only if this generalisation was borne out during the pre-race check on conditions, and there can be exceptions, especially if the course is set close inshore where wind patterns become confused by the land.

Tidal stream

A current of water across the course adds another important dimension to first leg strategy and variations in strength and direction must be recognised before the start. Remember, strength and direction of the current is certain – the wind is not – so the first yacht to tack towards the favoured side will take a progressive advantage over the fleet. Only a major shift or increase in wind speed will be great enough to counteract even a half knot variation in tidal stream, and in the Solent and many other parts of the world where the current can flow at between three - four knots, this is an essential element to be taken into consideration when race strategy is planned.

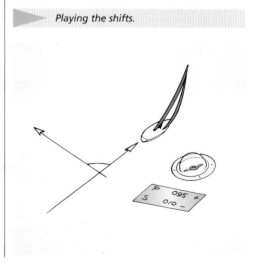

Playing the shifts.

The lee bow myth

It is a common misconception that when the bows are angled to weather of the tidal stream, the yacht is pushed dramatically to windward; unfortunately, this lee bow effect is pure myth. The confusion arises from the fact that when a yacht is faced with an offset tidal stream, the duration of the two tacks alters, for the yacht beating into an adverse current will take longer to cover the same distance than an opposing yacht takes on the opposite tack. But the current is nothing more than a moving carpet and yachts tacking to one side of the course or the other always remain relative to each other. Gains can only be made by exploiting variations in the strength of this current because of the effect this has on the wind over the ground.

Comeback strategy

After a bad start or collision, picking up places is as much a state of mind as anything else. Remain dejected or angry and you fail to spot the opportunities to regain that lost ground. Treat the situation calmly by turning attention to the breaks

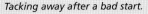
Tacking away after a bad start.

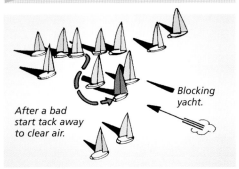
Blocking yacht.

After a bad start tack away to clear air.

A blocker ahead and to leeward will fend off potential interference. When tacking back, position yourself to weather of competitors nearby so that you remain free to play the shifts.

rather than misfortune, and a comeback is assured. After a poor start, the first task must be to break into clear air. A tack on to port, ducking under opposing yachts to break into clear air will lose less ground than remaining boxed in and bunched for much of the first leg, and if the tack back on to starboard can be timed to coincide with the positioning of another starboard tacker ahead and to leeward, it will block other yachts from tacking under your lee bow and disturbing the air.

Clear air is a high priority but so too are the shifts, and while it may be difficult to discern any pattern in the confused conditions midway down the fleet, the sooner you can time the tacks to coincide with the oscillations in the wind, the faster they begin to recover.

When approaching the windward mark the greatest gains can often be made by avoiding the majority of the fleet, all sailing in each other's dirty wind, stacked up on the starboard layline. Far better to approach this layline on port tack just short of the mark, allowing enough distance to prepare the spinnaker hoist, if necessary, crossing under the stern of starboard, right of way yachts to find a hole to tack in. Remember that in the

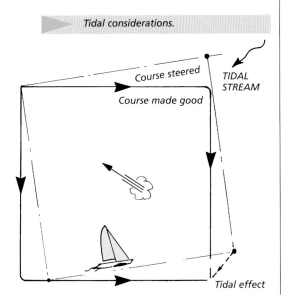
Tidal considerations.

Course steered

TIDAL STREAM

Course made good

Tidal effect

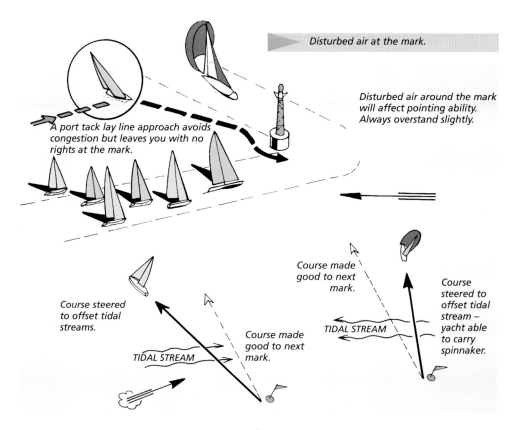

Disturbed air at the mark.

Disturbed air around the mark will affect pointing ability. Always overstand slightly.

A port tack lay line approach avoids congestion but leaves you with no rights at the mark.

Course steered to offset tidal streams.

Course made good to next mark.

Course made good to next mark.

Course steered to offset tidal stream – yacht able to carry spinnaker.

TIDAL STREAM

TIDAL STREAM

disturbed air around the mark, pointing ability will be impaired, so always overstand slightly to avoid being squeezed out at the mark.

The reach

Before rounding the weather mark, the fore-deck crew must know what sails are required for the following leg in time to set the pole and have the spinnaker ready to hoist the moment the yacht bears away. Course and true wind angle are simple enough to compute but an important aspect many fail to appreciate fully until later is the part played in this geometry by the tidal stream. Yet this factor alone can make all the difference between carrying a kite or not.

In order to counter an adverse current 45° off the lee bow, the helmsman will bear away from the rhumb line broadening the apparent wind, an effect that is both strengthened and increased further by the 'current wind' (the yacht's movement through the air caused by the tidal stream). On a course previously judged to be too shy for a spinnaker, the crew could have hoisted a chute the moment they rounded the weather mark and gained valuable ground on less observant crews ahead. Conversely, if the tidal stream is running 45° towards the weather bow, the spinnaker set that looked possible at first sight could be dashed by the fact that the helmsman has to head that much higher into the wind in order to maintain his straight line course.

Where conditions and course are marginal for a spinnaker, it often pays for the leading crew round the weather mark to stay their hand until the second and third yachts have hoisted their chutes and proved they can hold their course. When the apparent wind is so close abeam, less

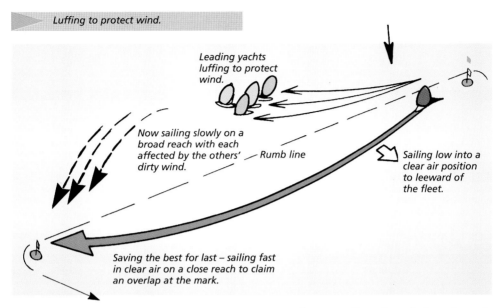

Leading yachts luffing to protect wind.

Now sailing slowly on a broad reach with each affected by the others' dirty wind.

Rumb line

Sailing low into a clear air position to leeward of the fleet.

Saving the best for last – sailing fast in clear air on a close reach to claim an overlap at the mark.

distance is lost for the short period you are two-sail reaching than from a beam-end-broach – which is often the reward for a premature hoist.

The task for the leading crew will be to sail the fastest course, maintaining a blocking position between the fleet and the next mark but for those astern what options are open to improve their position?

Saving the best for last is a principle that should remain foremost in the mind on any reaching leg. By deviating to leeward soon after rounding the windward mark, you not only avoid the inevitable drift to weather of the rhumb line as each of the leading yachts luff into clear air, but the faster sailing angle is kept to the last, giving you the speed to maintain, or claim, an overlap at the gybe mark.

Reaching low after the gybe will rob you of that all important overlap advantage at the leeward mark, so the leading yacht inevitably maintains a position covering

At the gybe mark.

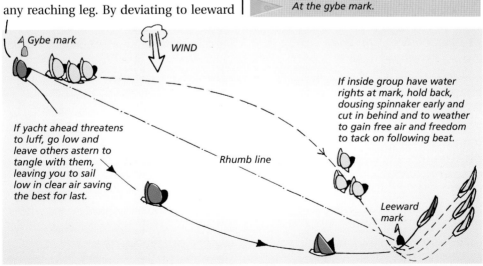

Gybe mark

WIND

If yacht ahead threatens to luff, go low and leave others astern to tangle with them, leaving you to sail low in clear air saving the best for last.

Rhumb line

If inside group have water rights at mark, hold back, dousing spinnaker early and cut in behind and to weather to gain free air and freedom to tack on following beat.

Leeward mark

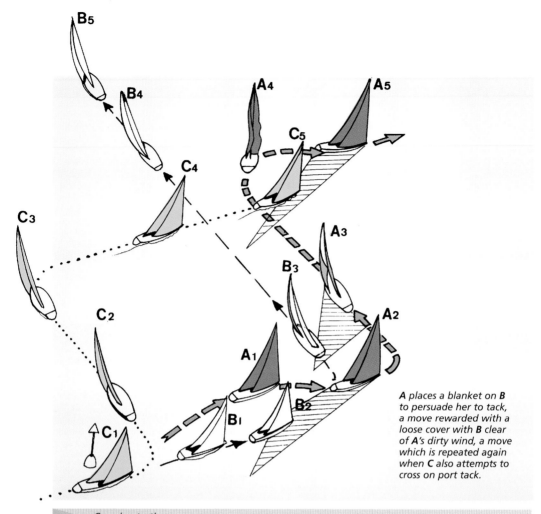

A places a blanket on **B** to persuade her to tack, a move rewarded with a loose cover with **B** clear of **A**'s dirty wind, a move which is repeated again when **C** also attempts to cross on port tack.

Covering tactics.

competitors nearest to weather. For those further astern, however, that final overlap advantage will not be as important as a close rounding of the mark to ensure a weather position on those astern and ahead. If there is a tight bunch making a final approach, the chances are that the luffing that will have undoubtedly occurred during the proceeding leg will in extreme cases have brought the leaders round to the point of almost running down towards the mark – the slowest point of sailing. By saving the best for last, approaching the mark from further to leeward on a broad reach in clear air, there is always the chance of breaking ahead of those further to weather. If an overlap cannot be claimed not all is lost, for by holding back, taking the spinnaker down early if necessary, it may be possible to cut in behind and to weather of the leading bunch, whose crews will be fighting for position around the mark and distracted from watching those catching them up. Often, a space is left close to the mark to slip in and round the mark, and finish up in clear air ready for the second beat.

The second windward leg
With the first round complete and pecking order established, the leading crew must cover their nearest rivals throughout the second beat, maintaining a position midway between the weather mark and the fleet, while those astern try to exploit any advantage from a change in

conditions or tactical slip made by those ahead.

Prior to rounding the leeward mark the tactician must ascertain which is the freeing tack to ensure that his yacht loses no time in getting in phase with the oscillating breeze, even if this means maintaining only a loose cover on those astern. For the fleet leader the situation becomes complicated when his nearest rivals split tacks, making it impossible to cover every eventuality. First instincts are to continue covering the nearest yacht even if this means tacking into a heading shift but this only plays into the hands of the third placed crew. If the yachts are close together and of equal speed, the only means available to the leading yacht to dictate the course from ahead is to place a blanket cover on the crew making the wrong tactical move to force them to go about. Then, like training mice, reward them for making the right decision with a loose cover to give them little or no disturbed wind. They soon get the message. If these herding tactics are played right, the leading yacht will be able to maintain its position midway between the windward mark and its nearest competitors, firmly in control of the situation.

For those further astern, however, the first priority after rounding the leeward mark will be to gain clear wind, get into phase with the oscillating shifts, and wait for those ahead to make mistakes. There is often much to learn from those further to windward, especially in light, fluky conditions when the shifting wind can be difficult to discern. Those leaders make good scouts, pinpointing the lulls and shifting wind.

The run

The downwind leg is no time to sit back and relax once the spinnaker is set; in contrast to the parading reaches, the run provides one of the best opportunities for following yachts to pull themselves up through the fleet. It can be a taxing time for the leading crew, who must not only protect their position from the blanketing effects of spinnakers lined up astern but also stay in phase with the shifting wind. Indeed, playing the shifts is as important downwind as it is on the beat, with strategy a mirror image of the tactics employed on the upwind leg. Thus, to start on the run in phase, take up the opposite gybe to the lifted tack immediately after rounding the weather mark. Monitoring the wind carefully throughout this leg also helps to make the best of the next beat. For instance, if the wind favours the starboard gybe, an immediate gain can be made on less observant competitors by remaining on port tack after rounding the leeward mark – or tacking on to starboard as soon as possible if the port gybe is favoured.

The blanketing effect from a spinnaker casts a wind shadow up to five boat lengths ahead, which the leading crew

Wind shadow.

Shadow cast by a yacht broad reaching can affect the wind for distance of five boat lengths.

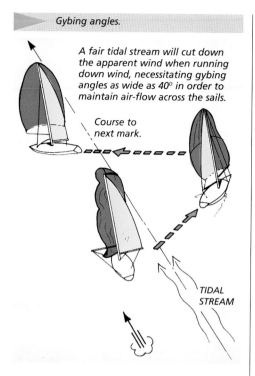

A fair tidal stream will cut down the apparent wind when running down wind, necessitating gybing angles as wide as 40° in order to maintain air-flow across the sails.

Course to next mark.

TIDAL STREAM

must evade at all costs, while at the same time duplicating a challenger's every move in order to maintain a covering position between their opponent and the next mark. On the other hand, those astern have the advantage of being the first to benefit from each fresh gust. They will want to trap the leaders in their shadow, to force them to gybe out of phase with the shifts and break off the cover. Just like chess, these moves and counter moves call for foresight and sharp thinking which, for many, becomes one of the more enjoyable aspects of yacht racing.

Tidal stream is another important factor to take into account on this downwind leg. If the current is favourable it reduces the true wind speed, necessitating wide tacks away from the rhumb line to increase apparent wind, especially in light airs when gybing angles as wide as 40° are justified. In areas like the Solent, where the current can run at three or four knots, this course angle is reduced

considerably. In very light airs the tidal stream can negate the true wind completely, causing the spinnaker to collapse or even blow aback. In these situations the best course is often to lower the running sail and set a lightweight reacher or flat spinnaker to cope with the apparent wind which will be fluctuating in a wide arc.

When fighting an adverse current the apparent wind effect is increased, allowing a much smaller gybing angle, but the effect of wind against tide can also create a short, choppy sea which, in moderate weather especially, may require a wider tacking angle than normal to ease pitching and keep sails filled.

The final beat

After rounding the leeward mark the sole pre-occupation for the leading crew will be to maintain an effective cover over their nearest pursuers, keeping themselves between the finish line and the fleet, copying the movement of their closest rivals as soon as a clear weather advantage can be gained. Never be the first to tack on a header. Rather, wait for those behind to make their move, then tack to cover once a weather overlap can be established to negate any chance of the underdog gaining a weather advantage, should the wind continue to shift round.

If yachts from another class are approaching the finish ahead, keep a wary eye open for any significant shifts in the wind that might favour one side of the course. This is especially important if the chasing group splits tacks, making it difficult to cover both extremes.

However, those leading yachts may also provide a useful pointer to any bias at the finish line. Whatever the case, never overstand the final tack, even if this means breaking cover on those astern, for this only gives away valuable distance – and

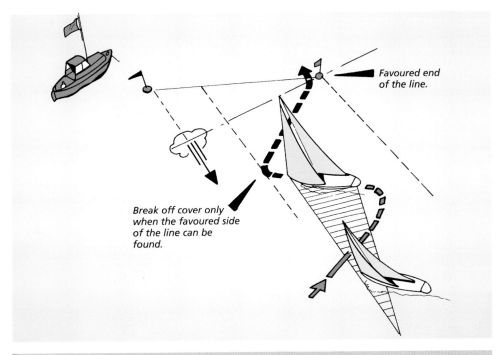

Favoured end
of the line.

Break off cover only
when the favoured side
of the line can be
found.

Favoured end at the finish.

possibly the lead – to a third yacht that may have split tacks to approach the finish unopposed from the opposite side of the course.

For those out of touch with the leading group but still mindful of a respectable finish, the temptation to take a flyer in the hope of a miracle can be strong. But winning a series calls for consistent results and unless there are good reasons to suggest an immediate and dramatic change in conditions, the risks involved are unwarranted. Greater success is likely from playing the shifts accurately while those ahead tack and counter-tack to cover their nearest rivals, often with total disregard for the oscillating wind.

Racing at night

American yachtsman Ted Turner has attracted many nicknames but *Night Raider* was one earned from respect for his ability to distance even the best

competition once dusk falls. 'Let's get 'em at night' was his favourite battlecry at the peak of his sailing career and he invariably did with an infectious drive for boat speed that kept him and his crew keyed up and motivated throughout the dark hours. In trans-ocean events you quickly become accustomed to a night routine, but in shorter overnight races, senses, easily dulled by the soporific effects of sea and night air, coupled with a sudden break in routine, can blunt the sharpest racing edge.

With vision limited to a beam of torchlight, crew work must be instinctive, for if sail setting or adjustments are sloppy during daylight, the night only compounds those problems, resulting in rapid backward steps through the fleet. The dark always illuminates any inefficiencies in yacht layout and crew routine. Faded sail codings, halyard and genoa track markings are indiscernable after dusk, and sails, sheets, sail ties, turtles, spare battens and other essentials always required in a hurry when racing, will remain hidden from view unless an alphabetical list noting storage locations is drawn up.

Crew comfort is important too. Only when fortified with a good evening meal, and a hot drink at the start of a watch followed by a second hot beverage midway through (prepared earlier and stored in vacuum flasks), will the crew give their best during the night hours. Also, temperatures drop at night more dramatically than many envisage, and this slows body movements even further unless the crew come prepared with an extra layer of clothing packed in their sea bags.

Skippers all have their pet watch systems. On *Flyer*, we divided the night into three four-hour watches (which is the longest period I find that most can concentrate effectively in darkness), and then reverted to six-hour shifts during the day so that individual watch times alternated every 24 hours. Among the off-watch, one or two remained on standby, sleeping in oilskins ready for any call on deck to help with sail or course changes etc.

Grabbing any meaningful sleep is difficult at the best of times, but when sailing upwind those off-watch not only have to contend with the continual slamming as the yacht hammers a path through the waves, but swap bunks on every tack to keep their deadweight where it is most useful – on the weather side. They will be disturbed further if the on-watch is continually turning lights on and rummaging around for elusive sails or gear. Hence the need for that alphabetical list showing storage locations. Sail changes too create a good deal of disturbance and, by minimising them, the

chance of mistakes, always greater at night, are also limited. I always believe in holding a ten minute moratorium before calling a change; this gives time to see whether the gust or lull is short-lived, have the standbys ready on deck, and ample time for the crew to become fully prepared for a polished performance.

The wind can change dramatically at night, especially close inshore, and crews that anticipate this and have the next sail ready on deck are likely to make the greatest gains. As in daylight, there can be no let-up in trimming of sails during these night hours. Each of *Flyer's* crew during the 1981-2 Whitbread was issued with a small but powerful waterproof torch (they fitted unobtrusively in the pocket and doubled as a safety light), with which to make continual checks on luffs and leeches to maintain optimum trim. We also made regular sweeps over the deck to spotlight any troubles before they became serious, as well as look for stray lines unwittingly trawled astern.

A torchlight shone on the sails is also one of the best ways to give shipping a visual warning of your presence. A well-lit, well-positioned compass, powerful deck lights to illuminate headsail tell-tales and a Windex are all essential items for racing at night. So too is a well-lit display of electronic sailing instruments, for while 'seat-of-the-pants' sailors can rely on feel and instinct to keep the yacht in the groove during the day, those senses become dulled at night.

- Has the wind changed slightly?
- Has its velocity increased?
- Did boat speed or VMG improve after that sail adjustment?

At night, sailing instruments are the only sure way to monitor the situation accurately. Upwind, the helmsman is helped greatly when compass course can be matched to a light or star ahead, but off wind the apparent wind angle, signalled with most accuracy by the Windex, becomes as important as course angle.

Before any change of watch, the fresh team has to be briefed fully by the retiring crew members on any change in conditions and the yacht's position relative to the surrounding fleet so that tactics and performance are maintained. There is nothing wrong in injecting a little rivalry between the watches to see which can gain most distance from their rivals! This can only help concentration and motivation. Indeed, keeping close tabs on other yachts around, or rather the bearing and intensity of their lights, provides the clues to monitor your own performance and any changes in the conditions.

When the beam from stern lights up ahead suddenly brightens, it is time to think about setting a new course, for the likelihood is that these leading yachts have found a hole in the wind. Likewise, if gains are made on yachts to leeward but lights to weather seem to be losing their intensity, it will probably pay to head up fast because those weakened lights are likely to signify a stronger wind or stream to weather. Continually monitoring immediate rivals through binoculars, checking their relative bearings every 15 minutes to gauge any advantages in course or speed, gives the best chance of spotting changes early – and if positive action is taken immediately and an accurate assessment made, large gains are assured.

Satellite/navigation aids take much of the worry out of sailing at night, and also release the navigator to play a more active role on deck. However, yacht electrics place a heavy drain on batteries, which must be recharged frequently. To avoid disturbing the off watch, limit engine running whenever possible, to 20 minutes each side of the changeover – then give the batteries a full recharge during the day.

ocean passages

14

Final preparations for an ocean passage start from the moment the yacht is commissioned or bought, as it takes months of practice to select and mould a cohesive team, plan logistics for re-supply, tune the yacht and undergo a good work-up period.

Back in the early days of the first Whitbread circumnavigations, crews thought it was enough simply to turn up on the start line. There were no prerequisite qualifying passages, and if a crew had completed the Fastnet Race beforehand, then that was a bonus. Conny van Rietschoten was the first person to bring a professional approach to the sport. Before both campaigns, his *Flyer* yachts covered more than 10,000 miles, including two transatlantic crossings to shake down

the crew and boats. In retrospect, he had both races in his pocket by the time of each start. Now top-level racers have taken this to such extremes, with ludicrously expensive two-boat programmes, that it is little wonder that top level events like the Volvo Ocean Race have attracted so few entries.

With the Global Challenge races, the one-design yachts are well organised, but the crews, many of whom have little more than a burning ambition to circumnavigate the globe at the outset, undergo anything between 1,500 and 5,000 miles of training before the big day. By the time they start, these crews have vastly more experience than many of those pioneering Whitbread racers!

If the plan is extensive cruising, then preparing the boat and crew for any eventuality is of equal priority. Mast manufacturers have enough experience now to design spars that minimise halyard chafe, one of the biggest problems experienced during early Whitbread circumnavigations, but yachts still need a good shake-down voyage to highlight shortcomings like this and with furling and electrical installations, which can be just as problematic.

Logistics

However thorough preparation may be, this effort is all to no avail unless the logistics for re-supplying the yacht at each port of call are given careful consideration. New sails will be required and others may need extensive repairs; there will be rigging to replace, deck equipment, engines and electronics to service. The yacht will also require slipping for painting, if not repairs, and stores will need to be replenished.

Experience gained from early multi-stop races showed us that it was unwise to rely on local sources of supply. It is difficult to match specifications in all parts of the world and this leads to last minute panics and hefty airfreight charges. However, when planned well in advance these essentials – and even the transportation – can be obtained at very advantageous prices which, when taken as a whole, may even undercut local sources of supply.

For his first round the world race, Conny van Rietschoten had two half-size containers filled with spares and equipment to precede *Flyer* to the ports of call. One was sent directly to Auckland, the half-way stop, while the other was shipped first to Cape Town and then on to Rio de Janeiro in time for the final leg. The freeze-dried food for each leg was sent directly to each port of call by the suppliers, and was supplemented by fresh and frozen supplies bought locally. The yacht also had a spare mast held in store ready to be air freighted out to the yacht should the original spar get damaged.

For his second campaign, all equipment and clothing – some three tons in all – was air freighted to each port of call, which cut out much of the duplication necessary when supplies are sent by sea. Also, by routing the crates via Holland each time before onward passage to the next stopover, it was simple job to replenish or change stores as required.

Course strategy

It is the elements, as much as the competition, that determine a trans-ocean race winner, and they can turn life upside down when cruising too! Take a wrong turn on the first stage and you have the rest of the voyage to reflect on the mistake, for the opportunities to regain lost ground are slim. Competition stiffens with every event as crews learn the lesson of past failures, so pre-event planning and course strategy, taking prevailing winds, currents and distances into careful account, has become an important ingredient for success.

Much valid information can be obtained from looking back at the routes favoured by the clipper ships that raced across the oceans a century before. Likewise, a great deal is learned from more recent history and later yacht races, which take into account the improved windward performance of modern designs. The courses across the Atlantic and others around the world have now become such well beaten tracks that the best routes are readily apparent. But the wind holds many surprises, calling for a good deal of knowledge and experience if changes in the weather patterns are to be exploited. Modern technology helps, but weather routers and meteorological information that is now readily available on the Web, coupled with computerised sailing instruments and precision barometers all help to pick your way through the pitfalls. This equipment and information is only as good as the person reading it however, and crews still make the most basic mistakes, steering straight into high pressure zones and on the wrong side of low pressure systems.

With events like the Global Challenge races where the yachts are all equally matched, the weather can play a deciding role in the outcome. Back in 1981, there was no worldwide-web or computer prediction programmes to guide the *Flyer* crew. Instead, Conny van Rietschoten enlisted David Houghton, then the Senior Forecaster at the Meteorological Office headquarters at Bracknell, England, and embarked on an ambitious plan to make a computer study of weather information gained over the past century. They hoped this would highlight regular patterns, particularly around the Azores, Doldrums, South Atlantic and Indian Ocean, and the data, stored on an onboard computer, would then help them analyse the prevailing conditions en-route. What they found was that while weather conditions across the North Atlantic had been well documented for many decades, the same could not be said for other parts of the world, especially the Southern Ocean.

The work was not completely wasted however, as Houghton joined *Flyer* for that year's Fastnet Race and gave the crew a thorough grounding on forecasting weather patterns. During the week long voyage, he schooled them all about nature's quirky ways, and this did more than anything else to limit tactical mistakes later. Indeed, compared with his earlier victory in 1978 when van Rietschoten and his crew got on the wrong side of weather patterns 14 times, they got it wrong just once second time around. Two decades later this experience remains a text book lesson for any crew planning to race or cruise around the world, for while much more information is now readily downloadable from satellite pictures to weather maps, those who disseminate the information best will get the best out of the voyage.

The fastest course

The biggest single factor dividing trans-ocean from offshore racing is the fact that you sail to the wind rather than the shortest course, for large deviations across an ocean are more than offset if Velocity Made Good (VMG) is improved. Ketch rigged yachts have a secret weapon in the form of a mizzen genoa which can be carried in conditions up to force 5 whenever the apparent wind angle swings beyond 55° and will add a knot or more to speed. This alone makes it worthwhile bearing off in marginal conditions, for any increase in distance is more than compensated by the extra speed.

Sailing across oceans, it is better to sail at the most advantageous angle to the wind than to a set course. Before the days of digital electronics, crews determined the best course from a VMG polar diagram showing the yacht's optimum speed around the compass in differing wind conditions. The polar plot opposite was produced for a 65ft yacht, the figures derived from computer predictions and empirical data. Nowadays, a yacht's computerised instrumentation can be programmed to give a live VMG reading for navigators to monitor performance.

Passage notes around the world

Ocean Passages for the World, published by the Hydrographer of the British Navy, is a bible for anyone planning an extended voyage. The book, with its advice on every major trans-ocean sailing route culled from the experience of more than a century of trading under sail, together with its maps depicting weather and tidal streams governing the seven seas, provides an invaluable reference. The one drawback for contemporary navigators is the fact that the book has never been updated to take account of the much improved light weather and windward ability of modern designs, or the better understanding we now have of the world's weather systems. Amid all the good advice within its pages, therefore, there are some anomalies, many of which have been highlighted in recent round the world races.

Another more contemporary reference book is *World Cruising Routes* written by Jimmy Cornell and published by Adlard Coles Nautical. This guide covers nearly 500 of the more popular sailing routes across the world and is geared specifically to the needs of cruising sailors.

English Channel to Cape of Good Hope

The Bay of Biscay

In describing the route favoured by the sailing ships, *Ocean Passages for the World* offers this advice:

On leaving the English Channel at once make westing, as the prevailing winds are from that direction. With a fair wind from the Lizard, steer a WSW'ly course to gain an offing of 10° or 12°W.

If the wind should be from W keep on the tack which enables most westing to be made to get a good offing, and keep clear of the Bay of Biscay, even standing NW until well able to weather Cabo Finisterre on the starboard tack. By making a long board to

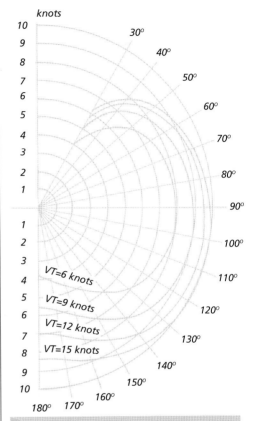

A typical polar plot for a 65ft yacht derived from computer predictions and empirical data, gives the crew a good indication of the design performance.

VMG table listing wind angles and boat speed required to better a straightline course.

Increase in speed required when tacking downwind to match boatspeed when sailing dead downwind.	
Degrees off course when tacking downwind	Percentage increase in speed required
5°	1.01%
10°	1.02%
15°	1.04%
20°	1.06%
25°	1.1%
30°	1.16%
35°	1.22%
40°	1.30%
45°	1.41%
50°	1.56%

the W nothing is lost, as the wind will generally be found to veer, so that a change of wind will be favourable, and even permit a vessel to pursue a course with a free wind; whilst if embayed in the Bay of Biscay, any change of wind to the W would necessitate beating to windward against the current.

It must be borne in mind that the prevailing winds and currents have a tendency to set towards Ile d'Ouessant, and into the Bay of Biscay when S of it. To get well to the W is therefore of the greatest importance. Ile d'Ouessant should, in no case, be sighted.

From 10° to 12°W, shape course to pass Madeira at any convenient distance, giving a wide berth to Cape Finisterre, in passing it, as the current from the Atlantic usually sets right on-shore there.

The book's advice to leave Ile d'Ouessant (Ushant) well to the east is not borne out from recent experiences. If the tides are favourable, cutting inside Ushant can save three or more hours. However it is imperative to remain well west of the rhumb line course to Cape Finisterre, or Fitzroy as it is now called, for quite apart from the adverse current inside the Bay of Biscay, the prevailing south westerly and north westerly airstreams prevent any significant sea breeze building up near the coast.

Fitzroy should also be given a wide berth, making a tack west if necessary, to leave this northern point of Spain at least 70 miles to port – a point proved during the 1981 Whitbread when *Flyer* broke off her duel with the Peter Blake skippered *Ceramco New Zealand*, to sail due west for two and a half hours before turning south again. The result was spectacular. Within 24 hours, *Flyer* was 75 miles ahead of her New Zealand rival after picking up better winds from one of the approaching lows out in the Atlantic that traverse a regular path across the ocean south of Fitzroy,

before sweeping north parallel to the European coastline. The lesson was not lost on Blake who played the tactic in the 1989/90 Race with his ketch, *Steinlager 2*, and gained a one day lead which his crew maintained for the rest of the race.

North east trades

The instruction within *Ocean Passages* to pass Madeira at any convenient distance is barbed advice for, like all the large islands within the Canaries and the whole of the Cape Verde group, it should never be passed on the leeward side. These land masses, and the high mountains of Madeira in particular, disturb the trade winds, creating 20 mile wide vortexes which, as our satellite picture shows, can affect the winds over a 100 mile area.

Once past the Canaries, you can generally expect blissful trade wind sailing almost to the Cape Verde Islands, though as if to show how fickle Mother Nature can be, there have been times when a high pressure system has suddenly developed without warning over Madeira and snuffed out the wind. Then the only option is to beat a course closer to the African coastline, then track south to avoid the worst of the calms.

The Doldrums

This area of frustrating calm dividing the north east and south east trades can hold yachts within its clammy grasp for seven hours – or seven days. Stretching from South America to Africa and varying in width from 150 to 300 miles, the Doldrums is best likened to a pot of boiling water, with the movement of air bubbling up indiscriminately, making it impossible to forecast. The area varies in position from 10° to 18°N and is controlled by two high-pressure systems to the north and south. It is the air from these, converging erratically into the Doldrums that rises up into cells of

This MetoeSat photograph provides the clearest picture of two parallel vortex streets extending some 800km downwind of the Canary Islands, illustrating the need to keep to windward of mountainous areas in the Trade Wind belts.

cumulonimbus cloud before condensing in these hothouse conditions and creating the tropical rainstorms, which are so particular to this area. This is the only refreshing aspect of sailing in these parts, but while the storms can lead to wind, it rarely lasts for long. It is possible to sail straight through unheeded when the northern high has reached its southern limit and begins to move north again, but if you reach the area when the high is at its northern extremity, it can hold you in its grasp for a week, drifting south with you. The answer is to track the movement of the two highs for a week and judge from this a longitude that best avoids their calming influence.

Equator and South Atlantic high

Ocean Passages for the World recommends:

In considering where to cross the Equator it is necessary to bear in mind that if a vessel crosses far to the W there will be a lesser interval of doldrum to cross, but it may be requisite to tack to weather the coast of South America, and these crossings vary during the year, as the direction of the southeast trade wind is more S'ly when the sun is N of the Equator than when S of it.

After passing Archipelago de Cabo Verde, stand S between the meridians of 26° and 29°W, being nearer 26°W from May to October, and nearer 29°W from November to April. The Equator should be crossed at points varying according to the season, as follows: In July, August and September, the S'ly winds will be met between 10° and 12°N. On meeting them, steer on the starboard tack so as to cross 5°N between 17° and 19°W. Go round then on the port tack, and cross the Equator, as in May and June, between 25° and 23°W. In October, November and December, the S'ly winds will be met between the parallels of 8° and 6°N. On meeting them, steer so as to cross 5°N between 20° and 23°W, then take the tack which gives most southing and cross the Equator between 29° and 24°W.

From the Equator southward. Having crossed the Equator as recommended, stand across the southeast trade wind on the port tack, even should the vessel fall off to about 260°, for the wind will draw more to the

The Doldrums are controlled by two high pressure systems and it is the air from these converging into the Doldrums that rises up and then condenses, creating the tropical rainstorms characteristic of the area.

The Doldrums

East as the vessel advances, and finally to due E at the S limit of the trade. When in the vicinity of Penedos de Sao Pedro e Sao Paolo frequent astronomical observations should be made, the current should be watched and allowed for, and a good lookout should be kept, as these rocks are steep-to, and can only be seen on a clear day from a distance of about eight miles. The same precautions are necessary if passing westward of Ilha de Fernando de Noronha, when approaching the dangerous Atol das Rocas.

This advice from the clipper ship days takes no account of the high pointing and light-wind performance of modern designs which have proved in successive round the world races that a windward course, bucking the southeast trades, to be the faster route. The decision on which route to follow has to be made before the Doldrums, for yachts planning to take the windward route south must make as much easting as possible during these calms to gain a favoured windward position in the trades. The tactic is to continue on port tack until the wind heads sufficiently to make the long starboard tack south.

Two weeks of continual pounding with decks heeled at 30° is tiresome, for with sheets cleated and few sail changes to perform in the steady winds, it is left to the helmsman to get the best performance out of the boat. Motion can be eased by sailing at 40° to the wind with sheets cracked off, and boredom is relieved if a rota system is introduced to provide one or more crew members with a 24-hour break, each day for the rest of the voyage. Any yearnings for the easy reaching conditions further west are countered by the fact that those who choose to sail the extra 1,000 miles of the clipper route remain further away from the Cape of Good Hope, a gap that only increases the further south you sail.

The effects of the South Atlantic high begin to be felt between 25° and 30°S and once within its vicinity, the tack on to port can be made. The centre of the high is monitored from the barometer readings and changes in the wind. The closer you sail towards it, the higher the pressure and lesser the wind. By passing to the east, the modern designs can sail close to its centre while still maintaining good speed, for the apparent wind is strongest to windward. It then becomes a fairly easy matter to maintain a position relative to the high within this windward air stream; tacking away if necessary should the centre threaten to sweep overhead, or sailing towards it if the centre starts to move away.

During the 1981/2 Whitbread Race, the position of the high to the west of *Flyer* was producing light reaching winds which lessened the apparent wind, and thus boat speed, so her crew decided to tack south for two and a half hours towards the centre of the High to regain their windward course towards Cape Town – a move that gained them two days on their rivals, who were left totally becalmed.

Another route down to the Cape is to stand in towards the Gulf of Guinea after passing through the Doldrums. Several yachts have tried it in the past without success, and one crew who ventured a little too close to land were arrested as spies by an Angolan patrol boat which escorted them into Luanda!

Closing on Cape Town, *Ocean Passages for the World* warns of the strong northerly current often experienced after passing the Greenwich meridian. This is best countered by staying a little to the south of the rhumb line.

Cape Town to Australasia

The mountain range that shields the waters from Table Bay to the Cape of Good Hope creates all manner of turbulence and sets a premium on local knowledge. Whenever a westerly wind prevails in Table

Bay, it pays to tack inshore towards Granger Bay to gain from a lift in the wind, then rock-hop to Sea Point and Llandudno. Here, the wind fanning down the valley blows south east, so you must stand up to two miles off the coast to avoid being becalmed inside Hout Bay, then remain within five miles of the coastline for the remaining distance to the Cape to avoid the adverse Agulhas current, which runs at up to three knots.

When the wind in Table Bay is southeasterly, then it pays to remain offshore past Clifton and Sea Point before taking an inshore course from Llandudno onwards.

After rounding the Cape, *Ocean Passages for the World* suggests:

Vessels are recommended to pick up the E-bound track from Cabo de Hornos at the point where it is met by the track from the North Atlantic bound to the Indian ocean, namely in about 40°S, 20°E. There is but little difficulty in passing the Cape of Good Hope E-bound at any time, though a greater proportion of gales will be met with from April to September, the winter season.

From October to April, E'ly winds prevail as far S as the tail of Agulhas Bank (about 37°S), with variable but chiefly W'ly winds beyond it. In May and September, at the tail of the bank E'ly and W'ly winds prevail, extending sometimes close in to the coast. Should a SE'ly wind be blowing on leaving Table Bay, stand boldly to the SW until the W'ly winds are reached or the wind changes to a more favourable direction. In all cases when making for the 40th parallel S of the Cape of Good Hope, steer nothing E of S so as to avoid the area SE of the tail of Agulhas Bank, where gales are frequent, and heavy and dangerous breaking cross seas prevail.

The course across the Southern Ocean to Australasia has proved a real poser for yacht racing crews in the past, as distance is only part of the equation. Navigators have to balance the shorter distance of the smallest navigable great circle route around the Antarctic continent (approx 60°S) against the extreme cold, continual ice and the strong possibility of running into unfavourable headwinds. The advice proffered by *Ocean Passages for the World* is:

Vessels bound to Australian ports would make the passage at about the parallel of 39° or 40°S, but those bound to Tasmania or New Zealand, would do so at between 42° or 43°S, especially from October to March. Between 39°S and 43°S the winds generally blow from a W'ly direction, and seldom with more strength than will admit of carrying sail. In a higher latitude the weather is frequently more boisterous and stormy; sudden changes of wind with equally wet weather are almost constantly to be expected, especially in winter. Ile Amsterdam may be seen from a distance of 60 miles in clear weather.

In summer many vessels take a more S'ly route, some going as far S as 52°S, but the steadiness and comparatively moderate strength of the winds, with the smoother seas and more genial climate north of 40°S, compensate by comfort and security, for the time presumed to be saved by taking a shorter route. Tempestuous gales, sudden violent and fitful shifts of wind,

Weather fax map of the Southern Ocean showing the two sets of lows that regularly traverse the Southern Ocean in an easterly direction.

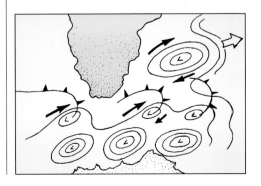

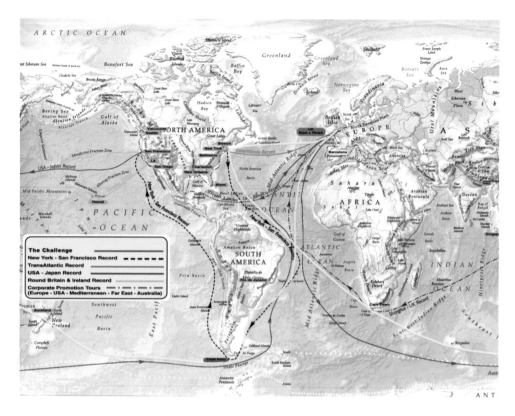

accompanied by hail or snow, and terrific and irregular seas are often encountered in the higher latitudes; moreover the islands in the higher latitudes are so frequently shrouded in fog that often the first sign of their vicinity is the sound of the surf beating against them.

There are two sets of lows that regularly traverse the Southern Ocean in an easterly direction. The larger of these centre over the icy wastes of Antarctica, while smaller, more vigorous and faster moving secondary lows follow a route further to the north. Uninterrupted by land, these create the very strong winds in the notoriously named latitudes – the Roaring Forties and Screaming Fifties. As with all lows in the southern hemisphere, which circulate in a clockwise motion, yachts to the north benefit from strong westerlies while those to the south face adverse headwinds – and a yacht has only to be caught once on the bad side of a low to drop 250 miles on the fleet, which is more than the distance they save by taking a shorter great circle course.

Those crews that have gone well south in the past have gained nothing from sailing the shorter distance, for, in addition to the unfavourable winds, the ice hazard and extreme cold made it impossible to race their yachts with any efficiency. The New Zealand yacht *Outward Bound* went down as far as 52°S only to find her sails and reefing lines became so stiff with ice that it was impossible to reef. 'Lifelines became encrusted with ice two inches thick, winches could only be freed by pouring hot water over them and our sails were always full of snow' was skipper Digby Taylor's comment.

Two yachts, *Berge Viking* and *Swedish Entry* ventured even lower – to 56°S – in the hope of cutting the distance sailed, but conditions became so cold that water breaking on the deck froze instantly. 'We had icebergs all around us,' said Pede Lunde, the skipper of *Berge Viking*. 'It was just impossible to sail the boat hard or set a spinnaker with the worry of all that ice about,' he added.

Ice is certainly a hazard, and *Ocean Passages for the World* warns:

Icebergs are most numerous SE of the Cape of Good Hope, and midway between Kerguelen Island and the meridian of Cape Leeuwin. The periods of frequency vary greatly. It may happen that while ships are passing ice in lower latitudes, others, in higher latitudes, find the ocean free of it. The lengths of many of the Southern Ocean icebergs are remarkable, bergs of 5 to 20 miles in length are frequently sighted S of the 40th parallel, and bergs from 20 to 50 miles in length are far from uncommon.

It may be gathered from numerous observations that bergs may be found anywhere S of the 30th parallel, that as many as 4,500 bergs have been observed in a run of 2,000 miles, that estimated heights of from 240m to 520m are not uncommon, and that bergs of from 60 to 82 miles in length are numerous.

Global warming has had the effect of increasing both the number and spread of icebergs. One large berg confronted the Global Challenge crew off the River Plate soon after the start of the second leg of the 1992/3 race. Nowadays, race organisers invariably include waypoints within the course across both the Indian and Pacific oceans to stop crews from venturing too far south.

It is important to monitor the weather charts for two weeks or more before entering the Southern Ocean, to find the line being taken by the secondary lows that traverse the ocean just above the 50th parallel. It takes some experience to read these weather maps for, with few weather stations and so little shipping in this part of the world, their accuracy can vary by as much as 2° of latitude. The charts are useful in showing general weather patterns as they approach, but detailed local analysis is better observed from the prevailing conditions.

The first sign of an approaching low is always marked by a fall in the barometer, followed by a backing wind. The further north this swings the nearer you are to the centre of the low. The skill comes in judging this right. Initially, it is tempting to bear off 10° to keep the spinnaker up, but it is far better to replace the chute with a reacher than steer low and face the strong possibility of having the low sweep to the north of you and face head winds on the wrong side.

Once clear of the coast it pays to sail due south to escape the Agulhas current and benefit from the strong westerly air stream. *Flyer* made the mistake of holding too far north during the 1977/8 Whitbread, following the track taken by *Sayula* and *Pen Duick VI* in the same race four years earlier, which led them straight into headwinds generated by the Indian Ocean high which extended quite far south that year. Those that chose to head south forged ahead under spinnakers and within 12 days, *King's Legend*, *Flyer's* great rival, had gained a 340 mile advantage.

Compass error

Sailing so close to the magnetic pole, the compass card dips and becomes so sluggish that it is hard to steer by in this part of the world. Some manufacturers produce special compasses for use in this southern extremity with a blob of solder on the underside of the card to counter the dipping effect from the earth's magnetic field. The card swims in a low viscosity oil to improve sensitivity. It is a real problem for yachts fitted with a compass balanced for the northern hemisphere since the magnetic pull can lead vessels well off course, so regular position checks are essential.

The Tasman Sea

Ocean Passages for the World recommends:

It is often necessary and in heavy W'ly weather, desirable, to make the passage down the W coast of Tasmania at from 120 to 250 miles from the coast, and often at the same distance round the S end of the island.

From the Indian Ocean, for New Zealand ports, it is normal to leave the trans-ocean route in about 110°E and to proceed S of Tasmania in 45°S to 47°S. Both in summer and winter, if bound to Auckland proceed round the N point of New Zealand.

As those who competed in the 1998 Sydney Hobart classic will readily attest, The Tasman can produce nasty steep swells that can break boats, as well as crews. Even with prevailing north westerly winds, the Tasman is a confused, uncomfortable sea but when a low pressure system is centred off the north east coast of Australia, it generates strong NE headwinds for the final 1,500 miles all the way to Cape Reinga on New Zealand's northern point.

Across the Pacific

Ocean Passages offers two courses to Cape Horn during December and February. The first joins up with the trans-ocean route at about 51°S, 148°W then follows this parallel to 115°W before inclining gradually south to round Islas Diego Ramirez and Cape Horn. The alternative is the shorter, faster, but colder, route down to between 54° and 55°S, but the book warns:

This course would, clear of ice, and with favourable weather, doubtless ensure the quickest passage, as being the shorter distance, but experience has proved that at nearly all times of year so much time is lost

Compasses are badly affected by the strong pull of the magnetic south pole and instruments must be balanced to compensate.

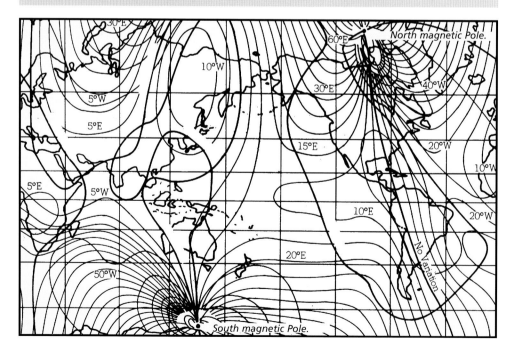

at night and in thick weather, and even serious danger is incurred on account of the greater quantities of ice normally met within these higher latitudes, that a parallel even as far N as 47° has been adopted with advantages. It is believed that a passage made between 47°S and 50°S will provide steadier winds, smoother water and less ice, and that a quicker passage may be expected in better weather, and with more security than in a higher latitude.

Icebergs are certainly more prevalent on this leg than in the Indian Ocean, and have caused several scares in recent races. Sailing through fog, *Traite de Rome* came up against a giant iceberg less than 200m ahead of it and her crew were forced to make an all-standing gybe to avoid it. In that race a number of yachts, including *Flyer*, sailed as low as 60°S, only to position themselves on the wrong side of several lows. Four years later, *Flyer* followed a higher course, dropping no lower than 56°21'S and, despite the continuing low quality of the weather charts, was caught only once in the calm centre of a low, when closing on the Horn.

Most of the sailing rules governing the Indian Ocean passage also hold true for the Pacific. Leaving Auckland it pays to head south immediately into the stronger westerly air stream, which normally begins to build up once the 40th parallel has been crossed. A rhumb-line course west of Chatham Island has proved to be the optimum course, for those that have strayed east have always lost out badly in the light airs that often prevail there.

Another trap occurs during the approach to Cape Horn, for boats that get too far south can finish up with a cold and very uncomfortable beat back up around this notorious headland.

The weather around the Horn where the grey-green waters of the Pacific mix with the brown Atlantic stream is almost always bad, blowing a full gale most days and a storm that can build up to hurricane force for three days every three months or so. Beware too, the deep cut between the mainland and Staten Island where the bottom plunges down to 176 fathoms within metres of the shore. Here, when the wind opposes the strong southerly running tidal stream, severe seas can build up and make for a very rough ride. The slamming can be so bad that it has forced Whitbread and Volvo crews to dowse their spinnakers and run under headsails through this narrow channel.

Once into the Atlantic, *Ocean Passages for the World* recommends:

At all times of the year stand N with the Falkland Current between Falkland Islands and Tierra del Fuego, and carry it up the coast, with the prevailing W'ly winds, to Bahia Blanca or Rio de La Plata.

The Falklands current is at its strongest along the 200m sounding so it pays to stay east of the rhumb line, a course that can also provide a windward advantage on the final approach to the River Plate region, where north-easterly winds predominate. The routing books talk of prevailing westerly winds in this area, but experience has shown that headwinds are just as likely, during January at least. You must also keep a weather eye open for the 'Pampero Limpio' – a local storm that sweeps up from the south to provide the unusual experience of sailing with spinnaker set straight into head seas.

Once past the River Plate competitors are faced with the adverse flowing Brazil current which can set a yacht back by 20 miles a day. The charts show a counter current close inshore but during the months between November and April, this northerly set is spasmodic and there is also little wind here. Far better to give the South American coast a wide berth and head north around 300 miles to the east.

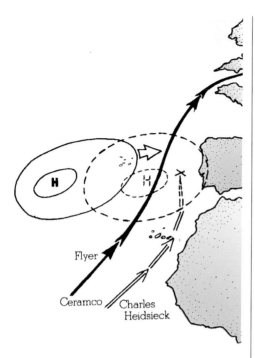

The key to plotting a course around the Azores High is to monitor its movement for a week beforehand. If it is moving east, then you need to stay well west as Flyer and Ceramco New Zealand did during the Whitbread race. Charles Heidsieck, by contrast, took an inshore track and remained trapped in light airs for a week. The delay cost her crew overall victory.

South America to the English Channel

With both the Doldrums and the Azores high to contend with, the final stage of these circumnavigations can be a nightmare for tacticians, who must not only cope with these areas of calm, but also attempt to cover their rivals to the finish. The game is to keep them positioned between yourself and the high-pressure systems, in the hope that they are first to suffer should these areas extend. But then, if you too become ensnared, the opportunity opens for others further astern to strike a course well to the west of the islands and take the lead.

After leaving the River Plate region give the area of calms around Rio a wide berth by steering a north easterly course 300

miles off the coast and cross the Equator somewhere between 28°-33°W. Any further east and you run the risk of running into the Azores high if this is moving that way. This was the fatal mistake made by Alain Gabbay and his French crew on *Charles Heidsieck* who committed themselves early to an easterly track and were then unable to take avoiding action when the high moved across their path.

Instead, your course should be governed by the position of the Azores high. If it is centred at its most western extreme, then you know it is only a question of time before it begins its erratic path eastwards. The key is to track its position on a daily basis for a week or more before you reach the area. If it is possible to squeeze past the high before the gate shuts, well and good. If not, then you need to anticipate the track and steer a course behind it.

Entering the Western Approaches, a rock-hopping coastal route up the English Channel will allow you to avoid the strong tidal stream when it is adverse, and head further out and ride the incoming 2-4knot current whenever the tides are favourable.

Westabout around the world

Sir Chay Blyth's pioneering solo non-stop voyage around the world against the prevailing winds and currents back in 1971 has now become something of a thoroughfare for fellow adventurers to follow. Chay's own Challenge yachts have between them made 50 circumnavigations this way, and an increasing number of yachts are chasing the Gold Rush records from New York to California. Add to these, the number of cruising yachts that head south each year to explore the Antarctic waters that the Chilean Authorities have laid a visitor's mooring in the lee of Cape Horn to allow crews to have their passports stamped by the lighthouse keeper!

Equator to South America

The route down the North Atlantic remains much the same as if heading for the Cape of Good Hope. The changes only start when considering where to cross the Equator. *Ocean Passages for the World* warns that while the doldrums area will be smallest far to the west, crews that choose the Caribbean route south can finish up in head winds and have to tack to clear the South American coast. The advice is:

These crossings vary during the year, as the direction of the southeast Trade Wind is more S'ly when the sun is N of the equator then when S of it.

After passing the Cape Verdes, stand S between 26° and 29° W, being nearer 26° W from May to October, and nearer 29° W from November to April. Between January and April, when the northeast Trade Winds are well to the S, continue on a S'ly course, and cross the parallel of 5° N between 18° and 20° W, and the equator. In May and June the S'ly winds will be met with between 5° and 10° N. On meeting them, stand on the starboard tack and cross the equator, between 25° and 23° W.

In July, August and September, the S'ly winds will be met between 10° and 12° N. On meeting them, steer on starboard tack so as to cross 5°N between 17° and 19° W. Go round then on the port tack and cross the equator, as in May and June, between 25° and 23° W.

In October, November and December, the S'ly winds will be met between the parallels of 8° and 6° N. On meeting them, steer so as to cross 5° N between 20° and 23° W, then take the tack that gives most southing, and cross the equator between 29° and 24° W.

Caution: the South Equatorial Current is not as strong in the winter of the N hemisphere as in the summer and autumn; but the mariner must remember that the strength of the current increases as it advances towards the American coast.

From the equator southward: having crossed the equator as recommended, stand across the southeast Trade Wind on the port tack, even should the vessel fall off to about 260°, for the wind will draw more to the E as the vessel advances, and finally to due E at the S limit of the Trade. On approaching the Brazilian coast between March and September, when the wind is from SE and the current near the coast sets N, it will be better to keep from 120 and 150 miles off the land until well S, and steer so as to be to windward of the port of destination; but from October to January, when the NE'ly winds prevail and the currents sets SW, the coast may be approached with prudence, and a vessel may steer according to circumstances for her intended port.

For Rio de Janeiro, from October to March, make Cabo Frio and give the coast a prudent berth, as a constant and sometimes heavy swell sets in. The islands at the entrance to the harbour should not be approached until the sea breeze is well set in, as a vessel may run into a calm and be exposed to the swell and current.

For Montevideo or Rio de La Plata, stand direct through the southeast Trades, passing about 200 miles E of Rio de Janeiro.

Rounding Cape Horn westbound: the usual track is to take as direct a course as possible from a position 200 miles E of Rio de Janeiro to about 45° S, 60° W, and from thence so as to pass 30 or 40 miles E of Isla de los Estados. This track lies between 120 and 200 miles E of the Patagonian coast, and is the most direct route for a large and well-found ship. The older navigators, however, recommend that sailing ships should keep within 100 miles of this coast, in order to avoid the heavy sea that is raised by the W'ly gales and to profit by the variableness of the inshore winds when from a W'ly direction.

Near the coast from April to September, when the sun has N declination, the winds prevail more from the WNW to NNW than from any other quarter. E'ly gales are of very rare occurrence, and even when they do blow, the direction being obliquely upon the coast, it is not hazardous to keep the land aboard.

From October to March, when the sun has S declination, though the winds shift to the S of W, and frequently blow hard, yet as it is a weather shore, the sea goes down immediately after a gale. The winds at this time are certainly against making quick progress, yet as they seldom remain fixed in one point, and frequently back or veer six or eight points in as many hours, advantage may be taken of the changes so as to keep close in with the coast.

When passing Isla de los Estados, the usual course is E of the island, but there is, off its E extremity, a heavy tide-rip which extends for a distance of five or six miles, or even more to seaward. When the wind is strong and opposed to the tidal stream, the overfalls are overwhelming and very dangerous even to a large and well-found vessel. Seamen must use every precaution to avoid this perilous area.

The experience from the past Global Challenge races is on leaving Rio or the River Plate to get offshore fast. South of Deseado Island and again in the Strait de la Mer there can be a good current inshore which *Nuclear Electric* exploited during the first British Steel Challenge race. It also pays to head south after Cape Horn and not north as *British Steel II* did in that first race.

The advice from Mike Golding, who skippered *Group 4 Securitas* on three west-about circumnavigations, is to play each low pressure system as they come through, heading down on starboard tack as close to the north side of their centres as possible, then tack to port and ride the lift until you can tack down towards the next depression coming through.

Sydney to the Cape of Good Hope

Ocean Passages for the World suggests that the only time to round South Australia is between December and March. The Good Book suggests: *During these months, proceed through Bass Strait, or round Tasmania; E'ly winds prevail in the strait and along the S coast of Australia at that season, and good passages have been made by keeping N of 40°S, and passing round Cape Leeuwin into the southeast Trade Wind, which then extends well to the S. A vessel from Bass Strait bound round Cape Leeuwin is recommended, with a favourable wind, to shape a course which will lead about 150 miles S of that cape.*

In adopting this route, advantage must be taken of every favourable change of wind, in order to make westing; and it is advisable not to approach too near the land, as it would become with SW gales, which are often experienced, even from December to March, a most dangerous lee shore, and the contrary currents run strongest near the land.

After rounding Cape Leeuwin, stand to the NW into the southeast trades, steering for 30°S, 100°E, and thenceforward make a nearly W'ly course across the ocean to the meridian of 40°E, keeping between the parallels of 27°S and 29°S; being farthest to the S in December, and to the N in March. From the meridian of 40°E, steer towards the African coast to join the northern route, making for the African coast about 200 miles SW of Durban, then keep in the strength of the Agulhas Current until abreast Mossel Bay; from thence, steer direct to round Cape Agulhas at a 7-8 mile distance.

June, July and August are the worst months, and January and February the best months for sailing vessels proceeding W-bound round the Cape of Good Hope, and it should be borne in mind that there is much less sea over the Agulhas Bank in depths from 110m to 130m, or less, during heavy gales, than is near its edge and S of it.

Mike Golding describes this leg of the Global Challenge Race as simply – 'More of the same.' Once around Cape Leeuwin, it is a mainly windward course similar to crossing the South Pacific, with your latitude dictated by the approaching westerly low pressure systems.

His advice is to give the Kerguelen Islands a wide berth. 'In my experience, this is a high risk area with the biggest seas making knockdowns a probability.' The possibility of taking advantage of the 3 knot Agulhas Current depends on the position of the South Atlantic high pressure system and the flow of smaller highs that break off to join the Indian Ocean high pressure system. In some instances, it is less problematic to simply steer a Great Circle course and approach the Cape of Good Hope from a more southerly position.

Cape of Good Hope to the American Eastern Seaboard

The route from Cape Town directly to the US Eastern ports is a modern one and *Ocean Passages for the World* offers little advice until reaching the old commercial routes around Recife northwards. Mike Golding's advice is to head out west and get into better gradient winds, then follow a Great Circle course to cross the Doldrums at its narrowest part 200-300 miles off the South American coast, then ride the Gulf Stream north.

Transatlantic – Westbound

Another Great Circle route Golding recommends hitching a ride with is the warm Gulf Stream out over the Grand Banks before picking up the North Atlantic Current on a direct course for the Western Approaches, making the most of the low pressure systems as they flow across the Atlantic.

jury rigs and repairs

Saving a yacht from sinking, setting up a jury rig, or merely overcoming structural problems hundreds of miles from land, are the ultimate initiative tests. Solutions can be bought ten-a-penny from armchair theorists, but sadly the few with real practical experience rarely seem to set their stories down on paper. This may be because the cold facts rarely reflect the high degree of leadership, ingenuity and teamwork required to overcome what are, in extreme cases, life and death situations.

Success invariably relies upon improvisation, adapting what is left from a shattered rig, cutting down a jockey pole to shore up damaged framing, or jamming sails and sleeping bags through a hole.

One such case was *Ceramco New Zealand*, the 20.7m Farr design skippered by Peter Blake, which lost its rig soon after crossing the Equator when a starboard intermediate shroud broke at a point where the rod was bent around the spreader tip. The spar snapped in two places but the crew managed to salvage the 15m top section and lashed this to the stump to set up a jury rig. It took them 24 hours to raise the section, make up new

The jury rig that carried Ceramco New Zealand 3,800 miles. The broken mast sections were salvaged and lashed together. The jockey pole was used as a supporting spreader and a lower spreader was taken from the centre section and fastened to the opposite side. A breadboard was used as a base plate for the mast and a cut-down jockey pole was rigged up below to act as a sampson post. A spinnaker pole was erected in the cockpit to act as a mizzen mast. The work took 24 hours to complete, but thereafter, Ceramco averaged 6.5 knots for the remainder of the voyage to Cape Town.

rigging and re-cut the sails. This enterprising crew then averaged 6.5 knots for the remainder of the 3,800 mile voyage to Cape Town, running 244 miles during one 24 hour period, to set what remains as a world record distance under jury rig.

Improvisation was key. A breadboard was used as a base plate for the mast, a cut-down jockey pole acted as a sampson post, and one of the spinnaker poles was erected in the cockpit as mizzen mast. The jaws of a large pair of bolt croppers were converted into a swage press so that running rigging could be adapted as stays. A jockey pole was set up on the port side to act as a spreader, and a lower spreader was salvaged from the centre section, complete with its root, and fastened on the starboard side. Luckily the gooseneck remained undamaged allowing the mainsail to be set down to the fourth reef on the boom, but holes had to be punched through the seams along the luff so that the sail could be laced to the spar. A trysail was set from the mizzen, and the fore triangle was filled with a cut-down reacher and No. 6 jib, the latter acting as a staysail. Had the crew been forced to run directly before the wind, they had in mind the idea of making a square sail from cut-down sail bags, using their spinnaker pole as a yard.

Another crew to show ingenuity was Richard Tudor's team aboard *British Steel II* during the British Steel Challenge following a bottle screw failure mid-way across the South Pacific, 2,000 miles from the nearest land. The mast broke at deck level, before disappearing into the Southern Ocean, dragging sails and rigging with it. The crew picked up fuel supplies from other yachts and a passing ship, but over a period did develop a schooner rig of sorts with a spinnaker pole set up close to where the mast should have stood, together with a second spar found abandoned during one of their fuel stops, from which they flew a series of staysails and cut down genoas. It was good enough for this crew to turn off their engine and sail unaided across the finish line, to pick up a finish time for the leg!

British Steel II *sailing under a schooner jury rig cobbled together from cut-down sails and a spinnaker pole.*

Prevention being better than cure, it is essential to carry out daily checks on the spars and rigging whenever it is safe to do so at sea, to spot the first signs of fatigue. A snapped strand on 1x19 wire, or hairline cracks in tangs and mast sections, and even score marks on rod rigging are all indicators. Unlike 1x19 wire rigging which invariably breaks a strand at a time, rod rigging provides few outward signs of fatigue. Incorrect installation is the most common cause of failure, and breaks occur most frequently close to the swage terminals and where the rod is bent, ie over a spreader tip. The slightest score marks also weaken the rod considerably and, if this occurs, it is imperative to smooth the marks out immediately with a file to restore its strength.

Hull damage

There is always a danger of hull damage in extreme conditions when a yacht falls off the top of a wave into the following trough. It is bad enough for the crew, but the unyielding power of the sea can break hull frames just as easily as human ribs! One to suffer this problem was South African solo sailor Bertie Reed, whose 49ft (15m) wooden monohull *Voortrekker* fell off a wave at the height of an Atlantic storm. The drop stove in the yacht's port bow, fracturing one of her laminated ribs. This forced Reed to lie hove to for more than a day while he shored up the damaged area with the aid of a cut-down jockey pole and the seat from his bosun's chair.

Yachts have hit semi-submerged containers that have fallen from a ship's cargo deck or a bulk of waterlogged timber, which are both hard to see and can cause extensive damage. Boats designed to cross oceans are now fitted with a crash bulkhead in the bow and a watertight door to seal the main bulkhead forward of the mast and limit flooding. Such situations

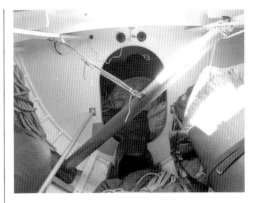

Hull damage shored up with a cut-down jockey pole aboard Voortrekker.

underline the strong need for a precise crew drill to ensure that everyone knows what to do, where the pumps are – and how to operate them!

Fire is another risk which invariably starts with a gas explosion. Gas is heavier than air and can settle in the bilge, so it is just as important to check this area at the start of each watch, and pump to disperse any gas build-up as it is to turn the cooker and grill safety valves off immediately after cooking.

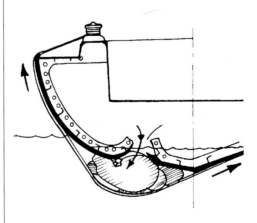

Ragged holes can be plugged with sails and sleeping bags, and held in place with a sail wrapped round the hull.

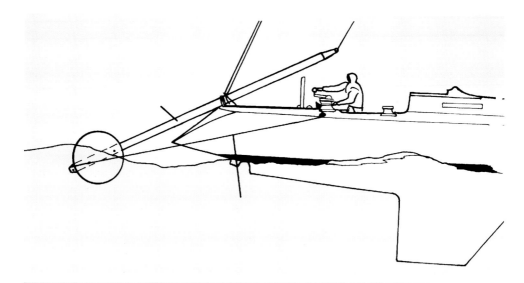

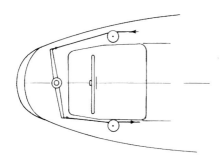

An emergency steering arrangement using reins that link the yoke on the rudder head to the primary winches.

Rudder breakages

Theorists have written at length about rudder breakages but unfortunately little of it is backed by practical experience. Some racing rules stipulate that yachts must not only carry an emergency tiller, but be able to utilise a spinnaker pole and floorboards bolted to one end to form a sweep over the stern should the yacht suffer total rudder failure. The effect this arrangement might have in steering a maxi sized yacht once the rudder has been lost is very limited, and while the sails can be balanced to sail upwind, the likelihood is that this could provide merely an interim solution until being taken in tow.

One skipper with practical experience of this problem, however, is Iain McGowan-Fyfe, whose 43ft (13m) Contessa production yacht, *Bubblegum*, lost its rudder 600 miles from the Horn. After some trial and error, her six man crew learned to control the yacht's course by utilising two round alloy plates U-bolted to one end of the spinnaker pole. The pole was then trailed astern, secured to the backstay at a point approximately one third of its length from the inboard end, which allowed it to sweep through a 90° angle. The makeshift blades were most effective when the pole was angled just below the surface of water, maintained by the boom topping-lift clipped to the inboard end. The sweep angle was controlled by two lines, led to the primary winches via snatch blocks, clipped to the gunwales. These were manned by two crew who learned to work in unison to wind and release the lines, one of them calling 'Give . . . Take . . . Give . . . Take . . . ' as they swung the sweep through wide angles to keep the yacht running in a straight line. This task was made easier by balancing the rig – changing down to a smaller headsail and playing the mainsail sheet continuously to release pressure as the bows began to head up, and sheeting in again as soon as the yacht started to bear away.

It took the crew half an hour to rig up this jury rudder and the only modification required later was a limiting line running from the backstay to the inboard end of the pole to stop it from riding up over the stern. They covered more than 100 miles a day under this jury system and McGowan-Fyfe believes they could have reached port had a Chilean naval ship, sent out to provide assistance, not taken them in tow.

The emergency tiller supplied with most yachts is often a simple alloy fabrication that fastens directly over the head of the rudder stock where this protrudes through the deck. This arrangement is not always practical,

(particularly on larger yachts which invariably require a yoke to straddle the aft deck) similar to the steering arrangement on a canoe, with steering reins attached to the outboard ends, leading back to the primary winches.

Another yacht to run into steering problems while bound for Cape Horn was *Outward Bound*, a 49ft (15m) race yacht skippered by Digby Taylor. Her wheel began to shed its spokes, forcing the crew to remove it from its pedestal and steer with their emergency tiller while repairs were made to the fractures around the boss. Using a glass fibre and polyester resin repair kit, the crew used a sail cover to set up a small tent on deck to protect the wheel from the elements during the repair and retain some of the heat generated from the small gas stove brought up from the galley to cure the resin. Small webs cut from a sheet of plywood were first glued in place around the boss to act as spacers between the spokes before wetting out several layers of glass fibre over the damage. The repair proved to be so strong that on arrival in Mar del Plata they decided to continue racing with it all the way back to the Portsmouth finish line.

heavy weather sailing and survival

The Fastnet disaster back in 1979 highlighted one principle lesson: experience is all-important when sailing in heavy weather. Out of the 303 starters in that 605 mile classic race from Cowes to Plymouth, it is significant that there was not one tragedy recorded among the 56 *Admiral's Cup* yachts competing.

A number suffered rudder breakages, but only one yacht, the Irish owned *Golden Apple of the Sun*, was abandoned. Her skipper decided to take advantage of a rescue helicopter hovering above to hitch a lift ashore to charter a boat and return to tow the crippled yacht back to port. *Golden Apple* was later recovered in the same condition as she had been abandoned which demonstrated that her crew would have been safe to stay on board.

Most abandonments, fatalities and sinkings occurred within the smaller end of the fleet. While the larger size of those Admiral's Cup yachts, which ranged from 39 to 51ft (11.8-15.5m) overall, may have had a bearing on these statistics, the experience within this premier sector of the fleet counted for much more. All continued racing unless overtaken by rudder or major gear failure first. None resorted to lying a-hull or trailing warps.

Unless faced with a major failure, it is fear, seasickness and cold, and not the conditions that invariably overwhelm a crew. Experience and practice are the all important ingredients to survival. Deliberate, practiced movements to reef the mainsail down and set a storm jib, an experienced hand on the helm and hot drinks to keep the cold at bay and morale up is what is required.

The damage is done when an unpracticed crew waste time first searching for the jib below, then struggle to hoist and sheet the unfamiliar sail on a pitching deck awash with green water. Invariably things go wrong. The foredeck crew, drugged by exhaustion and stung by the shouting from the cockpit as much as the spray, begin to make the most basic mistakes in their haste to recover a quickly deteriorating situation. The wrong halyard is pulled aloft; the sail is hoisted upside-down, a sheet comes untied and the flogging clew smacks someone in the face. It is in situations like this that the unpracticed, inexperienced crew make all manner of mistakes. By the time the yacht is eventually shipshape, the number of close calls leave everyone battered, bruised and exhausted, if not close to panic – which is hardly the frame of mind to perform well for a further ten hours before the storm finally passes overhead.

Good teamwork is essential. Each member of the crew must know what to do – and do it instinctively – and, at the same time, keep both eyes open for trouble. This is why Conny van Rietschoten placed so much importance in the two transatlantic crossings before each of his Whitbread campaigns. This is why Sir Chay Blyth and his training teams insist that every one of

their recruits, whether experienced sailors or not, must undergo a full training programme before embarking on a Global Challenge race. Knowing the 60-70 knot gales that will inevitably overtake them in the Southern Ocean, these crews have to mould into a cohesive team to work shorthanded through thick and thin, taking every eventuality in their stride. Indeed, it is testimony to this preparation, that after 50 circumnavigations, no situation has left a crew unable to help themselves.

Many cruising sailors assume that their requirements are less than those who go racing for pleasure because they plan their trips according to the weather and will not press their boats as hard. But as those 3,000 Fastnet sailors found, storms can build up to ferocious heights with little apparent warning. If you cruise for long enough you are bound to be caught out in bad weather sooner or later, and with a less than experienced crew and mediocre equipment, the chances of damage or disaster are all the greater.

Every yacht that sets sail on the open sea, whether it be club racer or cruiser, should be fitted out and equipped to the minimum standards laid down within the Special Regulations drawn up by the Offshore Racing Council (see *The Offshore Special Regulations Handbook* published by Adlard Coles Nautical). These ensure that yachts racing in Category 1 and 2 offshore events carry a storm trisail, storm jib and heavy weather jib, and a heavy weather jib in category 3 and 4 races in more sheltered waters. These sails should not merely be stowed on board as an insurance policy you hope never to claim on. A force 8 gale is not the right time to learn how to set and trim these sails – or worse, find that the sailmaker has made a mistake with their size. Like every other sail onboard, head, tack, and clew need to

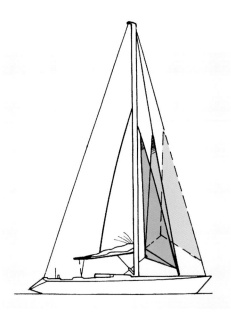

A yacht is often balanced best when the storm jib is set on the inner forestay. Where there is no inner forestay, a second genoa halyard clipped to an eyebolt on deck provides a compromise solution.

be marked accordingly, and halyard and sheet lead positions noted down.

Although the storm jib is designed for hoisting on the forestay, the yacht may be balanced better if it is set on the inner forestay where it will help to reduce lee helm, making the yacht easier to steer. Where there is no inner forestay fitted, a second genoa halyard clipped to an eyebolt on deck provides a compromise solution. The storm trysail must be fed into the mast luff track within easy reach of the deck. A storm tossed ocean is no place for monkey antics on the boom so if the regular mainsail luff feeder is out of reach, fit a second luff track on the mast.

Crew safety

The old adage, 'One hand for the ship and one for yourself' is common sense to the armchair critic, but to an inexperienced crewman weakened by fatigue, sickness and plain fear, logic is not always second nature. All yachts should carry a sticker at the top of the companionway shouting out the message – 'Safety Harness!' The wearing of a safety harness and lifejacket should be second nature. Permanent jackstays should be rigged the length and breadth of the yacht and crews encouraged to clip on before coming out of companionway hatch. Every crew member should also carry a knife, together with a torch during night watches and a personal EPIRB or flare in their pocket.

Shouting should be discouraged. A raised voice does little to hurry proceedings – it merely unnerves the recipient and, anyway, is often carried away unheard by the storm. Instead, routines need to be practiced until they became second nature with instructions from cockpits to foredeck carried out by sign language.

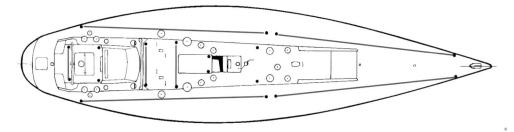

Permanent jackstays should run the length and breadth of a yacht, wherever the crew are likely to be positioned. Crew should be encouraged to clip on before coming out of the companionway hatch.

Steering techniques – upwind and down

The Southern Ocean is a cold and desolate place, but the strong westerly gales that sweep these seas unhindered by land provide the most exciting sailing conditions in the world. Sailing eastabout, the yachts are picked up by the stern and thrust forward on each wave. They start humming like an electric train, vibrating from stem to stern, and as the bow wave grows higher and higher, the noise drowns out all but the most excited hollering.

The first surfs are always the best. You just hang on and hold your breath. It is like riding a roller coaster down a vertical track, but it takes great nerve and skill to keep a yacht sailing fast in these conditions. Surfing on these crests at up to 30 knots, the slightest lapse in concentration is enough to allow the yacht to roll over in a vicious broach that keeps her pinned down on her side at the mercy of the next big wave. The helmsmen – and only the best should steer in these conditions – should be changed every 15-20 minutes before their concentration dulls – while the rest of the crew, working in a tunnel of spray reaching up to the first spreaders, grind themselves to a standstill playing the sheets continually as the yacht creams on, rolling, shaking and shuddering for hour after hour.

It is possible to carry specialist spinnakers in wind strengths up to force 10. The chicken chute is best hoisted on a pennant that lowers the head to three-quarter height to reduce its effect on heel and, though it looks like a pocket handkerchief compared to normal spinnakers, this half-sized chute can both stabilise the yacht and maintain remarkable average speeds. Racing in these conditions, the chasing yachts keep you on the knife-edge that divides wind-swept from wipe-out. A Martin-breaker line between spinnaker pole and the shackle at the end of the guy is essential to provide an instant release for the spinnaker should the loads become too high, and another should be set within the boom preventer to allow the mainsail to break free should the yacht broach heavily and drag the boom through the water.

Upwind, it is quite another matter. The helmsman must learn to pick his or her way over the waves, bearing off on the crests to avoid slamming down uncontrollably. The worst conditions come when a change in the wind direction generates an ugly cross sea. When one of these climbs above the underlying swell, it can form into a freak wave without a back to it. Then, even though the helmsman bears off as the yacht mounts the crest, the yacht still drops like a stone into the trough below. With these waves moving at 20 knots or more and the speed of the yacht sometimes hitting double digits, each crash is akin to hitting a brick wall at 30 knots. As one Global Challenge crewman put it, 'It is like someone putting a shotgun

The helmsman and mainsheet trimmer working in unison to minimise weight on the helm and the possibility of an untimely broach.

an inch from your ear and pulling the trigger.' Each bone-jarring slam is that loud. The shockwaves from a 35 ton yacht free-falling into the trough below are enormous. The first few times, crew will look nervously up at the rig, but are then caught out by the 'greenie' that follows; they quickly learn that self preservation comes first.

It is in conditions like this that the need for strength and durability in each and every item of equipment becomes far more important than savings in weight and windage – and why the Challenge yachts are built like Sherman tanks! If all else fails and the wave washes everyone off their feet, including the helmsman, these yachts look after themselves, keeping to course, giving crews time to pick themselves up and re-group for the next onslaught.

Talking with the helmsman is not encouraged, and if others on watch ever become bored by the infrequent change of sails, they can always amuse themselves by scoring the helmsman on the severity of their 'bangs'. If the emergency light at the stern flashes, that should score ten. Merely making the shroud covers ring does not

Going…Going…for a maximum score!

count. It can become much like scoring a skater for presentation and content, and occasionally, when the shockwaves wake everyone asleep below decks, the helmsman will earn maximum points from all the judges!

When caught out in conditions like these, trailing ropes or lying a-hull at the mercy of wind and waves are the worst things a crew can do. Those rules, handed down from sailing ship days, refer to the long-keeled heavy-displacement yachts that were built at the turn of the century or before, which remained sluggish to the helm even in the most favourable conditions. The biggest advantage modern yachts – both cruisers and racers – have in these wild conditions is manoeuvrability. They need speed and an attentive hand on the helm to manoeuvre through the waves; this cannot be done when trailing buckets and warps astern. If the storm is judged too strong to sail into – though no Challenge yacht has ever had to do this – then turn and run with the waves. This was a lesson

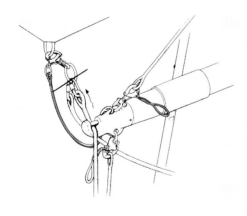

The tripping system used to release the spinnaker when a line squall is about to strike.

Mike Golding's Group 4 Securitas *crew facing extreme conditions at the start of the Global Challenge Race. They went on to win the race outright.*

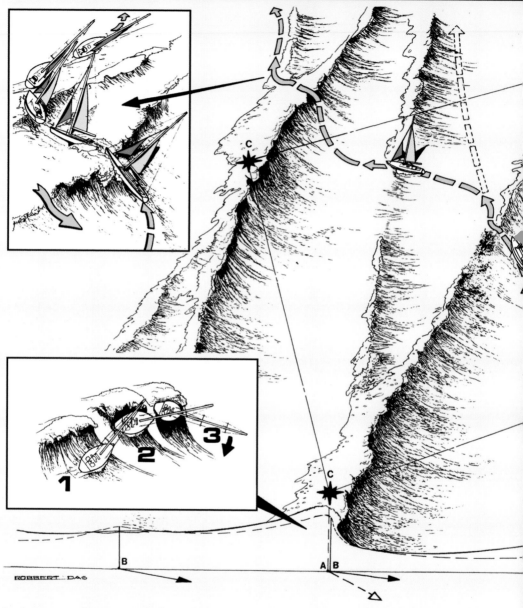

ROBBERT DAS

Freak waves are often generated when a change in the wind pattern builds up an ugly cross sea whose intersecting crests, C, then combine to form the foaming walls of water.

When cruising it is best to steer a close reaching course, heading up as the crest approaches then bearing away down the back of the waves. When racing and a close hauled course is called for, the helmsman needs the utmost concentration to judge each wave, heading the bows right up to avoid being knocked backwards, or worse, rolled over (inset). He must bear away sharply to avoid having the yacht slam down into the trough ahead.

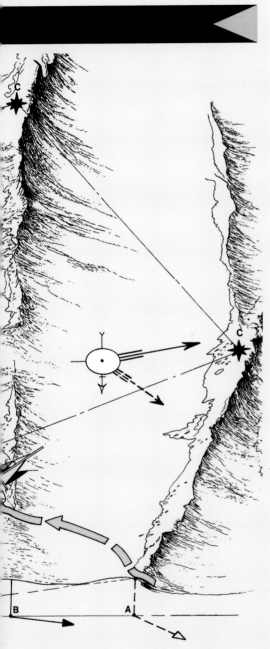

The one big advantage modern yachts have over latter day heavy displacement craft in these conditions is manoeuvrability. Never lie ahull or trail warps – a knockdown is likely. Keep the yacht sailing, easing her through the waves.

brought home to the crew on *Police Car*, once they had rounded the Fastnet Rock and started the run back towards Plymouth during the tragic race in 1979. Running before the wind at what they thought was a safe speed of between 5-6 knots, this seaworthy 40ft (12.2m) Ed Dubois design was knocked down three times, rolling more than 120° each time and dipping her mast beneath the waves. Eventually her crew realised that she was going too slowly to allow the helmsman to steer around the worst waves and they changed the trim of their storm jib (the only sail set) to increase their average speed to eight knots. Veteran New Zealand sailor, Chris Bouzaid, later described this experience in an article in the American magazine *Yachting*:

'*Every sea was different. Some of them we would square away and run down the front of. Others were just far too steep to do this. One imagines a sea to be a long sausage like piece of water moving across the ocean. However, this was not the case at all as these seas had too many breaks in them and were not uniform. We found that in many cases we could pick our way through the seas, finding a little valley between seas and ducking through, now that we had more boat speed. Once we got all of this together, we had very little trouble. We found that we were managing to avoid all the breaking seas, either by cutting through the sea and going beyond the breaks, or bearing away on the sea prior to the break to avoid having it hit the boat.*

During the next four hours, we were in fact only hit once by a breaking sea, and that was only because the helmsman (me) was talking to the other crew members and not concentrating on the job in hand.'

Heavy weather techniques.
Sailing to windward.

WHAT NOT TO DO

11 Never allow the yacht to luff up when surfing. This may result in a broach, leading perhaps to a dangerous knockdown.

12 The same applies as the wave passes. Luffing while the yacht is still surfing will throw her on her beam ends.

13 Never remain square to the wind once boat speed drops – the apparent wind will swing back and a Chinese gybe may result.

9 The helmsman then luffs up to main speed before bearing away again in readiness for a ride on the next wave **10**.

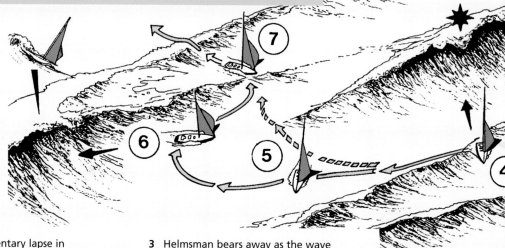

6 A momentary lapse in concentration on the part of the helmsman leads to the yacht deviating from the safe line, but he recovers the situation by bearing away to reach a safe position in the following trough, ready to meet the next wave **7**.

3 Helmsman bears away as the wave approaches, to keep the yacht level, and avoids the chance of broaching when the yacht surges forward and apparent wind increases.

4 Crewman notices a dangerous wave building up astern. Helmsman takes avoiding action by luffing sharply as soon as the preceding wave has overtaken the yacht, to finish up in position **5**.

WHAT TO DO

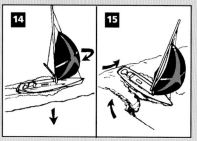

14 Start luffing the moment speed drops and the yacht starts to sink back into the water.

15 Bear way almost square to the wave just before the crest overtakes, then maintain a steady course while the yacht remains surfing to avoid gibing or broaching.

8 Surfing down a very steep wave, modern yachts can reach 25 knots+ before slowing down rapidly in the following trough as the wave crest draws ahead.

Read from right to left

(as the waves move faster than the yachts)

This drawing illustrates two approaches to sailing safely down wind. One is a 40ft (12.2m) yacht which is picking her way through the worst crests with just a storm jib set to keep the yacht moving just fast enough to be manoeuvred quickly. Assuming a wave speed of 25 knots she is making eight knots and is picked up by an overtaking wave every 20 seconds.

The second approach is to maximise on speed to maintain steerage and manoeuvrability. The maxi yacht in this illustration is flying a storm spinnaker and fully reefed mainsail. As a result, she is averaging more than 12 knots and can surf up to 25 knots. She meets up with the crests every 46 seconds.

Both approaches are much safer than running under bare poles or towing warps, which badly affect manoeuvrability.

1 Being overtaken by waves with a relative speed of 17 knots, the crew look out for the next crest, the moment the yacht begins to fall behind the overtaking wave.

2 The helmsman luffs up in the trough to maintain speed just as the crew spot a following wave building up on their port quarter.

WAVE SEQUENCE

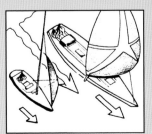

Assuming a wave speed of 25 knots, both a 76ft Maxi (23.2m) (top track) and a 40ft (12.2m) race yacht are sailing backwards relative to the waves. There is, however, a big difference in their speeds. The 40 footer with just a storm jib set makes eight knots and is picked up by an overtaking wave every 20 seconds, while the Maxi under chicken chute averages more than 12 knots with surfs up to 25 knots. She meets up with crests every 46 seconds.

Proof of the power generated by freak waves. The freighter Neptune Sapphire *was broken in half by such a wave off East London, South Africa, during a storm in 1973.*

Freak waves

There seems little you can do in the case of a freak wave, other than pray long beforehand that you never meet up with one. These waves are great mountains of water; vertical walls some five storeys high, topped with wild foaming crests, that appear from nowhere, rolling forward at 30 knots. Formed by one wave climbing the back of another, they rarely retain their height for more than a few seconds, but in that short time will break anything in their path.

Such waves are legion near the Agulhas Bank at the southern tip of Africa and are thought to have been responsible for the many ships that have disappeared without trace there. One of the most famous is the 9,400 ton steamer, *Waratah*, lost off Port Elizabeth on her maiden voyage during a storm in 1909. At first many refused to believe her loss. No wreck, boat, body or floating debris was found, and stories rebounded from one continent to another that she had broken down and was drifting on the ocean currents. Today there is little doubt that she followed the path of so many other ships, dipping her bows into the enormous trough that always precedes a freak wave and, buried by thousands of tons of water that would have broken her back, was taken straight to the bottom as the giant roller swept over to seal her fate.

Incredible though this story may seem, proof of the power generated by these giant waves can be seen in the picture of *Neptune Sapphire*, a freighter broken in half by such a wave off East London during a storm in 1973. The waves in this notorious area build up when a series of low pressure systems sweep in from the South Atlantic against the Agulhas current. This great river of warm blue water that stems from the surface drift in the trade wind belt and is driven thousands of miles through the Indian Ocean by the monsoon. Then it is deflected south by the African coast where it is squeezed between Madagascar and the mainland. Along with the Gulf Stream, it is one of the world's most powerful currents.

One hundred miles wide and 300m

deep, this body of water sweeps south along the 100 fathom line at between 4-5 knots until the bulge of Cape Aghulas heads it out into deeper waters. The one big advantage a yacht holds over a ship in these seas is size. Faced with such a wave, a yacht may be rolled over or pitch poled, depending on her attitude to the sea. She may be dismasted, have her crew washed overboard, water below flooding through an open or broken hatch, but if she is strong and well built, she is unlikely to sink. Her small size will allow her to bob about and squeeze out from under the full force of the water.

Flyer was overtaken by one of these waves during her transatlantic trial voyage back from America. Standing at the helm at the time, Conny van Rietschoten suddenly found a giant hole opening up before him. *Flyer* took off, spray from her bow wave climbing to spreader height on both sides. It lasted less than 30 seconds but the time seemed eternal as they hovered on the point of pitch poling. The yacht's downward angle exceeded 60° and brought the off-watch up out from their

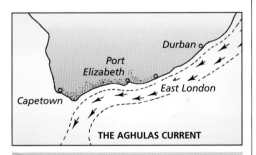

THE AGHULAS CURRENT

The infamous Aghulas Current – a great river of warm water stemming from the surface rift in the Trade Wind Belt that is deflected south by the African coast. 100 miles wide and 1,000 feet deep, this body of water sweeps along inside the 100 fathom line at 4-5 knots. A succession of south west gales opposing the current can produce freak wave conditions between Durban and Port Elizabeth. A weak counter current, however, running inshore, can provide a smoother passage.

bunks to see what was happening. They survived unscathed, the wave dissipating as fast as it had appeared, but it remained the topic of conversation on board for a long time after.

Sail control

Sailing with a genoa or reacher set in heavy weather, it is a sensible precaution to lift the sail with a second halyard attached to a cringle in the foot so that water breaking over the deck has a clear passage over the leeward side, and save the lower panels from being blown out or stanchions bent outboard by the weight of water that would otherwise be trapped.

Another good rule is to raise the main boom by putting in a reef at the outboard end to save the spar from dragging through the water whenever the yacht begins to heel. Booms come under immense pressure when dipped in the waves, especially when the boom vang or preventer limits swing. Small yachts without a hydraulic vang often rely on a purchase between boom and leeward toe rail to control mainsail leech tension and stop the spar from swinging across to decapitate the crew during an uncontrolled broach. In these cases it is important that the purchase can always be released quickly.

On larger yachts, the preventer line attached to the aft end of the boom, can be led outside the shrouds to a block at the bow, then back to a winch. This arrangement has the advantage of limiting the swing while, at the same time, allowing the boom to 'sky' when the vang is released to reduce the pressure on the spar in the event of a bad roll. Whatever the arrangement, it is important to have a small piece of thinner line spliced into the preventer to act as a fail-safe that, in the event of extreme pressure, will break before the boom does.

Spinnaker handling

Running with a spinnaker set in heavy weather calls for the utmost teamwork on the part of helmsman and sheet hands. As the yacht starts to surf down a wave, the helmsman bears off to counter the forward swing in the apparent wind and keep the yacht on an even keel before hardening up 20° or more as the crest overtakes the yacht and her speed drops back. The sheet hand, sensing whenever the yacht starts to heel, must play the spinnaker continually to keep the luff of the sail on the point of curling inwards and balance the yacht. He dumps the sheet by large amounts if the helmsman starts showing any signs of struggling with the helm.

It all calls for split second timing. A broach is almost certain to follow a lapse of concentration on either part. Yachts caught in this predicament can lie pinned down for several minutes and should the spinnaker subsequently fill with water, it may become necessary to jettison both sheet and halyard to get the yacht upright again.

The most awesome experience when running in strong winds is the death roll which, unless controlled immediately, invariably leads to a spectacular Chinese gybe. The problem occurs either because the yacht is being sailed by the lee, or the spinnaker is set over square. The helmsman's primary task is to keep the yacht under the masthead, steering into the roll as she begins to heel, before hardening up on a closer course to the wind or easing the pole forward and over-trimming the sheet once control has been regained. Another tried and tested way to

A Mumm 36 class yacht performs a spectacular spinnaker broach after the crew lost control of the sail.

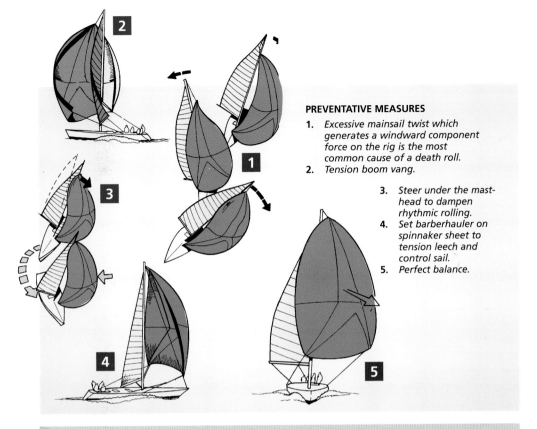

PREVENTATIVE MEASURES

1. *Excessive mainsail twist which generates a windward component force on the rig is the most common cause of a death roll.*
2. *Tension boom vang.*
3. *Steer under the masthead to dampen rhythmic rolling.*
4. *Set barberhauler on spinnaker sheet to tension leech and control sail.*
5. *Perfect balance.*

The death roll occurs either because the yacht is sailing by the lee or the spinnaker is set over square, or the mainsail is set with excessive twist.

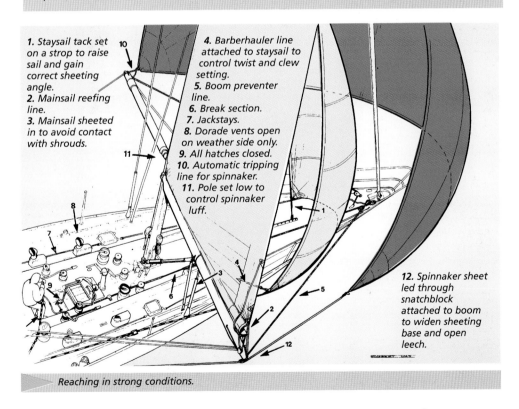

1. Staysail tack set on a strop to raise sail and gain correct sheeting angle.
2. Mainsail reefing line.
3. Mainsail sheeted in to avoid contact with shrouds.

4. Barberhauler line attached to staysail to control twist and clew setting.
5. Boom preventer line.
6. Break section.
7. Jackstays.
8. Dorade vents open on weather side only.
9. All hatches closed.
10. Automatic tripping line for spinnaker.
11. Pole set low to control spinnaker luff.

12. Spinnaker sheet led through snatchblock attached to boom to widen sheeting base and open leech.

Reaching in strong conditions.

improve control is to pull the spinnaker sheet down amidships with the aid of a barberhauler which will then stop the sail from oscillating wildly.

A further cause for rolling is excessive twist in the mainsail which tends to push the mast head to windward. Keep enough pressure on the vang to take out this twist but have a crewman standing by to release tension if the yacht broaches badly, otherwise the boom may break.

The death roll can be an expensive experience, especially if it results in a spinnaker wrap around the forestay as a knife is invariably the only way to release it. The best way to avoid this problem is to hoist a spinnaker net between forestay and mast to stop the chute from turning inside out through the fore triangle.

Reaching

Reaching in heavy weather calls for a small flanker or star-cut chute set on a low pole

to keep draft forward, while the sheet should be led well aft – through a snatch–block at the end of the boom if possible – to open the leech. Reefing the mainsail and setting a staysail to compensate often helps to balance the yacht better in strong conditions.

A low set inner foresail adds little to the overall heeling effect yet can help to maintain maximum speed in the lulls when other yachts look under canvassed. However the sheet must be held by an attentive hand, who will be quick to release the sail whenever the yacht looks like being overdressed. Just as one crewman must be ready to dump the staysail sheet so another must be ready to release the boom vang/preventer and mainsheet. If the top of the mainsail constantly flogs as a result, taking in a reef will reduce unwanted windage aloft.

Steering on a reach in fresh conditions is undoubtedly the most tiring, so much so

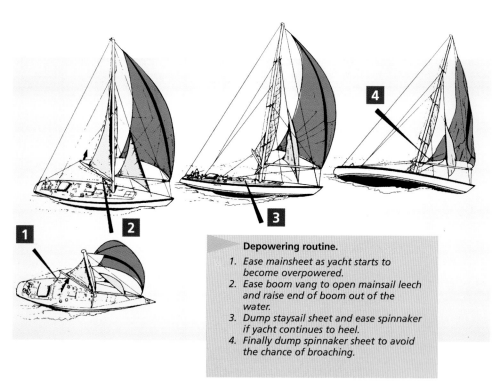

Depowering routine.
1. *Ease mainsheet as yacht starts to become overpowered.*
2. *Ease boom vang to open mainsail leech and raise end of boom out of the water.*
3. *Dump staysail sheet and ease spinnaker if yacht continues to heel.*
4. *Finally dump spinnaker sheet to avoid the chance of broaching.*

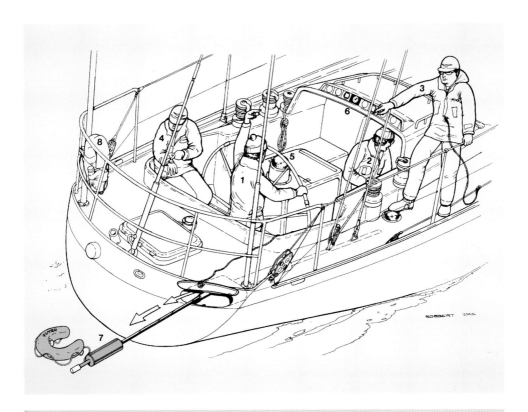

on some yachts that a second pair of hands, ready to help pull the helm up, is essential to maintain control. If the rudder suddenly starts to ventilate and stall out, a quick pump action on the helm will help to re-attach the flow of water over the foil and regain directional stability.

It takes good teamwork on the part of sheet trimmers and helmsman to keep a yacht on the fine edge between maximum speed and wipe-out, while the crew work progressively through a practiced de-powering routine to keep the yacht from broaching. Start by easing the mainsheet, then the boom vang. If the yacht continues to heel, free the staysail sheet then ease the spinnaker, dumping the sheet completely if a broach looks in sight.

Man Overboard!

Within a minute of falling overboard, there is a 215yd (200m) divide between the hapless crewman and his yacht sailing on at six knots. If the speed is ten knots, then that distance widens to 492yd (300m), which is further than the eye can often pinpoint a small object in a heaving ocean swell. The need, therefore, for clear, co-ordinated action the moment someone falls overboard is of prime importance,

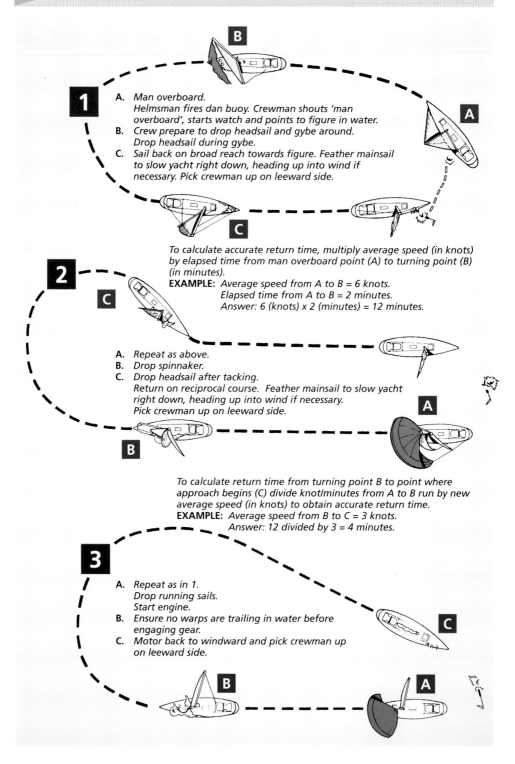

1

A. *Man overboard.*
   Helmsman fires dan buoy. Crewman shouts 'man overboard', starts watch and points to figure in water.
B. *Crew prepare to drop headsail and gybe around. Drop headsail during gybe.*
C. *Sail back on broad reach towards figure. Feather mainsail to slow yacht right down, heading up into wind if necessary. Pick crewman up on leeward side.*

To calculate accurate return time, multiply average speed (in knots) by elapsed time from man overboard point (A) to turning point (B) (in minutes).
EXAMPLE: *Average speed from A to B = 6 knots.*
Elapsed time from A to B = 2 minutes.
Answer: 6 (knots) x 2 (minutes) = 12 minutes.

2

A. *Repeat as above.*
B. *Drop spinnaker.*
C. *Drop headsail after tacking.*
   Return on reciprocal course. Feather mainsail to slow yacht right down, heading up into wind if necessary.
   Pick crewman up on leeward side.

To calculate return time from turning point B to point where approach begins (C) divide knot/minutes from A to B run by new average speed (in knots) to obtain accurate return time.
EXAMPLE: *Average speed from B to C = 3 knots.*
Answer: 12 divided by 3 = 4 minutes.

3

A. *Repeat as in 1.*
   Drop running sails.
   Start engine.
B. *Ensure no warps are trailing in water before engaging gear.*
C. *Motor back to windward and pick crewman up on leeward side.*

especially in the cold waters of the South Atlantic and Southern Ocean where life expectancy is very limited. There were three man-overboard incidents during the first Whitbread race and sadly two lives were lost. These were followed by single incidents in the two later races. Luckily for them, both crewmen were picked up in time, and their stories provide valuable lessons for others.

Recalling one crew's moment of drama on *Heath's Condor*, skipper Robin Knox-Johnston told me in Auckland that the helmsman rounded up before the spinnaker was fully taken down with the result that the sail twisted itself around the rigging. Further vital moments were lost when the blades of the folding propeller refused to open. However, once the crew had sorted themselves out, they were helped in their search by the flock of birds that had been following in their wake. Thinking the fallen crewman might be discarded food, the birds continued to swoop down on him inquisitively until disturbed by the yacht's return. The crew then plucked him back on board cold but otherwise unharmed.

As with that incident on *Heath's Condor*, it was a spinnaker sheet that flipped Paulo Martinoni over the side of the Italian round the world race yacht, *Rollygo*, while en route for the Horn. The spinnaker was hurriedly doused and the yacht turned about, but, because the incident happened at night, the crew soon lost sight of him and were only guided back by his shouts, throwing him a lifebelt with a light attached on their first pass which Martinoni waved aloft to guide them back again. All told, the Italian was in the water for little more than six minutes but with temperatures down to 6°C, he was suffering badly from hypothermia when pulled back on board and would not have survived for much longer.

Losing a crewman overboard is every skipper's greatest fear. The ones at greatest risk of falling overboard are fumblers, those who are always falling over themselves on deck, slow to react to the yacht's movement, and those prone to seasickness. Those who appear to take the greatest risks – climbing out along the spinnaker pole to free a snagged line, balancing themselves on the lifelines while leaning over to change a genoa sheet or shinning up a halyard to sort out problems aloft – are always at one with the sea; their catlike instincts and self confidence ensuring their safety.

Cold water can sap the strength of the toughest individuals within minutes, and though the victim may look okay from a distance waving arms energetically to attract attention, he may not have the strength to hold on to a rope by himself – and by the time this has slipped through his hands and the yacht has turned about to make a second pass it may be too late.

As a guiding principle, no second crewman should go over the side. However, if the victim is lying prone in the water, one crewman, attached to a line, must jump in to support his head above water and, if possible, start administering mouth-to-mouth resuscitation. The line should be tied with a bowline to form a large bight at one end that can be passed under the victim's arms to pull them alongside. Waterlogged clothing can double the weight of the body once clear of the water, and this added burden is often too much for many people when trying to pull themselves up unaided.

If the rope has been passed under the arms and round the body, then the rest of the crew may be able to pull the victim aboard with this if there is no ladder available. The alternative is to drop the head of the mainsail into the water to form a wide strop for the rescued crewman to lie

1. The moment a crewman falls overboard the helmsman:

a) Presses the emergency button at the helm which sets off the alarm and logs the time and yacht's exact position.
b) Pulls the lever in the cockpit to fire the dan buoy and attached life belt into the water.
c) A second crewman notes the time and shouts 'Man Overboard'!

2. The crewman nearest to the stern keeps the man in sight, continually pointing in his direction, never taking his eyes off the spot, to give the helmsman a visual bearing, while a second crewman sets up the portable radio direction finder to track the victim's EPIRB signal.

in, then take up on the halyard while others onboard take a tight hold on the lower folds of the sail. This stops them from being picked up by the wind or pulled down into the water by the weight of the body wrapped inside.

The rescue is made much easier if the yacht is beating or reaching under mainsail and head-sail only, for the helmsman can bear away almost immediately onto a broad reach then return to the spot on a reciprocal course under mainsail alone, gybing round in light/moderate conditions or tacking in strong winds.

The problems are heightened when the yacht is running downwind with the spinnaker set, for these sails must be doused and a check made that there are no ropes left trailing over the side before the helmsman can turn the yacht round, or put the engine in gear. In such situations, motoring back up to windward is the quickest way to return to the helpless crewman.

To calculate the return time, the navigator multiplies the average speed of the yacht by the elapsed time taken from the man overboard point A (when the helmsman started his stop-watch) to the turning point B, then divides this figure by

the new average speed to obtain an accurate return time.

As the yacht makes its final approach towards the victim on a broad reach, the mainsail is eased out to slow the yacht down and the prop shaft is disengaged as the helmsman is guided in for the pick-up by a man stationed on the bow. If the crewman is strong and in good heart, it may only be necessary to throw a line and haul him aboard, but two other crew (preferably one with medical experience) should be standing by wearing inflated life jackets ready to jump overboard should the victim show signs of fatigue.

The Global Challenge yachts are equipped with a hand-held radio direction finder to locate the pocket sized Emergency Position Locating Radio Beacon (EPIRB) carried by each crewman, together with a dan buoy with life belt attached which is stored in a tube and fired out over the stern. This buoy has a strobe light at the top of its mast which lights up once it has been deployed, to help pinpoint its position. Horseshoe lifebelts with lights attached are also ready to hand but kept in reserve, to be thrown when the yacht is close to the victim. In addition to their personal EPIRB, each crewman also carries a light and whistle.

Whales

Whales are a constant worry during ocean passages, especially in warmer latitudes when there is always the chance of running down one of these mammals slumbering just below the surface. Generally, whales do not pose an aggressive threat unless they are provoked first – then they can become killers!

Stan Darling, one of Australia's most successful ocean racing navigators, with successive Sydney Hobart wins to his credit, wrote on the subject in the Journal of the Australian Institute of Navigation:

Generally whales are pretty good at minding their own business, but they can be careless. A yacht recently collided with one, killing it with a tremendous gash over the head. Her calf made some ineffectual attacks on the yacht but shortly after along came a very angry daddy, and in a matter of minutes the yacht was on its way – straight down.

There have been many reports of attacks on yachts, including concerted attacks by killers. Strongly built boats might survive such attacks on the hull but are likely to be vulnerable to attacks on the keel, or around the rudder.

Right in the middle of a radio sked during a Transpac Race, a cruising yacht with six people on board, radioed that she was being successively attacked by killers, and was taking water by an increasing rate after each attack to the point where they could no longer cope and had to abandon. The nearest boat in the race diverted to the scene, picked them all up and continued its race to Honolulu with a greatly enlarged crew.

In 1952, a John Spencer plywood chine design on passage from New Zealand to Sydney for the Hobart race collided with a whale or killer in mid-Tasman and literally disintegrated without getting a radio message out. Being off the regular shipping routes that might have been the end of the story, but by a stroke of good luck, a tramp steamer picked them up after the crew had been in their liferaft for several days. Another yacht to suffer a similar fate was the Australian Admiral's Cup yacht Gingko *while making the crossing from South America to the UK. A single attack by a killer whale opened up the hull along the line of the keel and she sank within 12 minutes. This time the crew had only to wait 18 hours before being picked up.*

Iain McGowan-Fyfe, skipper of the Contessa 43, *Bubblegum*, can recount two equally harrowing experiences with whales while en route from England to Cape Town. One mammal, whose size dwarfed the yacht, swam underneath when they were close to the Equator and bodily lifted it clear of the water, the tail damaging the log impeller, propeller and flaps around the skeg, before dropping the yacht back on her beam ends into the sea. The whale was only scared away by the engine starting and the propeller slamming into reverse to cause the maximum amount of turbulence, a practical tip others have found equally successful. Two weeks later another school closed in on the yacht, one whale swimming close enough for the crew to reach out and touch its tail. This time, however, *Bubblegum's* batteries were flat so they could not start the engine. Luckily for them the whale swam away on its own accord.

Any attack by a whale is more likely to be an attempt to remove a rival mammal than an attempt to damage alien craft. For this reason any activity that identifies one as a non-whale, such as hitting the hull, starting the engine or switching on the echo sounder is worth a try. Iain McGowan-Fyfe's experience certainly seems to bear this out.

The 1979 Fastnet disaster: a rescue helicopter hovers over the yacht Camargue *as her skipper prepares to jump overboard and be picked up from the water.*

Abandoning the yacht

The yacht remains your best survival craft, and should never be abandoned unless it is on the point of sinking. That was the lesson learned from the Fastnet tragedy and other emergencies in the Sydney Hobart Race and rescue dramas in the Southern Ocean.

The Fastnet highlighted some serious deficiencies in liferaft design, and prompted Britain's Department of Industry to fund a research programme carried out by the National Maritime Institute into the behaviour of these craft in storm conditions. Their test work with scale models in a tank and lengthy observation of full sized liferafts in the storm-tossed winter waters off Iceland drew several important conclusions. These related to the design and construction of the craft (which manufacturers have since taken action to rectify), and their handling. The researchers found that the rafts are extremely unstable immediately after launching and must be boarded as soon as possible – just to hold them on the surface of the water in high winds! The first occupants must concentrate their weight on the weather side immediately after climbing aboard otherwise the raft will be little more stable than when empty, even after the water ballast pockets under the raft have filled.

With a full crew evenly distributed around the perimeter, the circular raft was stable beyond 75 knots compared to 35 knots when unladen. Fully laden rectangular rafts were slightly less stable because the straight buoyancy tubes tended to dig into the water rather than ride over it. This was particularly noticeable when loaded to 80% capacity, for while the circular raft was generally stable on breaking waves – tending to surf at times and becoming unstable but never

Liferafts under test with Britain's National Maritime Institute in 60 knot winds off Iceland...

...and in the test tank.

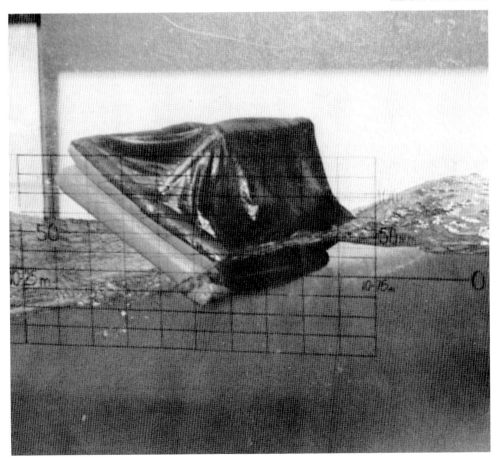

showing signs of overturning – the rectangular craft overturned on several occasions, and not necessarily on the largest waves. When loaded with a lesser capacity than this, it was found that the circular raft design showed no serious signs of instability if the occupants positioned themselves on the weather side. The other important consideration is the canopy, which the researchers found aided aerodynamic stability if the opening was closed once the occupants had climbed inside.

Immersion in water

If you find yourself immersed in water:

1. Float on your back if wearing a lifejacket. Hold your arms tightly around your chest, and lift your legs. This posture is sometimes called HELP – Heat Escape Lessening Posture – and is aimed at preserving deep body heat and slowing down the onset of hypothermia.

2. If without a lifejacket practice survival swimming (drown-proofing) or use a floating object to maintain buoyancy. Once again every effort must be made to preserve deep body heat otherwise death from hypothermia may be rapid. The best way to preserve heat is by holding your arms tightly around your chest and lifting your legs up towards the torso.

3. If in a group, huddle together to reduce heat loss. Do not remove clothes and do not swim to keep warm. Swimming and treading water will dissipate body heat rapidly, particularly in cold water.

Generally large fat people survive longer in cold water because their body temperature drops at a slower rate than that of thin people. Children are particularly sensitive to cold temperatures. Wearing warm clothes will greatly increase your survival time in water. The estimated survival time of an average adult in water at 20°C is

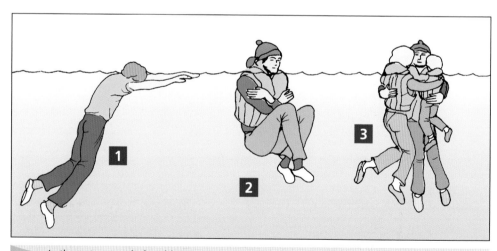

In the water – survival positions.

1. **Drown-proofing** – *an effective method of sustaining yourself for long periods in the water, but reduces survival time because head is immersed regularly which induces rapid heat loss.*

2. **The HELP method** – *Heat Escape Lessening Posture – reduces the amount of heat lost through head, neck, sides and groin areas. This posture doubles survival time in cold water but cannot be maintained without a lifeacket.*

3. **The huddle** – *when several people are in the water together huddling preserves body heat and maintains morale but cannot be maintained without the aid of lifejackets.*

1. Never leave the yacht unless it is about to sink
2. Wear a lifejacket and protective clothing
3. Board the raft as quickly as possible after launching
4. Stream out the sea anchor
5. Stay on the weather side if the raft is not filled to capacity
6. Close the canopy after boarding

SURVIVAL

Drowning, hypothermia, dehydration and shark attacks pose the most serious problems for most crews after they have abandoned ship or fallen overboard. Here, Dr Ron Proudford, a survival expert with the Royal Australian Air Force Special Reserve, offers this advice on staying alive. A survival kit stored in a waterproof container, such as a spare flare container, is essential for all craft venturing out to sea. It should be firmly attached to the liferaft and contain the following items:

1. At least four litres of water per person (stored in plastic or metal containers and 95% full to allow airspace for flotation and to prevent splitting).

2. One solar still and one desalinating kit per person.

3. High-energy food such as chocolate, nuts, dried fruit and sugar-based sweets.

4. One fishing kit.

5. Basic navigation aids such as a compass, chart, protractor, pencil and note pad.

6. A first aid kit.

7. A plastic sheet for cover.

8. Matches or, better still, a cigarette lighter.

9. Signal aids such as a heliograph (signal mirror), torch (plus spare set of batteries and bulb), whistle, distress sheets, sea dye marker, at least three night/day flares, a battery-powered transmitter/receiver and if possible a locator beacon.

10. A good quality knife, nylon cord, sewing needles and thread.

11. A liferaft repair kit.

12. A pack of waterproof playing cards to relieve boredom.

It is also sensible to pack a set of thermal underwear for each crew in the same container. Vacuum packed, they can be reduced to a fraction of their normal size and will provide a warm dry change of clothing once inside the liferaft. It is essential to wear a lifejacket at all times because of the possibility of being thrown out of the liferaft, and because they are very difficult to put on once you are immersed in water.

If trouble does strike: unless the vessel is sinking or on fire it is much better to remain with the yacht, simply because it is much easier for search and rescue teams to locate than a liferaft or survivors floating in the water. If the vessel is abandoned, try to remain in the area because this is where a search will most likely concentrate.

about five and a half hours and at 10°C only an hour and a half. These times will be greatly reduced if the survivor has consumed alcohol.

Shark attack

The chance of a shark attack can be significantly reduced by keeping a sharp lookout and adhering to these rules:

1. Use shark repellent if available.
2. Keep shoes and clothes on.
3. If in a group huddle together.
4. If a shark comes close, ward it off by shouting underwater and thrashing arms and legs. Do not remain motion-less while floating on the surface as this is likely to provoke an attack.
5. Do not defecate or urinate if a shark is nearby.
6. If in a liferaft do not clean fish or discard blood, offal or body wastes when sharks are around.

Priorities for survival

Long periods on board a liferaft or a small disabled craft can cause a number of serious mental problems such as boredom, loneliness and fear. The best way to deal with these and with the six physical stresses – thirst, hunger, fatigue, pain, heat and cold – is to select a leader and organise the group so that every person has a task to perform. To survive at sea four priorities need to be attended to – Protection, Location, Water and Food.

Protection

The first survival priority involves attending to injuries and disabilities; clothing and body for sea survival; and setting up a cover to provide more shelter from the elements. The main health hazards a survivor will face at sea are seasickness, boredom, sunburn, sun glare, heat exposure, dehydration, immersion, salt water sores, hypothermia and constipation. Of these, the two greatest problems to overcome are dehydration and boredom. Sickness greatly accelerates the onset of dehydration and must be overcome by taking anti-seasickness tablets every two to four hours, and by keeping the mind busy.

Location

This is the second priority because, in order to be rescued, you must first be seen or heard. Some location aids used in sea survival are:

- Emergency locator transmitters
- Night/day flare
- Distress rockets
- Strobe lights
- Distress sheets
- Whistle
- Torch
- Heliograph (survival mirror)
- Sea dye marker
- Reflector tape

One person should be made responsible for maintaining location aids so no time is lost in attracting attention should rescue personnel be identified in the area. Sweeping as much of the horizon as possible on a clear day with a signal mirror is highly recommended by the RAAF because although you might not see or hear distant aircraft, the crew will in most cases see the reflection. Hanging a metal object such as an empty kerosene can from the mast is another useful location aid because it will give a good radar return to a searching aircraft.

Water

Water is the third priority for survival. This is usually the most difficult need to satisfy at sea. Generally, you will require at least two litres of water each day to sustain normal body functions. However, this volume rises dramatically to six litres or more if you experience seasickness, or expose yourself to the heat. Without water most people will not survive longer than three or four days. Possible sources of fresh water at sea are rain, dew, sea water (sea water can be converted to fresh water using a solar still or desalination kit) and emergency rations. Consume your emergency supply of water last because you may be too weak to procure water from the environment. Never consume sea water, urine, blood from sea birds or fish, or tissue fluid extracted from fish. Wartime records show the mortality of castaways who drank sea water was ten times greater than the mortality of those who kept strictly to their limited supply of fresh water.

Food
This is the fourth priority for survival because the average adult can survive without it for about 25-30 days, providing they are in good health, do not exert themselves physically and have access to plenty of water (providing they are not attempting to survive in a cold environment where a good supply of high energy food is essential). As a general rule do not eat until your water problem is solved.

index

photography credits